GLOUCESTE

Pennsylvania Hall

....

CRITICAL HISTORICAL ENCOUNTERS

Series Editors
James Kirby Martin
David M. Oshinsky
Randy W. Roberts

Pennsylvania Hall

....

A "Legal Lynching" in the Shadow of the Liberty Bell

BEVERLY C. TOMEK

University of Houston-Victoria

New York   Oxford

OXFORD UNIVERSITY PRESS

Oxford University Press is a department of the University of Oxford.
It furthers the University's objective of excellence in research, scholarship,
and education by publishing worldwide.

Oxford   New York
Auckland   Cape Town   Dar es Salaam   Hong Kong   Karachi
Kuala Lumpur   Madrid   Melbourne   Mexico City   Nairobi
New Delhi   Shanghai   Taipei   Toronto

With offices in
Argentina   Austria   Brazil   Chile   Czech Republic   France   Greece
Guatemala   Hungary   Italy   Japan   Poland   Portugal   Singapore
South Korea   Switzerland   Thailand   Turkey   Ukraine   Vietnam

For titles covered by Section 112 of the US Higher Education
Opportunity Act, please visit www.oup.com/us/he for the
latest information about pricing and alternate formats.

Published in the United States of America by
Oxford University Press
198 Madison Avenue, New York, NY 10016
http://www.oup.com

Library of Congress Cataloging-in-Publication Data

Tomek, Beverly C.
  Pennsylvania Hall : a "legal lynching" in the shadow of the Liberty Bell / Beverly C. Tomek,
University of Houston-Victoria.
      pages cm. -- (Critical historical encounters)
  ISBN 978-0-19-983760-1 (alk. paper)
  1. Pennsylvania Hall (Philadelphia, Pa.)--Fire, 1838. 2. Antislavery movements--
Pennsylvania--Philadelphia--History--19th century. 3. Abolitionists--Pennsylvania--
Philadelphia--History--19th century. 4. Philadelphia (Pa.)--Politics and government--
19th century. 5. Philadelphia (Pa.)--History--19th century. I. Title.
  F158.44.T66   2013
  974.8'1103--dc23   2013030689

Printing number: 9 8 7 6 5 4 3 2 1

Printed in the United States of America on acid-free paper

For Phil Lapsansky and Ira V. Brown

.

CONTENTS
....

EDITORS' FOREWORD

....

The volumes in this Oxford University Press book series focus on major critical encounters in the American experience. The word "critical" refers to formative, vital, transforming events and actions that have had a major impact in shaping the ever-changing contours of life in the United States. "Encounter" indicates a confrontation or clash, oftentimes but not always contentious in character, but always full of profound historical meaning and consequence.

In this framework, the United States, it can be said, has evolved on contested ground. Conflict and debate, the clash of peoples and ideas, have marked and shaped American history. The first Europeans transported with them cultural assumptions that collided with Native American values and ideas. Africans forced into bondage and carried to America added another set of cultural beliefs that often were at odds with those of Native Americans and Europeans. Over the centuries America's diverse peoples differed on many issues, often resulting in formative conflict that in turn gave form and meaning to the American experience as it has evolved over time.

The Critical Historical Encounters series emphasizes formative episodes in America's contested history. Each volume contains two fundamental ingredients: a carefully written narrative of the encounter and the consequences, both immediate and long term, of that moment of conflict in America's contested history.

The antislavery movement was one of the most contentious and conflicted reform efforts in U.S. history. Lasting from the late colonial period until the Civil War, it evolved and underwent many changes as advocates of the cause struggled to find the best way to end human bondage. The most radical changes began in 1830, and by the end of the decade the movement had transformed in ways that even many abolitionists found unsettling. As slaves throughout the northern United States gained their freedom, abolitionists focused on the South, causing a firestorm of protest as Southerners decried outward interference with their domestic institution. At the same time, most Northerners turned on their antislavery neighbors, blaming them for the political and social unrest of the period. From their perspective, abolitionist meddling with the South threatened the strength of the nation by placing an already fragile union on even shakier ground. Also, many Northerners concluded that black freedom came with social costs to their own region, and they resented abolitionists for the increasing number of free African Americans and the resulting job competition and possibility of racial mixing.

Known as the birthplace of American abolition, Philadelphia faced these tensions acutely. Located near the border between the free North and the slave South, the city experienced a number of anti-abolition and anti-black riots in the 1830s. The most famous of these was the dramatic destruction of Pennsylvania Hall, an antislavery meeting place erected by Philadelphia's abolitionists just blocks from the State House (known today as Independence Hall) and the Liberty Bell—two of the most famous symbols of American freedom.

In the first full account of what happened at Pennsylvania Hall, historian Beverly Tomek engagingly recounts the dramatic confrontation, revealing how this fateful encounter illustrates the complexities of American abolition, let alone the challenges states faced as they envisioned the prospect of having a biracial post-emancipation society. Woven throughout Tomek's vivid narrative is an explanation of how tensions among abolitionists and resistance from the public at large collided in a violent clash that foreshadowed a critical split in the antislavery movement and provided abolitionists a martyr around which to rally support for their cause by emphasizing the importance of free speech, free expression, and human freedom.

James Kirby Martin
David M. Oshinsky
Randy W. Roberts

PREFACE

....

The strange mix of danger and excitement that often accompanied the mobs filled the air on that spring night in Philadelphia—April 17, 1838. William Lloyd Garrison knew the fury of the mob. Not long before, he barely escaped with his life as a similar group of enraged citizens showed up at an antislavery meeting in Boston ready to tar, feather, and hang him. Garrison managed to escape, but

The Burning of Pennsylvania Hall. By John Sartain.
Library Company of Philadelphia

in a separate incident another abolitionist newspaper editor was not so lucky. Murdered just six months earlier as he fought to defend his press from repeated assaults, Elijah P. Lovejoy was the most recent antislavery martyr—until tonight.

Perhaps Garrison's mind turned to Lovejoy as his Philadelphia abolitionist friends made plans to ferret him out of town before the mob could find him. For the time being, the enraged were preoccupied with another victim. The martyr this night was Pennsylvania Hall, a building that symbolized antislavery and racial "amalgamation" (mixing) to the attackers. Like many martyred bodies before, it was beaten and broken and then set on fire. Blocks away, from atop Independence Hall the famous Liberty Bell rang out to summon help. The building recently christened as a "Temple of Liberty" was ablaze, and freedom of speech was under attack. Ironically, the Constitution—the document that promised Americans the right of free expression—had been signed under that very bell just sixty-one years before. As the fire burned down and the mob went on the prowl, abolitionists knew Garrison had to leave the city. With the help of Pennsylvania's biracial antislavery community, he managed to escape the melee that he would later describe as a "legal lynching."[1]

Garrison's description of the assault as a "lynching" applies on many levels and exposes a number of similarities between the post-emancipation North and what would occur after slavery ended in the South almost 30 years later. When viewed from this perspective, the attack reveals much not only about the antislavery movement and the Jacksonian anti-abolition backlash, but also the racism that permeated the United States after blacks gained their freedom, whether in the North in the early 1800s or in the South after 1865. What happened on that fateful night in Philadelphia highlights the difficulty of shaping a biracial society.

Tracing this parallel, the story of Pennsylvania Hall shows how the antebellum abolition and civil rights movement faced unique challenges as reformers swam against the current in a society that was still trying to come to grips with emancipation in its own region and was unsure about, and often quite resistant to, the need to push for emancipation throughout the country. The people of the North were adjusting to black freedom and dealing with post-emancipation issues that the South would face after the Civil War, and Pennsylvania was central due to its position as a Northern border state that depended a great deal on trading and interacting with Southerners. In addition to the city's important trade relations with the South, Philadelphia attracted many Southern visitors on a regular basis. They came to visit family, see the sights of the city, and shop. Many Southern men who wished to become doctors went to Philadelphia's renowned medical schools. Finally, many Philadelphians had moved to the city from the South and maintained their family ties and allegiances to their native region. They resented abolitionists who refused to ignore the South's "peculiar institution" and leave well enough alone. This led to a number of social and political tensions as Southerners not only cried out against abolitionist "meddling" but also called upon non-abolitionist Northerners to help them repel the antislavery "attack" upon their way of life.

As Northern whites were trying to deal with the reality of black freedom and the push for racial acceptance and equality in their own region, the movement of more freed blacks from the South into the North was not an appealing prospect for most. Also, slaveholders responded to abolition efforts by defending their bound labor system as a good and paternalistic one and insisting that any challenge to the system could not be tolerated by anyone who loved and hoped to preserve the United States. Thus, most white Americans saw abolitionists as dangerous radicals who recklessly threatened the security of the nation for an undesirable goal.

Those whites who did not resist abolition altogether argued that black freedom must either come after a lengthy period of preparation in which slaves would be made ready for freedom through education and training, or be followed by removal of free blacks to Africa or other distant places. The first of these positions, known as gradualism, described the process by which Northern slaves had been freed, and many abolitionists saw it as a more fair way to confiscate private property in the form of bound laborers. Through a gradual process the slave would be prepared for freedom, and the owner would be repaid by the labor of the slave before he or she reached the age of emancipation. This position resulted in Pennsylvania's gradual abolition law in 1780. The group that had pushed for the law, the Pennsylvania Abolition Society (PAS), remained active in 1838 but was facing two serious challenges. On the one hand, many Philadelphians had started to resent the abolitionists because of the growing free black population in the city. Thanks to the efforts of the PAS slavery was illegal in Pennsylvania, but as an unintended consequence they had turned their state, and particularly the city of Philadelphia, into a haven for those in search of liberty, and whites blamed them for the increased black presence. The second position came from another group that opposed slavery but had different ideas about how to end it—the colonizationists. Adherents to this program were represented locally by the Pennsylvania Colonization Society (PCS), one of the strongest state auxiliaries to the American Colonization Society (ACS). While some colonizationists were concerned with the fate of slaves, others simply wanted to rid their state, and the nation, of all blacks—enslaved or free.[2]

Though they competed with each other, both gradual abolition and colonization enjoyed much more support in Pennsylvania, and throughout the nation, than did the movement for immediate abolition.[3] Even so, immediate abolition grew as a significant force throughout the 1830s and served as competition to the PAS in Philadelphia in 1838. Advocates of immediatism were the most radical of abolitionists. They argued that slavery must end immediately, that the freed should not be forced to leave their native land, and that slaveholders should not be compensated for their lost human property. They insisted that slaveholding was a sin and slaveholders must repent and free their bound laborers. They also argued that free blacks deserved the same rights and privileges of U.S. citizenship enjoyed by white Americans.

Pennsylvania was known as the birthplace of gradual abolition, and the state's colonization society was one of the strongest in the nation, but the epicenter of the immediate abolition movement had shifted northward to Massachusetts after William Lloyd Garrison established a newspaper there and declared an all-out war on both slavery and colonization. Whereas Pennsylvania gradualists had fought for black freedom quietly behind the scenes, mostly in courthouses and congressional chambers, Garrison and his followers pushed loudly and publicly. They hoped to use what they called "moral suasion" to convince slaveholders of the errors of their ways, but more often they put slaveholders on the defensive and found themselves under attack. Their tactics offended the general public as well as many "moderate" abolitionists, and Philadelphia's antislavery community was torn over how to deal with the new movement. By 1838 some of the city's abolitionists, many of whom remained also affiliated with the PAS, had formed their own immediatist societies such as the Philadelphia Antislavery Society and the Pennsylvania Antislavery Society. The reluctance of so many to leave the PAS, however, reveals their confusion over the changes taking place in the overall antislavery movement. Even so, both groups worked together to collect funds and oversee Pennsylvania Hall's construction.

The story of Pennsylvania Hall is the story of American antislavery in microcosm, and it sheds light on these competing agendas. The hall was built during a time when abolition was transforming and antislavery leaders were making some important choices. Step one involved choosing whether or not to stay with their gradualist organization or to join the new groups that were forming. The cooperation shown in raising money to build the hall provides an example of early efforts at bridging gaps and forging ties. Opening-week activities and the attack on the hall, however, highlighted the fissures. Soon afterward, immediatists split over a number of the very same issues that created tension between gradualists and immediatists to begin with.

The Pennsylvania Hall saga also reveals how complicated the immediatist movement itself was. Garrison represented one strain of immediatist thought, and several of the speakers in the hall shared his view. Accepting any gradual plan, they argued, or any plan that involved compensating the masters, made abolitionists complicit in the sin of slavery. In addition to this basic notion, Garrisonians held a number of other beliefs that even most fellow reformers found too extreme. For one matter, Garrison and his followers insisted upon "universal emancipation," which meant the emancipation of women from their subservient roles and civil rights for all Americans, regardless of race or sex. Also, Garrison had no problem questioning authority— whether secular or religious. He refused to vote or participate in politics because he insisted the entire political system was built upon a Constitution that, through its compromises and silence, sanctioned slavery. He also called ministers to task for refusing to expel all slaveholders from their congregations. These radical ideas appealed to only a small subsection within the immediatist movement.

Although Garrisonians thought of themselves as the only true immediatists, in reality some speakers in Pennsylvania Hall liked to think of themselves as immediatists too, even if they did not agree with Garrison on several key tactical and philosophical points. In general, the points of division involved varying answers to a number of key questions. At base was the question of what exactly "immediatism" even meant. Did it mean, as Garrison insisted, that slavery must end overnight? Or did it mean, as longtime PAS member David Paul Brown interpreted in his keynote speech, that plans must be made immediately to smooth a path for the final extirpation of the system? Beyond this basic question were the three that would ultimately split the movement in 1840: What role should politics play in the antislavery movement? If slavery was a sin but slaveholders sought fellowship in the churches, what role should those churches play in abolition? And finally, perhaps the most divisive question of all, what role should women play in the movement?

Women had been participating in abolition in both Britain and the United States from the beginning with little problem because they had confined their efforts to activities that did not take them out of the safe domestic realm. They held their own meetings away from the men, and they focused on such activities as shopping at "free produce" stores—stores that refused to sell goods produced by slave labor. Their sex-segregated meetings and domestic endeavors did not offend onlookers. The rise of Sarah and Angelina Grimké in 1836, however, shook the entire antislavery movement. These sisters came from a slaveholding family and used firsthand experience to write riveting speeches. Both women and men wanted to hear the sisters speak, but gender-mixed audiences were known as "promiscuous" audiences and were frowned upon. In an almost unprecedented move, they also embraced their black antislavery colleagues, interacting socially with them as equals. Such behavior led to charges of "amalgamation" that angered people in their wake across the Northern states.

As the Grimkés and other women spoke out against slavery, they found themselves having to defend their right to speak at all. Garrison supported unequivocally the right of women to speak publicly and to participate in the movement as they saw fit. Some abolitionists, however, argued that women had the right to speak out, but they insisted that the "women question" (the debate over whether or not women should specifically address their own rights) distracted from the matter at hand—the abolition of slavery. The tension over this question festered among abolitionists during the opening ceremonies at Pennsylvania Hall and came to a head soon afterward, eventually contributing to a bitter schism in 1840.

Finally, the work of the mob and the authorities during and after the attack reveals much about the general nature of society in the post-slavery North. Even though Northern states had abolished slavery, they were suffering the pains of social reconstruction as they tried to figure out how to make room for free blacks or chase them away. Though slavery was not as central to the Northern economy as it was to the Southern economy, it had almost as deep an impact on the social order of the region. Economic matters aside, race-based slavery afforded an important method of social control in a biracial society. At best most whites thought of blacks as outsiders; at worst they thought of them as a social problem.[4] In short, North American slavery created a racial caste system that influenced the thinking of whites in all states to varying degrees. Most Northerners, just like their Southern counterparts, had developed racial attitudes that had helped justify slavery for generations. As slavery ended in their region, they felt many of the tensions and, to a lesser degree, some of the resentment that Southerners would feel after the Civil War. As Southerners would a generation later, Northern whites in the 1830s were trying to adjust to the notion of black freedom. Blacks, hoping that their freedom would be followed by acceptance, were trying to make their way in a society that many whites argued had no room for them. This tension often led to mob action.

Historian David Grimsted has studied the riots that plagued the United States from 1828 to 1861 and concluded that they served as "a piece of the ongoing process of democratic accommodation, compromise, and uncompromisable tension between groups with different interests." Pennsylvania Hall was caught between several groups with highly divergent interests. Its friends wanted to awaken people throughout the North to their cause of ending slavery once and for all, but even they were split on how to achieve this goal. The Hall's enemies wanted to stop the abolitionists from discussing the issue. The enemies, like the friends, came from a number of different groups, any of which could have led the attack. Contemporary observers and historians have blamed a range of culprits for the attack, and looking at the different theories will offer a window through which to view a number of relevant topics, including the growing sectional animosity, the role of different socioeconomic classes during the period, and important changes in civil services, such as police and fire departments, that came about as a result of the violence and lawlessness that began in the Jacksonian era and continued throughout the antebellum years.

Ultimately the destruction of Pennsylvania Hall contributed to an awakening of the Northern public that was essential to the defeat of slavery. In a happy ending this would mean that the general public, awakened by the light from the burning hall (as a number of abolitionists immediately predicted would happen), embraced the cause of black freedom and equality. In reality, what opened the eyes of most whites who even contemplated the broader implications of the destruction of this "Temple of Liberty" was what such mob action meant for their own freedom. In short, abolitionists were able to argue that the assault on the hall represented an attack upon free speech. As Grimsted has argued, mobs like the one that burned Pennsylvania Hall essentially handed abolitionists a tool that "assured progress for their movement." "The South," he added, "was so slave-committed that it demanded the cessation of white freedom where it touched that issue." After silencing any questioning of slavery in the South, slaveholders and their allies demanded the same silence from the North. Thus, "every mob against abolitionists offered added 'proof' that the peculiar institution demanded that slavery of a sort be integrated and made a national commitment." Abolitionists realized this and used the destruction of Pennsylvania Hall to great advantage.

Grimsted has argued that riots were "exclamation points that can't be rightly read without sifting through the complicated immediate sentences that led to them as well as the many quieter chapters on the same subject that preceded and followed." This story will address all angles of the Pennsylvania Hall riot. It will start with the quieter chapters that set an important context before proceeding to the narrative-driven account of the pivotal moment itself and then ending with the "complicated sentences" that analyze the significance of it all.[5]

ACKNOWLEDGMENTS

....

A number of people have helped me in my effort to tell the story of Pennsylvania Hall. It all started many years ago when Phil Lapsansky told me he thought someone should write a book about the mobbing. I met Phil at the Library Company of Philadelphia, where for the past forty-one years he has offered guidance and suggestions to those of us interested in African American history. Other friends at the Library Company and the Historical Society of Pennsylvania have also played key roles in seeing this book to completion. The Library Company granted me the Albert M. Greenfield Fellowship in African American History to fund the research for the project. Connie King made the Library Company welcoming and made me feel at home there, as she always has. Jim Green also offered advice and assistance. Nicole Joniec helped me with all of the images. Lee Arnold and Tamara Gaskell at the HSP provided valuable insight and encouragement. Other research fellows who helped make the time I spent in Philadelphia tremendously enjoyable were Alice Taylor, Alea Henley, Jessica Linker, Jessica Roney, Jonathan Nash, Michael Goode, Cassandra Good, and Jane Calvert. Also during the course of writing this book I was lucky enough to meet Ira V. Brown, even if only by mail. Ira laid the cornerstone for the field of Pennsylvania abolition and he generously shared his expertise and advice on this project. In addition to our correspondence, this book could not have been written without his path-breaking work on the state's immediate abolition movement.

Many other friends helped in various ways. Alice Taylor read parts of the manuscript and gave very useful feedback. GG Hunt, my former division chair at Wharton County Junior College, secured travel funds so I could conduct research and present papers on the topic. Lou Ellen Callarman, Shirley Parkan, and the rest of the inter-library loan staff at the Victoria College/University of Houston-Victoria Library cheerfully and patiently helped me gather research materials from many distant places, and Lou Ellen checked in regularly to see how my progress was going. Richard Blackett, Hal Smith, Judith McArthur, Vikki Bynum, Gregg Andrews, Vernon Burton, Amanda Shelton, Manny Ness, Brian Walter, Angela Murphy, Theresa Jack, Marjorie Brown, and Karen Guenther also offered encouragement. James Kirby Martin not only reacted enthusiastically to the project but also introduced me to Brian Wheel, my editor at Oxford University Press. Both of these men, along with Karen Omer and my readers at OUP, helped me refine the manuscript and tell the story in a way that I hope reaches many readers. The OUP readers include, but are not limited to, Vernon Burton, Clemson University; Gary T. Edwards, Arkansas State University; Mark Elliott, University of North Carolina at Greensboro; J. Matthew Gallman, University of Florida; Emma Lapsansky, Haverford College; John Navin, Coastal Carolina University; Richard Newman, Rochester Institute of Technology; and Gregory Smithers, University of Aberdeen.

Finally, I could not have finished this book without the help of my family, including my husband, Bobby; my sons, Joey, Andy, and Grady; my sister, Brenda Hermes; my mother, Alberta Titus; my father, Hal Scull; my brother, Bruce Scull; and my mother-in-law, Vlasta Tomek.

I dedicate the book to the two men who had the most impact on this project from a professional standpoint. I have benefitted immensely from the privilege of knowing these scholars and counting them among my mentors and my friends. I just wish Ira could have seen the final product.

CHAPTER 1

....

Pennsylvania's Antislavery Background

Charles W. Gardner looked with pride at the spacious lot at the corner of Sixth and Haines streets, near Franklin Square. The location was both symbolically and strategically ideal. Men of the previous generation had framed a new government just blocks away, where the Liberty Bell sat perched atop Independence Hall. From there, they had issued a Constitution that guaranteed Americans the right to freely express themselves. Also nearby sat Quaker meeting houses that had sheltered abolitionists for generations as they voiced their opposition to slavery. Indeed, this neighborhood had witnessed many momentous events. The men who laid the groundwork for the nation had walked these streets, as had those who put in motion the nation's abolition movement. And now, in the spring of 1837, Gardner and his associates owned a small piece of this world.

Gardner had come a long way since his early days as a New Jersey shoemaker. He thought of the years he had spent traveling throughout the Upper South as an itinerant Methodist preacher. That adventure almost cost him his freedom. As an African American, he often found himself focusing on the critique of slavery that John Wesley, the founder of Methodism, shared with his followers. Unfortunately not many in the South wanted to hear about this side of the faith, and white Methodist leaders tried to force him to stop delivering his fiery antislavery sermons. Instead he added fuel by arguing not only against slavery but also against the American Colonization Society (ACS). Leaders of this group traveled similar routes and held meetings in churches, where they argued that slavery in the United States could be ended only if the freed slaves could be "returned" to Africa. Though Gardner was black he had never been to Africa in the first place, and he had no desire to leave his homeland for an unfamiliar place. He was born in New Jersey and had every intention of spending his life in the mid-Atlantic region.

Many leaders of the ACS wanted American blacks to follow their advice, not to question their logic, so they resented men like Gardner. Baltimore colonizationists seized their opportunity to silence this opponent by having him arrested. The preacher had traveled to the Southern city knowing that free blacks were allowed to remain there only ten days before facing imprisonment. He had not intended to overstay his welcome, but nobody plans to become ill. The sickness had immobilized him and stranded him in the hostile city, where local colonizationists had him arrested.

If his opponents meant to silence him they failed miserably. Further determined to oppose both slavery and colonization, Gardner settled in Philadelphia in the early 1830s. He was thrilled to accept a position as pastor of the First Presbyterian Church in 1836, and he soon became a leading figure in the city's black community. He also gained prominence as one of Pennsylvania's most active black abolitionists, even though he never gained material wealth.[1]

Soon the abolitionists who embraced Gardner would begin tearing down the buildings on their lot so they could create a special site where they hoped to fuse the Constitution's guarantees with their Quaker predecessors' dreams of true freedom for all Americans. As Gardner watched the progress of the project he noted how far the abolition movement had come.

The Home of Gradual Abolition

Philadelphia's abolitionist history began well before Gardner arrived in the city. Indeed, it began even before the American Revolution. In the 1670s George Fox, the founder of the Society of Friends, or Quakers, visited the New World, where he observed slavery first hand. Realizing the error of human bondage but also deciding that slaves would need to be prepared for independent life, he began to argue that masters should free their slaves after a period of service. Soon after that, Quakers in Germantown issued the first formal outcry against slavery—the 1688 Germantown Petition. Within a decade the Philadelphia Yearly Meeting took a stand against slavery by speaking out against involvement in the slave trade, but they fell short of calling upon all slaveholders to free their slaves.

From the very beginning the American abolition movement faced important tactical questions that Gardner and his friends were still trying to answer in 1837. The most important of those questions was whether they should use dramatic action to open the eyes of slaveholders and force them to acknowledge the errors of their ways, or whether they should gently appeal to those slaveholders and convince them with reasoned arguments to abandon bound labor.

Those who chose dramatic action followed in the footsteps of one of history's most eccentric abolitionists—a four-foot-tall vegetarian who reportedly lived in a cave. After seeing slavery first hand in Barbados, Benjamin Lay headed for Philadelphia on a mission to convince Quakers to have nothing to do with human bondage. Feeling ignored, he decided to show his neighbors how it felt to be a slave. Perhaps he learned from the slaves he met in Barbados that the worst part of their condition was not the physical brutality but the separation families faced when children were taken away and sold. Realizing that experiences made stronger impressions than words, he kidnapped a child from the close-knit Quaker community. This stunt likely turned off more people than it enlisted to the cause. Undeterred, Lay wrote a book that accused many individual Quakers, as well as the Society as a whole, of being connected to the slave system. *All Slave-Keepers that Keep the Innocent in Bondage* was published in 1737 in Philadelphia by a local printer named Benjamin Franklin, one hundred years before Gardner and his associates began raising money to build their abolition hall. It caused an immediate stir, leading many Quakers to try desperately to distance themselves from Lay.

In a final dramatic act that would get him disowned from the Society altogether, Lay carved out the center of a book that resembled the Bible and placed inside it a bladder filled with red liquid that some witnesses said was blood. Others reported it was pokeberry juice, but whatever it was, it served to make his point. He showed up at the 1738 Philadelphia Yearly Meeting, the Quakers' main annual gathering, wearing a military uniform and carrying the Bible in one hand and a sword in the other. This was enough for the Quakers, whose peace testimony led them to avoid all things military. It was not enough for Lay, however. Standing in front of the group he told them that their connection to slavery was a sin and that God would be perfectly justified in thrusting a sword through their hearts. As he uttered these harsh words, he stabbed the Bible with the sword and sent the liquid spewing all over those nearest him. Instead of converting his fellow Quakers to abolition, however, his dramatic behavior led them to reject him completely.[2]

Gardner never understood men like Lay. Too often, as he had seen during his own lifetime, this kind of behavior only irritated onlookers. In many cases those who were offended took their irritation out on their black neighbors. As a black man living in one of the most violent periods of U.S. history, he was tired of suffering for the radical actions of others. Gardner admired more level-headed abolitionists, many of whom modeled their behavior and tactics after John Woolman rather than Benjamin Lay.

Whether eighteen-year-old Woolman had been in the 1738 Yearly Meeting to witness Lay in action or not, he decided that radical and offensive behavior alienated possible followers. Woolman, who agreed with Lay that slavery was a sin that must be eradicated, used a softer approach and was able to win Friends over to the abolition cause, leading many to free their own slaves. Patiently counseling his fellow Quakers in public and private and accepting partial victories when that was all he could obtain, he managed to strike a balance between pressing the need for immediate action and accepting a slower pace of change out of concern for the unity of his religious society. His willingness to accept partial victories and to act in a manner mild enough to prevent social upheaval illustrates a very important aspect of Quaker reform.

In their quest for religious freedom the Society of Friends had pioneered the concept of civil disobedience, but they had also learned that civil disobedience taken too far could easily lead to backlash that would hamper or even destroy the cause. To Gardner it was a matter of common sense. As a man who faced the real possibility of suffering such backlash head on, he agreed with many of his Quaker associates that it was often best to work in stealth mode and push quietly for their goals rather than confront the opposition in dramatic fashion.

Of course, not all abolitionists agreed, and they continued to debate the merits of Lay's drama and Woolman's moderation. Gardner was aware of the tension as he stood on Sixth Street admiring the lot, and his musings foreshadowed an intense drama soon to occur on that very spot.

Woolman's tactics prevailed in the early years of the antislavery movement, a period described by historians as the era of "Gradual Abolition." Beginning around 1750 Woolman began to warn his fellow Quakers that if people allowed their neighbors to own slaves, then they were guilty by association. Thus, slavery was a sin the entire society shared. Quaker leaders began to consider the issue at their yearly meetings—annual gatherings where the leadership of local groups assembled to adopt policies for the international Society of Friends. In 1757 the London Yearly Meeting adopted Woolman's stance and expressed clear opposition to any connection with slavery. A year later the Philadelphia Yearly Meeting followed, and by 1760 the Society of Friends was officially an antislavery organization. In 1765 the Philadelphia group adopted the idea of freedom as a natural right, essentially endorsing the notion that slaves should be immediately emancipated. Even after unequivocally committing to abolition, Quakers proceeded moderately in the implementation of their reform agenda.[3]

Although the early Quaker abolitionists did not offer black leaders like Gardner positions of equality in their movement, they did concern themselves with the welfare of free blacks. They believed from the beginning that true freedom would have to include a program of black uplift through education, indentures, vocational training, and moral oversight. In 1766 a group of Friends bought slaves with the intention of freeing them after a period of indenture, and four years later another group, led by a teacher named Anthony Benezet, began what would lead to a long tradition of Quaker efforts to offer education for free blacks. Benezet became one of the most important early abolitionists, and his influence reached far beyond Philadelphia. Many of those convinced by Benezet's writings and example were not Quakers, and his influence provided a crucial first step in taking the antislavery message beyond both the Society of Friends and the borders of Pennsylvania.[4]

The era of the American Revolution saw a spread in antislavery rhetoric and further awakening of Americans to the evils of human bondage. As colonists cried out against their own "slavery" at the hands of the British, some began to realize the hypocrisy of fighting for their own freedom while denying liberty to others. With this thought in mind, the group that would become the Pennsylvania Abolition Society (PAS) met in the Sun Tavern on Second Street in Philadelphia on April 14, 1775. Originally calling themselves the "Society for the Relief of Free Negroes Unlawfully Held in Bondage," the group, which was composed mostly of Quakers, began by focusing on the fate of a woman named Dinah Nevill and her children, all of whom were illegally enslaved. The immediate goal was to identify cases in which people were legally free yet held in bondage and sue under existing law to secure their freedom.

Meanwhile, in 1776, as the members of the Second Continental Congress were declaring independence from England, the Philadelphia Yearly Meeting took the ultimate step of prescribing disownment for Friends who refused to free their slaves. By 1783—fifty years after Lay's final appeal—the Philadelphia group was able to report that no members owned slaves. Beyond these measures, abolition took a backseat to other political developments in North America, and the PAS operated largely under the radar until the end of the Revolution. Five months after the war ended, however, the group began to meet formally again after hearing stories of people who had committed suicide rather than allowing themselves to be illegally re-enslaved. With that, the PAS began fighting to ensure that the law was upheld and those who were legally free would be left free.

As the colonists fought for independence, colonial leaders began to write what would become their state constitutions and laws, and some Pennsylvania legislators took that opportunity to advance the work of abolition to a new level. In 1778 they began debating a bill that provided for gradual abolition of all slaves in the state. Despite opposition and a heated debate, the bill passed and in 1780 the Pennsylvania Assembly enacted the first abolition act in the United States. This bill had its limits, leaving slavery to exist in Pennsylvania until the 1840s, but it was an important first step to ending slavery not only in Pennsylvania but in the nation. Allowing slave owners to recapture their investments by keeping their current slaves and freeing their offspring after a period of indenture, the law provided for gradual rather than immediate freedom. The generation of adults enslaved when the law passed would die as slaves, but their children would see freedom after they reached adulthood. Owners also had to post bonds on all manumitted slaves, to provide for their care should they become indigent. This move ensured that the burden of emancipation would not fall on non-slaveholders, and it provided incentive for owners to train their slaves and teach them basic skills to support themselves once freed.

In addition to those provisions, the legislature also passed laws regulating black conduct. Lawmakers prohibited the freed from vagrancy, interaction with those who remained in bondage, and racial mixing. These laws reveal much about the concerns of whites who wanted to end slavery but were uneasy about a biracial society, and they illustrate the similarities between the post-emancipation North and the South after the Civil War. Though a generation apart, to some extent both sections faced the challenges of reconstructing their societies in the wake of emancipation, and in both cases the primary goal was to keep the existing social order intact. Border North states like Pennsylvania faced this challenge more acutely than New England states like Vermont or Maine because of their proximity to Southern slavery.[5]

While white supremacy was not necessarily as ingrained into Pennsylvania society in 1780 as it would be in the South in 1865, there was a clear racial hierarchy that even most reformers observed. It was assumed that whites were and would remain at the top of the social order and that blacks would have to be somehow molded to fit in without causing too much upheaval. Adding to the challenge, not all Pennsylvanians supported black freedom, and many refused to believe that blacks and whites could live together in peace. Others feared that abolition in their state would help fuel American sectionalism by offering what both slaves and their owners rightly perceived as a safe haven for blacks who could find their way there.

Despite the grumbling that could be heard from both their neighbors to the South and some of their fellow Pennsylvanians, the PAS continued to push forth their agenda of freedom. Once the abolition law took effect they helped slaves gain their rights, using technicalities when they had to, and learning all of the loopholes and defects in the legislation. Though they did not take the bold step of calling slaveholders to task in states where slavery was still legal, as immediatists like Gardner and his friends would do in the 1830s, they did prohibit any slaveholders or public defenders of slavery from joining the society.

As the PAS grew it began to attract well-known non-Quakers such as Benjamin Franklin and Benjamin Rush, and the leaders began to keep detailed manumission and indenture data to provide evidence in court. This step was necessary due to the increasing kidnapping of free blacks under the guise that they were fugitive slaves, an action made fairly easy by a Fugitive Slave Clause in the newly adopted U.S. Constitution of 1787. This clause stated that any person legally held to service or labor in one state would be returned to that state if he or she escaped into another. Though the framers of the document carefully avoided the word "slave" throughout, clauses like this one secured slavery in the United States and set the precedent for fugitive slave laws that would require free states to aid in the capture of runaway slaves.[6]

The PAS reacted to this development in a variety of ways. Some members began to buy slaves and sign them to indentures with the ultimate goal of freedom. Others studied the clause carefully in search of loopholes and collected important data in preparation for court battles. Some began to push for further state action to secure black freedom. Their efforts made it much more difficult to evade the original abolition act and led to an even stronger act that forbade slave owners from taking pregnant slaves outside the state to give birth, something they were doing to deprive the newborns of their eventual freedom by denying their Pennsylvania citizenship. The new act also prohibited separating families by more than ten miles and taking blacks from Pennsylvania by force or fraud to keep them in, or sell them into, slavery. The goal was to prevent kidnappings and to stop whites from evading the abolition law. At the same time, PAS members continued to try in vain to convince the legislature to solve the problem once and for all by declaring slavery altogether illegal in Pennsylvania. Their efforts to push the matter, combined with their ability to gauge where to stop before taking the matter too far, showed Woolman's influence.

The PAS had a broad abolition agenda. On the one hand, they focused on ending the African slave trade, certain that such a move would lead to the eventual demise of slavery itself. They took pride in the fact that their president, Benjamin Franklin, played an important role in securing a clause in the federal Constitution that said that the national government would not interfere with the slave trade for twenty years but implied that it would be ended at that point. Meanwhile, they continued to fight the trade and fought against a bill that would have allowed officers of the U.S. government to hold slaves while in Pennsylvania. They even tried, though unsuccessfully, to take a case before the state supreme court to test the constitutionality of slavery under the 1790 state constitution. They also petitioned against the expansion of slavery.[7]

Free Blacks in Post-Emancipation Pennsylvania

Even as they continued to fight bondage, the PAS began to look further into the future, adopting in 1787 a "Plan for Improving the Condition of the Free Blacks" to help prepare the freed for their place in society and perhaps help alleviate the fears of some of their white neighbors. To this end they assumed responsibility for providing free blacks education, vocational training, apprenticeship opportunities, assistance in obtaining employment, and advice for moral improvement. Three years later they created a series of committees to oversee the transition to freedom, much like the Freedmen's Bureau would do in the post-emancipation South. The Committee of Education was the strongest and longest-lasting of these.

The Committee of Education began its work by reaching out to the Free African Society for assistance in conducting a survey of the black community. Richard Allen, a leader among the first generation of black abolitionists and civil rights activists, had helped found the society in 1787. Best known for his role in establishing Mother Bethel Church and the African Methodist Episcopal Church, Allen helped set the bedrock for the largest, most successful free black community in the nation, often serving as liaison between the PAS and the black community.

Through the Free African Society, churches like Mother Bethel (the first independent black Christian church in the world, founded in 1794) and the African Episcopal Church of St. Thomas (the first African Baptist church, founded in 1792), independent schools, mutual aid societies, political action groups, and literary and reform societies, Allen and other black leaders, including Absalom Jones, Cyrus Bustill, and James Forten, worked to help recently freed people and newcomers to the city gain a foothold in society by securing employment, obtaining education, and learning the middle-class rules of conduct essential in gaining acceptance and, they hoped, respectability. Gardner met some of these men when he arrived in Philadelphia and they introduced him to their white friends in the PAS. While Allen and Gardner helped the white abolitionists collect information about the black community in their ongoing effort to defend blacks from maltreatment, wealthier men like Forten supported the Abolition Society through advice as well as monetary donations. Though none of Gardner's black friends ever joined the society, their work paralleled that of the PAS. Membership in the abolition society was by induction only, and even though black leaders served as intermediaries between white abolitionists and the black community, it never occurred to the members to invite their black associates into their ranks.

Even so, abolitionists of both colors were determined to help blacks find better opportunities. The PAS created the Committee of Employ to oversee job placement for adults and the Committee of Guardians to assist the youth. To help black parents secure job training for their children, the PAS founded the Committee of Apprentices. Each of these committees was short-lived due to lack of enthusiasm among potential clients. Obviously what the PAS saw as benevolent assistance many free blacks saw as paternalistic meddling, despite the involvement of black leaders. Black and white leaders also tried to direct the "moral improvement" of the community. The PAS's Committee of Inspection worked in cooperation with the Free African Society to come up with a plan for improving the condition of free blacks. Black leaders also developed temperance societies and self-help groups with their own uplift agendas.[8]

Black and white community leaders recognized the volatile situation that was brewing, and they did their best to foster smooth relations between the city's white and black residents. They shared a belief in the improvement and perfectibility of mankind, and they hoped to convince the masses—black and white alike—of the merits of hard work and good behavior. Whether they were white or black, social leaders of the time worked to suppress vice, train the poor, assist the indigent, educate the masses, and reform all aspects of society to create an uplifted world. The problem, however, was that racism had taken such a strong root in U.S. society that no amount of uplifting would convince most whites to accept their black neighbors.

As historian Gary Nash has shown in his pioneering study of Philadelphia's free black community, after the city gained a reputation for welcoming free blacks in the 1780s it saw "the first gathering in one American community of a large number of former slaves." By 1783 this black community consisted of over eight hundred people, made up of blacks who had been freed in the city as well as others who had moved there after gaining their freedom elsewhere. Some of these residents were poor workers in search of job opportunities but others, like James Forten, were veterans who had fought for their country during the American Revolution and managed to gain wealth through hard work. Regardless of their class, Nash argued, "individually and collectively, black Philadelphians faced the momentous task of completing the passage from bondage to freedom," and they did so under the weary watch of white neighbors who expected the worst and assumed that blacks were either naturally inferior to whites or had been made so by the debilitating effects of slavery. As skeptical whites questioned whether blacks were capable of citizenship, black and white abolitionists tried to prove the affirmative without agitating their detractors.[9]

At first the gradualist program seemed to be working. Soon groups from New York, Delaware, and New Jersey joined the fight to end slavery in their respective states, and in 1794 these groups united with the PAS to form the American Convention of Abolition Societies. Clearly the dominant force in this joint endeavor, the PAS had been pushing for such a union since 1790, and the convention first met in Philadelphia City Hall. They would meet in twenty-five sessions between 1794 and 1829, and one final time in 1837 as Gardner and his friends were building their hall. The PAS and the New York Manumission Society participated in every meeting, though eleven states and the District of Columbia participated at one time or another. All but four of the yearly meetings were in Philadelphia, and when the group disbanded in 1837 the PAS assumed responsibility for all American Convention records.

In general, gradualists followed Woolman's lead by seeking workable solutions and remaining firm and sincere in their efforts, even if they had to be prudent and careful in their tactics. The American Convention focused on protecting free blacks' legal rights, promoting abolition, and uplifting free blacks. They kept careful manumission records to prevent kidnapping, encouraged opponents of slavery in the South to push for state laws to end the institution, attacked the foreign slave trade, urged state laws to prohibit interstate slave trading, and fought to outlaw slavery in the District of Columbia. They also pushed to keep slavery out of the Western territories. With the growth of the American Convention, support for emancipation spread beyond the state, but Pennsylvania remained at the vanguard of the movement.

CHAPTER 2

....

Free Produce and the
Origins of Modern Abolition

Charles Gardner was not alone in his excitement over the activity at Sixth and Haines. Blocks away at his newspaper office at 223 Arch Street, Benjamin Lundy also anticipated the new hall. As he looked around the office he thought about the task ahead. His newspaper, the *National Enquirer and General Register*, was the city's antislavery newspaper and had been offered a new home in the basement of the hall.

Pennsylvania abolition was undergoing a renaissance, and Lundy was excited to be part of it. In the decade since he arrived in Philadelphia the city's abolitionists had embraced the free produce movement with enthusiasm and they eagerly supported the *Enquirer*. Sure, they engaged in tactical debates from time to time, as did all abolitionists throughout the United States. For the time being, however, they were working together to build what would surely be one of the most important buildings in a city filled with significant landmarks. Full of optimism as he thought about what he and his friends were starting to call Pennsylvania Hall, Lundy chose not to dwell upon just how badly things could go.

Lundy had visited Philadelphia a decade earlier, two years after attracting the attention of the gradualists who met in Baltimore for the 1826 American Convention of Abolition Societies. Like Gardner, Lundy began his abolition career in this border South city where he published one of the nation's first antislavery newspapers, *The Genius of Universal Emancipation*. He also owned and operated a unique grocery store, and that was what had attracted the attention of the gradualists.

Like most of his friends in the Pennsylvania Abolition Society (PAS), Lundy was a Quaker who admired John Woolman's early anti-slavery efforts. While most Pennsylvania abolitionists had focused primarily on challenging slavery in the courts, Lundy had taken up a different tactic, one invented by Woolman himself: he had refused to buy or sell any goods produced by slave labor. Woolman began this "free produce" movement by refusing to wear any clothing made of the cotton and dyes grown by slaves. Following his example, others like Lundy also refused to use slave-grown sugar. Of course, most cloth and sugar in the United States came from raw materials grown by slaves, so the trick was being able to find untainted goods. Lundy worked hard to find suppliers who could provide products untouched by the moral taint of slavery.

Lundy's customers realized that they would not likely make enough of an economic impact to make slavery less profitable, but that was not the point. Sure, in one sense free produce was a boycott. If people refused to buy goods produced by slave labor, slavery would lead to economic loss rather than profits, so slave owners would free the slaves. The problem, however, was that for this boycott to work it would have to appeal to a majority of American and British consumers, and it did not. In that sense the movement would be viewed as a failure, but the truth is that it was never just a boycott in the traditional sense to those who participated. Certainly adherents would have loved to make an economic impact large enough to end slavery, but they realized the unlikelihood of that happening. Whether their neighbors would join them or not, they knew that their own consciences were free. The products cost more and were inferior in quality, but they believed the benefits to their souls outweighed the inconvenience.

Though free produce had been around for generations it did not become a major tenet of Quaker abolitionists until it was embraced by Elias Hicks. Hicks led a split among Quakers in 1827 and encouraged his followers to focus more on obeying their "Inner Light" (the Holy Spirit's appeal to their consciences) than the rules of church and society. For Hicks, the conscience should always be a person's guide, and his conscience told him to avoid slave produce. He remained dedicated to this principle even on his deathbed, when someone placed a cotton blanket on him and he insisted that it be removed. Influenced by Hicks and the writing of English Quaker Elizabeth Heyrick,

Hicksites adopted free produce as a major part of their abolition agenda. James and Lucretia Mott of Philadelphia were two early adherents to Hicks's teachings, and James gave up a successful cotton textile business, choosing to deal in wool instead. The Motts both worked hard to bring free produce to the forefront of Pennsylvania's abolition movement. Though they gained the support of some gradualists, many others remained more concerned with improving the conditions of free blacks and protecting them from re-enslavement than with theoretical issues and moral boycotts.[1]

Lundy was most influential in taking free produce beyond the confines of Quaker abolition. Like Gardner, he was a craftsman from New Jersey who had abandoned his career, choosing instead to travel throughout the Ohio Valley and the upper South as an itinerant speaker. While Gardner preached Methodism and brought abolition into his lectures when he could, Lundy dedicated all of his time to witnessing against slavery. At just the moment that Northern abolition and manumission societies were beginning to bog down with their legal issues, Lundy was gaining support from manumission societies throughout the border South, eventually ending up in Baltimore, where he opened his free produce store in 1824. Like Woolman and most of the gradualists, Lundy remained flexible and willing to employ a number of tactics to secure black freedom, including resettlement or colonization, especially to Haiti or the Caribbean. He sometimes tied resettlement to free produce, hoping that resettled communities would someday grow cotton to compete with that produced by slaves.

Lundy's focus and outlook comported with the traditional abolition of the PAS and Woolman. He appealed to reason and to the consciences of his listeners and readers, remaining certain that the way to end slavery would be to convince slaveholders in the South to free their slaves voluntarily. He argued that Americans in the Northern states had a duty to assert their "moral strength" and show their Southern neighbors the error of their ways. In this sense he was the father of a tactic known as "moral suasion"—a tactic often associated with his protégée, William Lloyd Garrison.[2]

After the American Convention delegates visited Lundy's store, they adopted a resolution in support of free produce. Soon free produce organizations began to spring up in Delaware and Pennsylvania. In 1828 Lundy traveled to the home of gradual abolition and called a meeting to consider the merits of his moral boycott. As a result the Free Produce Society of Pennsylvania was organized in Philadelphia and several free produce stores opened in the city. The movement would reach its peak in 1838 with the formation of the American Free Produce Association at Pennsylvania Hall. By bringing free produce to the forefront and making slavery a moral issue, Lundy transformed the antislavery movement. He provided a bridge between gradualism and the radical abolitionists of Garrison's generation. Even as gradualists supported his efforts, they also worried that his enthusiasm would spread and eventually disrupt the social unity of the nation.

One major way free produce set the stage for the immediate abolition movement was by opening the door for women to participate in abolition. With its focus on such domestic endeavors as spinning yarn into cloth and guiding the family's choices in the realm of household consumption, it gave them a way to participate in an important abolition cause while remaining within their traditional sphere of influence. It also gave some women a new career option. Once the movement gained momentum it attracted enough support that Philadelphia was able to sustain a number of free produce stores, many of which were owned and operated by women.

Free produce led abolitionists to begin crossing racial as well as gender barriers. As it fueled the smoldering gradualist movement it drew in new support first from women like Lucretia Mott, a Hicksite Quaker who essentially became the matriarch of American antislavery, and then from black leaders like Richard Allen. Under Mott's guidance the women organized a female free produce association in 1829. Allen and his group followed, founding the Colored Free Produce Society in Allen's church in 1830. Leaders included Robert Purvis and James Cornish. A year later black women founded the Colored Female Free Produce Society.

Free produce reenergized the abolition movement, offering a more radical argument that unhesitatingly declared slavery a moral issue. While gradualists tried to reach out to slaveholders and convince them that ending slavery would benefit them in the long run, free produce adherents simply told them that what they were doing was wrong, clear and simple. This forceful stance paved the way for a new movement that had plenty of room for all abolitionists—black and white, male and female. It left black leaders believing that racial justice could be achieved.

Of course, it was not that simple. Slaveholders did not like being told they were wrong. They appealed to Northern friends to help fight off the abolitionist assault. They found a particularly receptive audience in Philadelphia, where many local whites needed little prodding to convince them that ending slavery was not in their own best interests. Despite Philadelphia's antislavery legacy, many white residents remained sympathetic to the South. Others wished not to endanger the Union and by 1830 had come to see abolition as an incendiary movement.[3]

Anti-Abolition Backlash

Resistance to the antislavery agenda surfaced immediately. When the PAS submitted to the first U.S. Congress a petition calling for national abolition in 1790, their efforts met with criticism in the Philadelphia newspapers. An anonymous writer going by "Rusticus" submitted a series of letters to the *Gazette of the United States* in which he argued that slavery would end once it ceased to be profitable and that interference with the process would lead to disaster unless followed by removal of free blacks. His idea of "disaster" was the threat of a biracial society that would include racial mixing, something referred to as "amalgamation" during this period. For people like Rusticus, racial purity was a crucial component of a successful republic and freeing blacks would get in the way of that goal. Abolitionists disagreed. They envisioned a republic with room for both white and black and believed that freeing slaves would be the best way to prevent a large-scale uprising or racial warfare. Detractors, on the other hand, argued that freeing blacks would lead to such chaos. The problem was a fundamentally different vision of the American future, and the abolitionists held the minority view.[4]

In Pennsylvania, those who did not share the inclusive vision began to panic when the state's reputation as a haven for blacks led to an increase in the free black population. In the first ten years after the abolition act, voluntary manumissions caused the slave population to drop from 10,000 to just above 3,000 in the state, but as the slave population shrank the free black population grew. By 1810 the free black population in Philadelphia (including the separately incorporated but geographically connected towns of Northern Liberties,

Southward, and Moyamensing) made up 9,653 of the city's population of 91,877, or 10.5 percent. Between 1810 and 1820 the city's
population grew to 113,000 people, and the free black population
grew to 12,110. This increase gave the city one of the largest concen-
trations of black residents in the North at the time. The trend continued in the following decades with more and more Southern blacks
seeking refuge in the city. In 1820 over 35 percent of the state's free
blacks lived there, and only about one-twelfth of the city's free blacks
had been born in Philadelphia.

What these numbers mean is that Philadelphia harbored a large
concentration of free blacks and many of them were immigrants from
other states, especially the nearby slave states of Virginia, Maryland, and
Delaware. Others came from as far away as the French colony of Santo
Domingo (which became the free nation of Haiti during this period).
White Philadelphians began to feel overwhelmed by the flood of black
immigrants, many of whom were recently freed or were fugitive slaves,
seeing them as foreign and threatening because of their differing life-
styles and lack of education. The proportion of blacks in the city began
to decline after 1812, but at that point it was a matter of perception
rather than reality as whites exaggerated the size of the black community and remained concerned that those who did migrate to the city
between 1790 and 1815 lacked important urban skills and were often in
poor health. These migrants faced deteriorating conditions and fewer
opportunities. Founders of mills and factories generally relied on native-
born and white immigrant workers and chose to exclude blacks, leaving
African Americans to positions as common laborers and seamen.[5]

Despite the obstacles, a number of free black Philadelphians acquired skilled positions or launched their own businesses. The city
contained a small but influential community of black professionals,
including ministers, teachers, and doctors. Others made respectable
and independent livings as barbers, tailors, shoemakers, carpenters,
bakers, and shopkeepers. By 1816 many of the city's black men had
risen to the rank of artisan, with one in every fifteen engaged in some
sort of craft. A number of free blacks made solid livings as caterers.
As a result, a visible black middle class began to form in the city. As
historian Emma Lapsansky-Werner has pointed out, the Philadelphia
black community was economically well off compared to other black
communities, but success could be a double-edged sword.[6]

As they watched the black population grow in numbers, many white Philadelphians began to regret the loss of social control that slavery had offered. In the North and the South alike, black bondage offered a way to maintain a clear racial order. In the absence of this regulating force, whites found it harder to control their black neighbors, giving rise to panic and resentment. In the post-emancipation North, as would also be the case after slavery ended in the South, freedom for blacks meant fear, distrust, and hatred on the part of many whites. Black success would also lead to jealousy and resentment. As a result, white Philadelphians began to present petitions to the state legislature calling for measures to make the city less attractive to black migrants. In addition to the fears of racial mixing and potential large-scale violence, they insisted that the black population contributed disproportionately to the city's crime rates and almshouses, though historians have proven that this was not the case. Beginning in 1805, then, lawmakers offered a series of proposals that called for restrictions upon black mobility, the imposition of special taxes on black residents, and the indenture of black felons through city auctions. Many whites saw removal of blacks to Haiti or Africa as the solution.

For most working-class whites, the main problem with the growing black presence was the resulting job competition. On the one hand were unskilled black laborers who sought to make a living in Philadelphia. They found themselves in competition for these jobs not only with native-born whites but also with ever-increasing numbers of Irish immigrants. The life these workers faced at the bottom of the U.S.'s labor pool was one of perpetual hardship and a constant struggle to get by, and the workers often turned on each other in resentment. On the other hand, Philadelphia contained one of the largest populations of skilled black workers in the nation. Black artisans competed in an atmosphere intensified by industrialization and mechanization as steam-powered machines displaced skilled workers regardless of skin color.

Philadelphia's elite African American families also faced the wrath of their white neighbors. While poorer whites saw blacks of their own class as competitors for jobs, they resented blacks of higher socioeconomic classes just as much, if not more. James Forten, for example, employed whites in his highly profitable sail-making loft, and he owned a number of rental properties, some of which he rented out to white tenants. Many whites of all classes saw his success as evidence that he had ventured outside his "proper" place at the bottom of society. They did not like men like Forten becoming "uppity" and climbing to the top of the social and economic ladder. They also argued that as black men sought to compete with their wealthier neighbors they would be more likely to marry white women. Clearly black efforts to forge an autonomous existence earned them the wrath rather than the admiration of many white Philadelphians. Though race riots did not become a serious threat until after 1830, this resentment made its way into popular culture through caricatures and cartoons that appeared in the 1820s.

In this climate both black leaders and gradualists could be described as victims of their own success. Even though historians have described the tactics of gradual abolitionists as moderate, many contemporaries in both the South and the North saw them as radical and threatening enough. For one matter, the very presence of antislavery agitation in the United States put slaveholding states on the defensive, and many Southerners in turn called upon their friends and families in the North to protect them from abolitionist agitation. At the same time, abolitionist efforts led to growth in the free black population throughout the free states, creating a situation that had the potential to drastically transform society. For these reasons the Pennsylvania abolition bill, often cited as weak or "watered down" by historians and contemporary critics, immediately faced numerous attempts at repeal. Despite this resistance, the act was never repealed and abolitionists and free blacks pushed for the ultimate end to slavery.

Between 1804 and 1817 both groups were under attack from many directions. Some argued that since the state had passed the gradual abolition law there was no further need for the movement. Others argued that further efforts had simply led to an increase in the black population and that this trend would continue because slaves and free blacks alike saw the state as a beacon of liberty. In 1809 a PAS member warned that their past success had created a situation that had to be handled cautiously: "hitherto, the approving voice of the community, and the liberal interpretation of the laws, have smoothed the path of duty, and promoted a satisfactory issue to our humane exertions" but now "prudence has become necessary to our security, and persuasion to our success."[7]

In addition to resentment over the growing black population, opponents argued that abolition was causing sectional animosity.

Pennsylvania's commitment to abolition angered its neighbors, especially Maryland, with whom it shared its southern border. Maryland slave-holders resented PAS interference with their rights to chase fugitive slaves into Pennsylvania, and abolitionists resented Maryland's disregard for Pennsylvania's state sovereignty. At the same time, the PAS found itself in conflict with South Carolina over a law that led to the imprison-ment of innocent free blacks. Much like the Maryland law later used to detain Gardner, the South Carolina law restricted the rights of free blacks who traveled into the state. It required black seamen to remain in jail while their ships were docked in South Carolina's ports. The men were released only to board the ship as it left the state. Abolitionists pointed out that the law led to the imprisonment of black Pennsylvanians simply for entering South Carolina, and they pointed out that, given the number of concessions their state had granted slave interests, the least they asked in return was protection for their own citizens who traveled in slave states. This request was posed just as legislators were engaged in heated debate over whether Missouri would be admitted as a free or slave state. To white Northerners not committed to abolition on principle, the im-mediate urgency was not to antagonize their friends, family, and business associates in the South.

The Abolitionist Response

The PAS remained determined to fight against slavery but they also had to do something to answer their critics and help free blacks suc-ceed in the face of this backlash. The group's immediate reaction to the growing hostility around them was to work even harder on their uplift agenda. They began by buying a lot on Cherry Street between Sixth and Seventh Streets, blocks from where Gardner and his friends would build their hall in 1837. This location became the home of Clarkson Hall, a building that would eventually house a boys' school, a girls' school, a high school, and several night schools. It would also serve as PAS headquarters for many years.

Gradualists also continued to fight against slavery and for the rights of free blacks. Introducing a memorial to the state legislature in 1811 calling for stricter penalties for kidnapping free blacks, they helped push through what some historians have described as the na-tion's first personal liberty law. This act, passed in 1820, imposed fines of $500 to $2,000 and prison sentences of seven to twenty-one years for those convicted of kidnapping free blacks and required judges to file reports on all fugitives returned to slavery. Arguing that the District of Columbia, unlike the states, was the direct domain of Congress, they pushed for abolition of slavery there, and they vigorously opposed the spread of slavery into new territories.

At the same time, gradualists continued to protest provisions of the 1807 Slave Trade Act that left confiscated slaves brought illegally into the country in the possession of the state in which they were landed. They argued that this provision left the fate of people who were legally free in the hands of those who would benefit from the opportunity to leave them in slavery. Congress eventually took heed, but the result was not quite what abolitionists had expected. Rather than freeing the recaptives outright, Congress provided that, beginning in 1819, they would be returned to Africa. Instead of their point of origin, however, they would be sent to the American Colonization Society (ACS)'s African colony of Liberia.

PAS members had mixed feelings about this development. Gradualists were still trying to decide exactly how to react to the colonization movement. Repatriation was not a new idea in 1817 when the ACS was formed. By that point a number of resettlement schemes had been put forth by both black and white leaders, often with the argument that slaveholders would be more willing to free their slaves if they had some place to send them after freeing them. The territories of the American West, Haiti, and Africa had all been suggested as possible locations for such a colony but after the ACS was founded, Africa became the main focus. As the society gained support in Pennsylvania, the PAS was forced to consider the merits of its scheme.

Gradualists knew from observation how the general public was reacting to the growing free black population in their state. They had been buying slaves to free them since 1766, but they had stopped this practice in the wake of the backlash. They had also stopped accepting slaves given to them by slaveholders as a means to free them, knowing that by bringing more former slaves into the city and state they risked jeopardizing what public support they still enjoyed. They also realized that if they pushed too hard it could result in further unrest, violence, and even discriminatory laws preventing free blacks from migrating to Pennsylvania.

At this point the PAS was essentially walking on eggshells and risked undoing the progress they had made by enlarging the black population even more. History had taught them to stick to Woolman's tactics of knowing when to push forward and when to consolidate their gains. Could colonization offer a way to make abolition more viable? In the best case, colonization would aid emancipation by making it more palatable to non-slaveholding whites who resented the growth in the free black population. In the worst case, colonization would strengthen the bonds of slavery by removing only free blacks and thus taking away an important antislavery constituent.

The PAS and the American Convention of Abolition Societies set out to decide which case was most likely. After hearing arguments on both sides and debating the issue for years, they ultimately concluded that colonization had promise if and only if it were voluntary. Blacks who wanted a new start and were interested in seeking that beginning in Liberia should have the freedom to do so, but under no circumstances should blacks, slave or free, be forced to relocate. The problem for most abolitionists was that many slaveholders were on the board of the ACS, so they could never be sure what the group's true motives were. They added that any plan of removal must be preceded by a program of racial uplift and must have as its ultimate goal complete emancipation.

What helped most gradualists decide how they felt about the colonization movement was the reaction of the free black community. Before the ACS entered the scene, a black sea captain named Paul Cuffe had appealed to Philadelphia's black leaders for support in taking American blacks to the British colony of Sierra Leone. He had met with some success, gaining the endorsement of James Forten, Richard Allen, and Absalom Jones, but his plan fell through upon his death in 1817. By the time the ACS came to Philadelphia seeking support, some free black leaders had learned that most blacks agreed with Charles Gardner's rejection of white-initiated resettlement and had determined to fight the ACS. Like the PAS they questioned the ACS's motives, especially given the number of slaveholders who supported African repatriation. They renewed their efforts at self-help, and the PAS agreed, deciding to focus on its own program of racial uplift.[8]

While the free produce movement was infusing new life into antislavery, the anti-abolition backlash was growing and expanding.

As new states were added to the United States, some of them sought to keep African Americans out altogether. The Northwest Ordinance of 1787 had barred slavery from the Old Northwest, and Illinois, Indiana, and Ohio, some of the states that developed in this area, worked to keep free blacks out as well by adopting anti-immigration laws that banned them from settling within their borders and using "Black Laws" to keep tight control over those who did manage to move in. Ohio, for example, required black immigrants to post bonds of $500 to guarantee their good behavior and to furnish court documents that proved they were legally free and not escaped slaves. The laws had been passed in 1804 and 1807, but strict enforcement did not begin until 1829, when authorities in Cincinnati decided that the black community had grown too much and decided to prevent further growth through the Black Laws.

Many blacks considered leaving as mobs of whites began to roam the streets of their neighborhoods, terrorizing them. Having their minds made up for them, over 2,000 free blacks left Cincinnati for Canada. This story was repeated throughout the North and the Northwest as more and more blacks gained their freedom, either legally or through escape. As in Pennsylvania, whites throughout the country saw free blacks as job competitors and were put off by the idea of integration and racial "amalgamation." Where they could, they pushed for social separation that foreshadowed the Jim Crow system of the post-Civil War South. Many hoped that blacks would volunteer to be colonized in Africa or elsewhere, and many went so far as to insist that blacks who would not offer to leave should be forcefully expelled.

As more and more new states adopted exclusionary measures, the repression began to take hold in older states as well. Massachusetts and Pennsylvania legislatures considered barring free black immigration outright, and Pennsylvania and New York revised their state constitutions to restrict voting rights. In both states blacks could vote, at least in theory, until new constitutions took that right away. In Pennsylvania this process was under way as Pennsylvania Hall was under construction, and one of the goals of the people meeting in the hall would be to resist this measure. In addition to these legal measures against blacks, widespread mob action throughout the North made blacks miserable on a regular basis, pushing some to seek asylum in Canada or Africa, or at least to move on to the next state hoping for better prospects.

It was in this context that Richard Allen and Baltimore free black Hezekiel Grice began to call for a national convention where blacks could collectively consider their fate in the United States. Allen made the official call for the meeting, which was held in Bethel Church in September 1830. Blacks from Pennsylvania, New Jersey, New York, Connecticut, Rhode Island, Ohio, Maryland, Delaware, and Virginia participated, electing Allen as president and organizing the "American Society of Free People of Colour for improving their condition in the United States; for purchasing lands; and for the establishment of a settlement in the Province of Canada." They also wrote and put forth an "Address to the Free People of Colour of these United States," explaining that their goal was to work for self-elevation of the black race. They rejected the white-led ACS, but they shared Lundy's belief that blacks should consider emigration to other places. While Lundy continued to favor the Caribbean, black leaders ultimately chose to support an independent black-led effort to create a settlement in Canada.

Black leaders continued to meet annually between 1830 and 1835. Eventually rejecting Canadian emigration, the delegates continued to organize against the ACS's African settlement scheme. They also worked to create plans that would support their main goal of self-elevation through education and moral reform. Eventually their work led them to establish the American Moral Reform Society. By 1835 the convention movement began to wane, primarily due to debates about whether black leaders should build their own institutions or work harder for integration into white society.[9] For a time at least, that question would be settled by the emergence of a biracial movement for immediate abolition.

CHAPTER 3

....

A Biracial Movement for Immediate Emancipation

As he contemplated his move into the new hall, Benjamin Lundy also considered whom he might bring to Philadelphia to help him move the paper into its new home. He knew his choice had long-term consequences because he was tired and ill, and the person who helped him move would also be asked to take over editorial duties at the *Enquirer*. Perhaps with a bit of regret, he thought about the last time he hired an assistant.

After visiting Philadelphia in 1828 and helping the free produce movement get started, Lundy had traveled to Boston on a mission to raise money for the *Genius of Universal Emancipation*. While he was there he met two young journalists—William Lloyd Garrison and John Greenleaf Whittier. Whittier had been quiet and reserved but Garrison exuded enthusiasm, so much so that Lundy made the fateful decision to hire him as his assistant. He had no way of knowing that the decision would cost him his newspaper.

Garrison later claimed that he was immediately taken by Lundy and his cause. After meeting the icon of antislavery journalism, he quit his job at a national reform newspaper in hopes that Lundy would hire him to help at the *Genius*, but that did not happen for over a year. As he waited in anticipation for Lundy to send for him, he boarded with Whittier. At some point he dabbled with the colonization movement and was asked to deliver a Fourth of July speech for the ACS at the Park Street Church. To the horror of his hosts, however, he used the occasion to deliver a radical statement calling for not only the abolition of slavery but also civil rights for African Americans in the

26

United States. As he watched from the pews, Whittier recognized the revolutionary nature of his roommate's words, later offering him encouragement as the hosts of the speech expressed horror.

While this Park Street speech marked an important milestone along Garrison's path to immediatism, the final stop in his journey occurred when he attended a celebration of Britain's abolition of the slave trade sponsored by the African Abolition Freehold Society. As he sat listening to the black speakers at this event he began to see the nation's "race problem" through the eyes of black Americans. Soon after, he became acquainted with Elizabeth Heyrick's free produce pamphlet. After embracing immediate abolition, Garrison went on what was basically a religious crusade.[1] Had Lundy realized just how far the young man would go to forcefully convert the masses, he may have steered clear of this modern-day Benjamin Lay. As it was, he had no idea what Garrison had in mind. All he knew was that he needed an energetic assistant—and Garrison was nothing if not energetic.

The Ascendancy of Garrison

As soon as Lundy sent for Garrison, the young editor moved to Baltimore to help the mentor whose views he had transcended in many ways. While Lundy continued to follow Woolman's lead and consider all tactics, including resettlement, Garrison decided upon a different approach. Taking his cue from a militant black abolitionist named David Walker, who wrote in 1829 that colonization was a slaveholders' scheme to secure slavery by removing free blacks, Garrison decided to fight both slavery and the American Colonization Society (ACS).[2]

Unlike other white abolitionists who tried to walk a fine line and challenge slavery without imperiling the Union or scaring off the indifferent, Garrison began pushing unhesitatingly for racial equality and an end to the prejudice that held blacks back in the United States. This was in many ways a recipe for disaster as he headed to the border South city—a major slave-trading center—to work with Lundy. Garrison spent six months assisting Lundy on the *Genius* before he landed in jail for libel after one of his many editorial attacks upon a slave trader. He welcomed his prosecution for libel because he realized that it would take his cause beyond antislavery and show indifferent whites that their freedom of speech was as tenuous as the freedom of free blacks and that slavery was the root cause of their own oppression because slaveholders, as they fought fiercely to protect their "property," would stop at nothing to silence anyone who did not agree with them.

Though Garrison's title was Assistant Editor, in many ways he took over the paper and used it to push strongly for immediate emancipation. Even so, Lundy continued to advocate Haitian colonization in the columns of the paper, and Garrison tolerated it because he realized that there was a clear distinction between Lundy's plan, which he saw as voluntary and humanitarian, and the ACS's scheme, which he insisted would lead to mandatory deportation and strengthening of slavery in the United States. He knew his stance would provoke hostility from colonizationists as well as slaveholders, but he insisted that controversy would only open more and more people's eyes to immediatism. He does not appear to have considered how his behavior would affect Lundy and the *Genius*, or the antislavery movement in general.

Garrison reveled in his arrest and used his legal situation to great advantage. He was sentenced to six months in jail or a fine of $50 plus court costs, which altogether totaled $70. Whether he could have paid the fine or not, he preferred to make a statement by serving the time. He was, in the words of the presiding judge, "ambitious of becoming a martyr." The jailor and his family treated him kindly, keeping him in their own quarters to protect him from the other prisoners, since he looked even younger than his 24 years. When Lundy made his daily visits, Garrison met him at the front door. He also ate with the family and was allowed to keep a desk in their parlor. Such circumstances made it easy to make a principled stand. He spent his days composing a pamphlet that told about his trial, describing the situation in terms that highlighted his struggle to defend the rights of free press. This pamphlet caught the attention of wealthy philanthropist Arthur Tappan, who sent Lundy a note for $200—$100 to help Garrison gain his freedom and $100 to help fund the re-establishment of the *Genius*. A week later, after 49 days in jail, Garrison was free. He kept the receipt as a keepsake—a trophy of sorts. Though he remained supportive throughout Garrison's confinement, Lundy had had enough of his inflammatory tactics and made it clear that he alone would work on the newly rescued *Genius*. The two men parted on friendly terms, though there is no record that they made any effort to reconnect.[3]

Lundy's advice, however, did lead Garrison to Philadelphia in 1830 upon his release from the Baltimore prison. The young editor was looking for a place to start an antislavery newspaper of his own and was considering the Quaker city. During his time there Lundy's Quaker abolitionist friends received his protégé warmly and arranged for him to lecture at the Franklin Institute. There Garrison introduced his doctrine of immediate emancipation and blasted colonization as a false reform in front of an audience made up of Quakers, including the Motts, and black leaders, including James Forten. Lucretia Mott, kind and supportive of his aims, helped him practice and improve his dry delivery, and Forten offered him guidance in his crusade against colonization and provided much-needed financial backing. All in all he was treated kindly in Philadelphia, gaining the support of the nation's abolitionist matriarch and the wealthiest African American activist in the country.

After leaving Philadelphia, Garrison embarked on an East Coast speaking tour that led him to Boston, where he established contact with a number of reformers who would help him take the cause forward. One famous antislavery minister was impressed with Garrison's enthusiasm but not his radical approach. He offered to support Garrison and help him become "the Wilberforce of America" if only he would allow them to guide him to a more nuanced stance. Essentially, traditional reformers, including gradualists, and colonizationists, recoiled at Garrison's willingness to put the political union at risk and his insistence on addressing racism head on. Garrison had no desire to be a puppet of these tepid abolitionists.

During this tour Garrison began to plan his newspaper and decided to make Boston his headquarters. From there he offered the first issue of the *Liberator* on New Year's Day, 1831. This move heralded the official birth of immediatism. The editor tackled a number of taboo topics, perhaps the most shocking of which was his forceful criticism of laws preventing whites and blacks from intermarrying. This would gain for him a reputation for supporting "amalgamation"— a reputation that would precede his arrival when he returned to Philadelphia.[4]

Immediate Abolition

Soon after beginning the *Liberator*, and just as the first National Negro Convention was about to meet, Garrison began to push for a national antislavery society based on immediatist principles. He, Lundy, and their generous benefactor, Arthur Tappan, attended the first black convention in 1830, where delegates discussed the need for just the type of organization Garrison sought. At this early juncture African Americans were leading the drive for large-scale organizing on the national level, much to the chagrin of white onlookers.

Two and a half years passed before the founding of the American Antislavery Society (AASS) in Philadelphia in December 1833. Much happened during these two years. To begin with, the immediatist cause gained a number of important white converts, including Arthur Tappan's brother Lewis, from New York; Garrison's former roommate, John Greenleaf Whittier, from Massachusetts; Beriah Green, of Ohio; and Theodore Dwight Weld, a student at Lane Theological Seminary in Cincinnati, Ohio. The Tappans joined the crusade for a national organization, which they hoped would be headquartered in New York, but others assumed it would hail from Philadelphia. Clearly, a biracial organization was rapidly developing, preparing to issue a forceful call for an immediate end to human bondage.

Meanwhile, a slave named Nat Turner led an uprising in Virginia that resulted in efforts to suppress the *Liberator* under the argument that Garrison's agitation had instigated the revolt. This, in turn, led Southern leaders like Virginia governor John Floyd to keep files on radicals like Garrison. The city of Georgetown, D.C., passed a law deeming it illegal for free blacks to take copies of the paper out of the post office. Those who did faced a $20 fine and 30 days in jail. If they could not pay the fine, they faced the threat of four months in slavery. In Raleigh, North Carolina, a grand jury indicted Garrison for provoking insurrection, and in Columbia, South Carolina, a vigilante association offered a $1,500 reward for the apprehension and conviction of whites caught circulating "seditious" papers like the *Liberator*. Georgia went a step further by offering $5,000 for anyone who could bring Garrison to the state to face trial for libel. Southerners from many places appealed to Boston mayor Harrison Gray Otis for help in quieting Garrison, insisting that he was imperiling the Union as well as their lives. The more people called for suppression, however, the more Garrison was able to emphasize the importance of free speech and freedom of the press. Unlike gradualists, he insisted, he would never violate his principles for the sake of political compromise. As a result, more people, including Philadelphia's female abolitionists, began to offer financial support to the *Liberator*.[5]

While waiting for the national organization to come about, New England reformers in 1832 founded the first biracial immediatist group in the United States—the New England Antislavery Society (NEASS). Garrison wanted the group to come out forcefully and uncompromisingly for immediatism, but delegates disagreed over whether it was expedient to state immediatist principles in the articles of incorporation. They also debated whether or not to include gradualists, a move that, on the one hand, would lead to a broader base but, on the other hand, could blur the new group's goals and stance. Though they never came out and labeled slavery a "sin" like Garrison wanted, the group eventually dedicated itself to the twin goals of ending slavery and securing equal rights for free blacks immediately.

As the abolition movement grew and expanded in the North, it faced its final defeat in the border South. During the winter of 1831–32 legislators in Virginia engaged in a series of "slave debates," considering gradual abolition measures like the Pennsylvania law. When all was said and done the legislature not only rejected abolition but also passed a stringent slave code and recommended the expulsion of free blacks from the state. With this measure died the hope that abolitionists could reach out and appeal directly to Southerners to end slavery voluntarily.

Virginia's decision to expel free blacks sent them seeking refuge elsewhere, and this only fueled the growth of racism in the North. As a result, the abolitionist goal of civil rights gained even more importance. Garrison knew this. Direct contact with blacks led him to his awareness of the depth of, and need to eradicate, racism. This consciousness started to develop as he listened to the black speakers in Boston and intensified as he interacted with the free black community of Baltimore. It reached new depths while he was in Philadelphia. In addition to the support he gained from James Forten, he also gained the trust and friendship of Forten's son-in-law, Robert Purvis. He stayed with Purvis while in the city to attend the black convention in 1832, and Purvis and Forten both helped him with his magnum opus, *Thoughts on African Colonization* (1832). This work solidified Garrison's reputation as a "radical" and put him at war with the highly popular colonization society.

As his war with the colonizationists heated, Garrison decided to tour England and seek moral and monetary support for immediatism and for the *Liberator*. While there, he competed with Philadelphia's leading colonizationist, Elliott Cresson, for the antislavery limelight. The competition created intense hatred between the two men. At the same time, however, the pamphlet brought Garrison support at the grassroots level, winning over many former colonizationists to the immediatist cause. Indeed, by the summer of 1833 the NEASS employed three full-time field agents and boasted nearly fifty local groups and several thousand new members. At the same time, the ACS's collections dwindled.

Garrison came under attack as soon as he stepped off the ship on his return from England in October 1833. The first newspaper he picked up hinted at the need for vigilante action to prevent him from forming a New York City immediatist group. Garrison knew nothing about the proposed society, which the Tappans had been planning while he was in England. They had announced their meeting five days before his return and the newspapers, with a little encouragement from Cresson and the colonizationists, had labeled it part of a fanatical plot by Garrison to spread his heresy. This threatened attack led the Pennsylvania Abolition Society to warn against a proposed meeting in Philadelphia to establish the national organization, but Garrison remained determined to meet in 1833.[6]

The American Antislavery Society

The official call for the convention to establish a national immediatist organization went out in November 1833. Though New York abolitionist Elizur Wright promised a low-key event lacking any "show" that would lead to "the physical interruption of the mobocracy," local abolitionists remained skeptical, questioning "the propriety and wisdom of that movement, *at this particular juncture*." The PAS warned that in light of "the present tumultuous and distracted state of the political mind" and the fact that "our brethren of the South are in a state of phrensy [sic] on this subject," a national convention on principles of immediate emancipation would be unwise, especially before clearly explaining "our meaning of the term." Pointing to the mob that had tried to prevent the formation of the New York City Antislavery Society a few days earlier, they insisted upon the necessity of gaining more public support first by clearly explaining their purpose and goals through pamphlets, addresses, and other media. They concluded by wishing the New Yorkers "Divine Sanction" should they pursue this course despite their warnings. Ignoring these warnings, abolitionists descended upon Philadelphia in December 1833 to establish the AASS.[7]

Garrison worked hard to enlist the support of Whittier, a Quaker whom he hoped would influence Philadelphia Quaker abolitionists, but Whittier hesitated. Aware that abolitionists "were everywhere spoken against, their persons threatened, and in some instances a price set on their heads by Southern legislators" and that "Pennsylvania was on the borders of Slavery," he feared the possibility of "the breaking up of the Convention and maltreatment of its members." "Quite unwilling to undergo a martyrdom," he still felt the pull of Garrison's summons. As a Quaker, he attended partly out of respect for "the traditions of that earlier abolitionism which, under the lead of Benezet and Woolman, had effaced from the Society of Friends every vestige of slave-holding." Clearly, Whittier saw this new society as an extension of, rather than a departure from, the abolitionism he had imbibed all his life.[8]

Whittier met Garrison in Boston and they rode to Philadelphia together, going first to the home of abolitionist Evan Lewis on Fifth Street. A member of the PAS, Lewis put himself in charge of local arrangements and attended the convention not as a representative of the gradualist group but on his own accord. Several other PAS members did the same. Other delegates also stayed with Lewis during the convention. Like Lewis, the Motts opened their home to guests in town to attend the convention, as did James McCrummell, an African American abolitionist who apparently hosted Garrison. When Whittier and Garrison arrived at Lewis's home they found about forty other abolitionists from throughout the North. They held an informal meeting led by Lewis Tappan where they determined the need to find a well-known Philadelphian "of distinction and high social standing" to preside over the convention. Whittier, given his Quaker connections, was the logical choice to lead a committee to recruit this person. The committee then went to the homes of Thomas Wistar and Roberts Vaux, two prominent men "known as friendly to emancipation and of high social standing," where they were received "with the dignified courtesy of the old school" and rejected "in civil terms."[9]

The local leaders knew what the abolitionists were up against. They saw the response of the local newspapers from the moment delegates started to arrive in the city. They also heard the warnings of the police, who insisted that all sessions be held in daylight. Finally, they knew Garrison had a large hand in the convention and they wished to keep their distance. Lewis Tappan explained to the group that "There is good evidence to believe that many professed friends of abolition would have been here, had they not been *afraid* that the name of WILLIAM LLOYD GARRISON would be inserted prominently in our proceedings."[10]

The convention met for three days at the Adelphia Building on Fifth Street below Walnut beginning on December 4, 1833. Delegates faced harassment by passersby but the police managed to head off trouble by remaining at the hall and preempting crowd action. Some historians have argued that organizers did not publicly announce the meeting because they feared mob action, but abolitionist J. Miller McKim insisted that their proceedings "were not secret" even if they were "not thrown open by advertisement to the public." Spectators included ACS officers, Southern medical students, and many women, most notably Lucretia Mott, who actively participated in the debates and boldly offered suggestions to the delegates. In all, sixty-three delegates, three of whom were black, attended from ten states. Seven women joined Mott as spectators. It was a grassroots group that took the abolition movement well beyond the bounds of genteel top-down gradualism. Contrary to popular expectations, anti-abolitionist grumbling remained at a low simmer and no mob attacked.[11]

The group's constitution called for immediate emancipation but acknowledged that states had the right to control slavery within their borders. It stated as the group's primary goal the use of moral suasion to work within the bounds of the U.S. Constitution as they sought to convince Congress to end the domestic slave trade—an act that fell under federal jurisdiction since it crossed state boundaries. It also called upon Congress to abolish slavery in the parts of the country under Congressional jurisdiction, namely the District of Columbia and the territories, pledging to fight against the extension of slavery into any future states. Finally, it called for black uplift in a way that sounded much like the PAS. Rejecting physical force in all cases, the immediatists "disclaimed any right or intention of interfering, otherwise than by persuasion and Christian expostulation, with slavery as it existed in the States." The roster of officers included a number of local abolitionists, but regardless of the local participation, most Philadelphians continued to see immediatism as a poorly defined, outwardly imposed movement. Even in the absence of mob action, the hostility was enough to convince the group to hold their annual meetings in New York City and to choose New York as their headquarters.[12]

Despite the new constitution, for many abolitionists and detractors alike the question remained: "What does 'immediatism' mean?" Immediatists themselves were torn on this issue. Some, especially the New York and Pennsylvania groups, believed that they were fighting for the process of emancipation to *begin* immediately, even if it would ultimately have to be *accomplished* gradually. The Garrisonian interpretation—the one best understood by the public—was that "immediatism" meant *immediate release* of all slaves. Unitarian minister, poet, and gradualist William Ellery Channing warned abolitionists of the danger of such a vague watch word, but its vagueness helped ensure its broad appeal. In Philadelphia, the PAS struggled with what to do about the new group—ignore it or work with it.

Vigilante Action in the North

Throughout the North most of the general public had no trouble deciding how to react to the immediatists: they used violence to try to intimidate them. Beginning in the spring of 1834 anti-abolition Northerners embarked upon what some abolitionists and their children would later describe as a "reign of terror" across the Northern states. That May a mob in Middletown, Connecticut, attacked abolitionists. In July a mob in New York attacked three black churches, assaulted blacks in the streets, and set fire to a dozen homes, including the home of Lewis Tappan. Late that summer, long-time PAS member and president Joseph Parrish drew the ire of a mob in Columbia,

Pennsylvania. The excitement lasted for two or three nights and resulted in property damage. The event alarmed Parrish, who was already
nervous about dramatic confrontations, and it led him to discourage
public action for a while.[13]

Perhaps the most notorious mob action of 1834 occurred in
Philadelphia and was directed at blacks rather than abolitionists.
Blacks lived throughout the city, but by the early 1830s one part of
Philadelphia held a particularly high concentration of black residents.
That neighborhood sat precariously in the middle of Philadelphia
proper, Southwark, and Moyamensing. While these areas were connected, they were technically separate cities, each with its own municipal government. Because of this situation, watchmen and constables
who acted slowly when trouble occurred were able to justify their
neglect by citing uncertainty over jurisdiction. This situation became
particularly problematic after 1831 when abolitionists and Southern
interests began to compete for Philadelphia whites' loyalty. At that
point, the neighborhood became a frequent target for violence. According to historian Sam Bass Warner, Southern trade connections
and "the customs of the adjacent slave states of Maryland and Delaware" affected Philadelphia's racial climate. Immediatist efforts to
revive the city's abolitionist legacy heightened existing tensions and led
to a series of increasingly violent riots. The first took place in August
1834.[14]

On the surface the 1834 Philadelphia race riot appears to have
been a fight between young men for control of a carousel. On South
Street above Seventh, the Flying Horses drew both black and white
patrons, bringing them into close social contact. In early August someone began to spread rumors that blacks were insulting whites at the
carousel and that a group of young black men known for frequenting
the carousel had attacked the headquarters of the Fairmount Engine
Company and had taken some of the equipment. As the story circulated throughout the neighborhood, young men on both sides of the
racial divide gathered at the carousel, and on the night of August 12
they began to fight. Within hours, the carousel and the building that
housed it were completely demolished. After that, whites associated
with the melee began to prowl the streets of black neighborhoods, attacking people and property. Over the course of the next two nights
they broke into the houses of blacks and destroyed everything. They

vandalized two African American churches and beat every black who came into their path, killing one elderly man and injuring many others. When all was said and done, they destroyed an estimated four thousand dollars' worth of property. The confusing municipal boundaries made it difficult to stop the rioting. Blacks in Southwark and Moyamensing were in many cases left to fend for themselves. Ironically, given what would happen four years later at Pennsylvania Hall, blacks in Philadelphia proper fared better because Mayor John Swift immediately gathered the watchmen, swore in a posse of three hundred constables, and called in two militia troops to face the rioters. They took twenty prisoners and dispersed the mob. They also successfully defended a group of blacks who had taken refuge in a black-owned meeting hall. In this case, Swift acted firmly and brought in the help he needed to respond to the outbreak.[15]

The riot resulted from a combination of racial and class tensions. Trouble actually began three days earlier when a gang of about fifty young white men went looking for a fight and found one of James Forten's younger sons. The child was out on an errand for his parents when the gang attacked him and hit him on the head. He escaped and a white neighbor who knew and respected Forten followed the gang and took note of their plans to return to the neighborhood two days later. Forten and the neighbor reported the incident to the mayor, who then assembled forces and met the attackers upon their return, arresting several.

Did the gang target the child due simply to his color, or did they know he was the son of one of the wealthiest men in town—a man who employed working-class whites in his business? There is no way to answer this question with certainty, but studies have shown that during the riot that followed, the attackers passed through other black neighborhoods to target this particular part of the city, which housed most of Philadelphia's black churches and wealthier black residents. Of the thirty-seven homes destroyed, some were substantial brick houses, and the looted property included items that only the well-off could afford, such as mahogany furniture, featherbeds, and china. James Forten received death threats during the riot, and the mayor and sheriff took the threats seriously enough to send the horse patrol to guard his home.

The committee in charge of investigating the riot concluded that the disturbances resulted from two main issues. First, white laborers were angered because they perceived that some business owners preferred to hire black workers "and that, in consequence of this preference, many whites, who are willing and able to work, are left without employment, while colored people are provided with work, and enabled comfortably to maintain their families." This explanation defied reality but reflected whites' perception of their economic situation and the jealousy they harbored toward successful blacks. The truth was that blacks, not whites, faced discrimination in hiring, but Forten was known for hiring both blacks and whites. The key issue here, then, was the notion that black families could be "comfortable" when some whites could not. The Forten family was indeed quite comfortable and owned many luxuries.

The other cause for the riot, according to the report, was that "certain portions of the colored people" actively pushed for black freedom and equality. The report cited their efforts at aiding fugitive slaves, but the significance of black leaders in the abolition struggle went way beyond that. Forten and other black abolitionists had fostered the birth and growth of the immediate abolition movement, and Forten was one of the largest contributors to Garrison's newspaper. Also, by the 1830s black leaders, including Forten, were leading the charge against colonization. In essence, then, the city's black population came under attack because they were too successful economically and too active socially in the eyes of many whites.[16]

Matters deteriorated further in 1835, for blacks and for abolitionists. That year mobs attacked in Worcester, Massachusetts; Utica, New York; and Canaan, New Hampshire. Southern vigilantes waited in New York and other Northern cities to assassinate abolitionists or at least to capture them and transport them to the South to face vigilante justice. Expecting violence, some began to barricade their doors and windows. Historian David Grimsted contends that the period between July and late October 1835 was one of "maximum mob mayhem."[17]

That summer Philadelphia saw another race riot. This time trouble began with the successful defense of a runaway slave. With much of the white community already agitated by the abolitionist victory, tempers flared after a mentally ill black servant murdered his master.

After word began to spread about the murder, a group of white young men and "half-grown boys" returned to the neighborhood where the Flying Horses had stood, and where James Forten owned rental properties. Once again Mayor Swift brought the police in to protect the part of the neighborhood under his jurisdiction, but Southwark authorities left the mob to rampage through the portion of the neighborhood under their control. This time the mob spared the elderly and women, saving their fury for the young black men they found. Once again they broke into and ransacked black homes. They set fire to a black dwelling and refused to let firemen intervene, going so far as to cut fire hoses and throw stones at the firemen. As the fire began to spread, white onlookers helped to extinguish the blaze out of fear that the whole city might burn.[18]

Even with the violence of crowds, immediatists found a number of reasons for encouragement that year. The women of Boston organized a biracial abolition society, and over one hundred New England clergymen declared slavery a sin. Also, divinity students at Lane Seminary in Cincinnati, Ohio, followed Theodore Dwight Weld into the immediatist fold after an eighteen-day revival converted most of the student body to the cause. James Gillespie Birney, a Kentucky slave owner, emancipated his slaves and resigned his agency with the ACS, offering his services to the AASS. He would become a major figure in the abolitionist movement, eventually running for President of the United States under the antislavery Liberty Party. In addition to more and more colonizationists joining the abolitionist cause, George Thompson, a well-regarded English abolitionist, came to the United States to help raise money and gain even more converts. Perhaps best of all, from the immediatist perspective, the ACS was $40,000 in debt. Many abolitionists hoped that the loss of support and dearth of funds meant that the colonization society's days were limited.

Along with progress, however, came dissension among the immediatist ranks. Lack of clarity from the beginning created a fault line that continued to deepen. Garrison's view of immediatism required adherents to agree that slavery was a sin that had to be rectified without delay, and he wanted the clergy to prove their support by taking action against church members who committed this sin. Of course, many rejected this dogmatic approach, insisting that the best way to bring their congregants into the fold was to keep them in the church and influence them with gentle nudging. Garrison saw this as half-hearted support. He also refused to accept assistance from reformers who did not agree entirely with his doctrines. This stubborn stance began to irritate other immediatists, and Philadelphia abolitionists who wanted all along to keep their distance shunned him and refused to invite him to speak in the city. The Motts remained steadfast friends, however, hosting him in their home and introducing him to receptive members of the Philadelphia reform community whenever the opportunity presented itself.[19]

The Postal Campaign

The connection between Northern liberties and Southern slavery became increasingly apparent in 1835 and 1836 as abolitionists initiated postal and petition campaigns that met resistance from both Southerners and members of Congress. It began with a postal campaign in which abolitionists sent literature south in the summer of 1835, turning the wrath they had already generated in that region into hysteria. The result was lynch law against abolitionists, which included the lashing of Amos Dresser and the imprisonment and eventual death of Reuben Crandall, the plundering of federal mail, and the burning of abolitionist effigies.

Southern leaders cried out against what they perceived as an attack upon their "states' rights" at the same time that they insisted the federal government reign in the abolitionists. Unwittingly bolstering Garrison's assertions that his cause was about free speech as well as antislavery, they argued that the Constitution was not only a compact that barred Congress and the state governments in the North from "interfering" with slavery, but also a contract that promised the federal government would take active steps to protect slavery, even if it meant stifling the civil rights of dissidents in the North. They also made economic threats, promising to boycott merchants and cities like Philadelphia that were known for abolitionist sympathy. When appeals to law and economics did not work, mobs throughout the South attacked people they suspected of carrying abolitionist literature.

In the North the postal campaign fostered further anti-abolitionist rioting and mob action against Garrison and other activists. In September 1835 Garrison found a mock gallows at his door. The incident shook his wife up. The young man who had reveled in his own incarceration a few years earlier and seemed to be spoiling for martyrdom, however, dismissed her concern and told her not to worry: "he who loses his life for Christ's sake shall find it."[20]

A month later matters grew even more serious as Garrison survived a close call at the hands of an angry mob during the anniversary meeting of the Boston Female Antislavery Society. An announcement that George Thompson was to speak at the meeting sent the public into a mad frenzy and prompted a local newspaper to advocate lynching him. Undaunted, the women remained determined to proceed with the meeting, but the owners of the hall made them change venues because they feared their property would be damaged or destroyed if a riot ensued. Nearby merchants shared this fear and petitioned the mayor in hopes of preventing the meeting, while local anti-abolitionists called upon their fellow citizens to defend the Union against the abolitionists. They offered a $100 reward for someone to capture Thompson and bring him to the tar kettle, where they hoped to dispense their own brand of justice. As the mob swelled into the thousands, the women left their meeting arm in arm with white women protecting black women. Thompson was not at the meeting, so the mob focused on Garrison, who was forced to make a dramatic escape. Once again he landed behind bars, this time for his own protection. The "brush with martyrdom" left him "elated." Leaving Boston after the incident, likely to appease his wife, Garrison returned unmolested two weeks later. Apparently disappointed, he wrote, "I did not prove to be so great a curiosity, as I anticipated."[21]

The mobbing did have the unintended consequence of bringing Edmund Quincy and Wendell Phillips into the immediatist fold, again proving that anti-abolition attacks could backfire. Indeed, Garrison masterfully used the mobbing to benefit the cause by emphasizing that it was, above all, an attack upon free speech. He gained the attention of Harriet Martineau, a Unitarian and social commentator from England who is often described as the first female sociologist. She had been staying in Boston with Channing's friends and followed the events of the mobbing with great interest. She insisted on meeting with Garrison. Perhaps as much psychologist as sociologist, she realized that he was forcing America to reform through an ordeal by fire—a forced rebirth that required a violent shake-up. She later described what ensued as a "martyr age."[22]

Other abolitionists faced similar treatment. On the same day of the Garrison attack, a mob targeted a group of abolitionists in Utica, New York. This action prompted wealthy colonizationist Gerrit Smith to leave the ACS and join the immediatists. Around the same time, angry mobs in New England set out to get Thompson and Whittier, threatening them on more than one occasion.

Whittier recounted a dramatic escape of his own in 1835. Traveling with Thompson, he went to Plymouth, New Hampshire, where Thompson gave three lectures without incident. On the way back they stopped at Concord, New Hampshire, where a meeting had been scheduled at the courthouse for the next evening. Arriving at their venue, however, they found it closed under the threat of a mobbing. Retiring to the home of a friend, the abolitionists became separated and the mob found Whittier walking with the editor of the local paper, but they mistook him for their main target—Thompson. They attacked him with rotten eggs and stones, ruining his suit. After escaping this mob, the two men headed back to Whittier's estate in Haverhill, Massachusetts, stopping along the way for breakfast at an inn where they overheard the innkeeper telling a story about how Thompson and Whittier had been beaten up and were on the run. After looking at a handbill the innkeeper was passing around that called for Thompson's apprehension, Whittier innocently asked, "How is the rascal to be recognized?" The innkeeper replied, "Easily enough. He's a tongue-y fellow." Whittier and Thompson then finished their breakfast and got into the carriage to leave. As it was taking off, Whittier leaned out and yelled to the innkeeper, "This is George Thompson and my name is Whittier." He refused to even try to have his coat cleaned, saving it as a relic of the attack, just as Garrison had saved the receipt from his Baltimore jail fine.[23]

What was it about the immediatists that spurred their neighbors to attack them? For one matter, abolitionists were civil rights leaders pushing not just for the end of slavery in the South but also for racial equality in the North. Though slavery was fading away in the Northern states, whites had yet to come to terms with black freedom. Many supported the removal of free blacks to Africa or other distant parts of the world. Some were willing to tolerate their black neighbors as long as they remained "in their place" at the bottom of society, but very few were ready to accept the notion of racial equality. Another factor that fueled the anti-abolition backlash was that abolitionist agitation angered Southerners who in turn appealed to the Northern public.

As abolitionists sent their literature south, Southern whites called upon the Northern populace to silence their radical neighbors. White Southerners argued that a threat to their property in slaves could open the door to endanger property rights in general, including Northern property rights. Also they claimed that abolition literature encouraged their slaves to rise up against them and fight for their freedom. Of course, they never admitted it directly, but historians Charles Sellers and William Freehling have shown that slaveholders also feared that abolition literature just might break through and open the eyes of some Southern whites. For all of these reasons, the flood of abolitionist pamphlets to the South had to be stopped. Grimsted argued that the abolitionists' mail campaign "changed the South's soothing 'someday' about slavery's end to a firm 'Never!'" He added that "It also led to strident demands that either laws or mobs silence those who publicly questioned the institution."[24]

The Petition Drive and the Gag Rule

Even while they tried to flood the southbound mail with pamphlets and newspapers, abolitionists were busy bombarding Congress with petitions to end slavery in the District of Columbia, stop the spread of slavery into the territories, and end the domestic slave trade. This angered Southern congressmen as much as the postal campaign infuriated Southerners in general. The loudest representative of slave owner interests, South Carolina Senator John C. Calhoun, pushed Congress to institute a series of gag rules against the flood of petitions. He also called for a bill to punish federal postmasters who delivered materials deemed incendiary.

With his insistence that Congress help him silence the abolitionists, Calhoun pushed Ohio Congressman Thomas Morris too far. A native of Bucks County, Pennsylvania, Morris was also a Democrat and supporter of President Andrew Jackson. As he sat in the Senate and watched Calhoun lead a drive to destroy American civil liberties like freedom of speech and freedom of the press, he could not join most of his fellow Northerners as they sat in silence and looked the other way. Instead, he grew furious at the idea that slave owners had become drunk with power and were, right before his eyes, seeking to bully their fellow legislators just as they did their slaves. To the dismay of Calhoun and the shock of others in the Senate chamber, Morris rose to oppose the gag rules.[25] Congressman and former President John Quincy Adams reacted similarly, and the two men became heroes to many abolitionists.

The spectacle that ensued generated more antislavery support, but many who defended the abolitionists' right to free speech still rejected what was increasingly being called Garrison's radicalism. William Ellery Channing, for example, criticized the attacks upon abolitionists' civil liberties but also called Garrisonians to task for their behavior. Like Channing, Morris, and Adams, many Americans were awakening to the abolitionist cause, but these supporters did not wish to consider themselves "radical abolitionists."

CHAPTER 4

Radicalism in the Gradualist City

Sarah Mapps Douglass noticed the activity at Sixth and Haines in the summer of 1837. She had grown up in the neighborhood—the same neighborhood where her mother had lived all of her life. She took pride in her family's deep roots in the city. Her grandfather, Cyrus Bustill, had anchored his family in Philadelphia by building a bakery at 56 Arch Street, just across from Betsy Ross's house, after returning from the Revolutionary War. During the war he gained fame by baking for the troops, and after it he gained wealth by selling his baked goods to Philadelphians. Though their ancestors included whites, Native Americans, and Africans, Sarah and her family, like all Americans with any amount of African ancestry, were considered black.

Cyrus Bustill and his family never applied for membership in the Society of Friends but they attended Quaker meeting and lived the Quaker lifestyle. At one point when Sarah was young her mother Grace, Cyrus's daughter, considered applying for membership but was warned against it, told that she would certainly face a humiliating and heart-breaking rejection. Even so, Grace continued to attend meeting. Though they attended Arch Street Meeting with the other Quakers, the Douglasses had to sit in a separate pew. Looking back, Sarah remembered wishing as a child "that the meeting house would fall down, or that Friends would forbid our coming, thinking then that my mother would not persist in going among them." As she grew into adulthood she found herself skipping meeting despite her mother's pleas. Many Sundays, Grace Douglass found herself sitting alone in the "negro pew."[1]

While even the Quakers excluded her family from true fellowship, Sarah Douglass felt a new hope stirring that summer. And the building going up just blocks away from her home and church gave her a reason to dream. She and her friends with the Philadelphia Female Antislavery Society (PFASS) had helped raise funds to buy that lot and build what many were already projecting would be the grandest structure in the city. In return for their dedication, and for buying one hundred dollars worth of stock in the venture, the women expected to rent the hall at a reasonable rate for their future meetings.

The women had been meeting at the Pennsylvania Abolition Society (PAS)'s Clarkson Hall—the same building that housed a number of schools, including Sarah Douglass's. Following in the footsteps of her grandfather and her mother, Sarah was a teacher in the PAS school. She had not minded allowing her friends to meet in the schoolroom where she taught, but the new hall would be so much nicer. It would have much more room. Plus, it just might offer a warmer place to meet in the winter if indeed the men did as they were considering and included the innovation of gas power in the new hall.

Sarah's excitement over the new hall and the prospects for real fellowship with her abolitionist colleagues was heightened by her experiences a couple of months earlier at the first Antislavery Convention of American Women, which had met in tandem with the annual American Antislavery Society (AASS) meeting in New York from May 9 to 12. At first she had been reluctant to attend the meeting, but her friends Sarah and Angelina Grimké had convinced her to go. Oddly enough these sisters were members of a South Carolina slaveholding family, but, like Douglass, they had never fit in with those around them.

The Grimké sisters began their journey from the slaveholding world of South Carolina to the forefront of American abolition in the 1820s. It began with Sarah's conversion to Quakerism and move to Philadelphia in 1821. She traveled to the city in 1819 with her father, who was ill and sought treatment from Quaker physicians. When he died, the Orthodox Quakers took Sarah in and she became part of their Arch Street Meeting. Angelina joined her sister in 1829 and both joined the PFASS in 1835. Through this group and the Quaker church they formed a deep and lasting friendship with Sarah and Grace Douglass. While other white Friends, even those who were abolitionists, continued to tolerate segregation in the meetings, the Grimké sisters broke the rule by joining Grace on the Negro pew.

When the PFASS began corresponding with female abolitionists in Massachusetts and making plans for the national meeting of abolitionist women, the sisters took for granted that the Douglasses, leading figures in Pennsylvania abolition, would attend. Perhaps they never stopped to consider their black friends' humiliating history of rejection. After learning of Sarah Douglass's hesitation they realized what was at stake for their black friends, but they also knew how important it was for them to attend the meeting. Angelina wrote to Douglass telling her that she understood her hesitation to attend, but she called upon her to help fight the racist resistance that almost certainly awaited in New York—both inside and outside the convention. Arguing that black women "have a work to do in rooting out this wicked feeling, as well as we," she told Sarah "you *must be willing* to come amongst us, tho' . . . feelings *may* be wounded by the 'putting forth of the finger,' the avoidance of a seat by you, or the glancing of the eye." The only cure for the ignorance that caused white women to behave this way was familiarity, and getting to know women like the Douglasses "will help your paler sisters *more* than anything else to overcome their own sinful feelings." Grimké concluded by pointing out that the Douglasses and Fortens had valuable insights that would greatly benefit the work done at the convention.

After this show of solidarity the Douglass women decided to attend the convention. When they arrived they saw that they were not alone: one in ten of the delegates were black. Unlike at their church, and in American society in general, these women enjoyed not only acceptance but equality at the convention. Grace was even elected a vice president.[2]

The Douglass women attended the convention as part of the delegation representing the PFASS, a group whose existence was made possible by Lundy's free produce movement. The free produce movement opened the door for women to participate in abolitionist efforts at a time when gradualist societies like the PAS did not. As was the case with blacks, some PAS members did not invite women to join because they did not see a place for them in the movement. Others, however, just never really thought about it before, blinded by the racial and gender conventions of the time. Once free produce opened the door for women to participate in abolition, women began to create their own antislavery societies in Philadelphia, Boston, Fall River, and many other communities throughout the northeastern United States. Just as important, many male abolitionists welcomed them in the AASS, at least at first.

The Rise of the Grimkés

Before immediatism, women had contributed to antislavery in ways that did not upset moderate reformers. Free produce did not challenge the standard notions of separate spheres, so it offered a way for women to participate without upsetting the prevailing order. Other efforts, like that of a teacher named Prudence Crandall to keep a school for black girls in Canterbury, Connecticut, were equally easy to defend for the same reason. Society accepted women as teachers, so although Crandall's efforts to teach black students crossed racial lines and led to multiple attacks by anti-abolitionists, she remained within the traditional female sphere of influence, making it easy for the abolitionists to defend her.

Another noted female abolitionist, Lydia Maria Child, also paid close mind to prevailing gender stereotypes as she contributed to the movement. At roughly the same time of the Crandall attack in 1833, Child issued her *Appeal in Favor of that Class of Americans Called Africans*, a pamphlet that focused on traditional gender roles in speaking out for the slave. The first book-length work on American slavery written by an American woman, Child's account introduced a unique angle by critiquing slavery from a gendered perspective as she pointed out the ways slavery hurt the family and left women vulnerable to sexual exploitation. This account influenced abolitionists of various persuasions, even those like William Ellery Channing who were put off by Garrisonian radicalism, and it set the stage for the Grimkés to come along and confirm many of Child's assertions with their own first-hand observations.[3]

Women began joining the immediate movement soon after the AASS was founded, forming the PFASS as the first women's auxiliary in 1833. The four women who had attended the founding convention of the AASS—Lucretia Mott, Lydia White, Esther Moore, and Sidney Ann Lewis—gathered just days after to establish their own group in response to an AASS resolution urging women to organize auxiliary societies in support of immediatist goals. The group, which was biracial from the beginning, adopted a constitution that pledged to fight to end both slavery and race prejudice. It also promised that all members would abstain from using goods produced by slave labor. The group met monthly at the PAS's Clarkson Hall and raised money, which they shared with the AASS. They corresponded with abolitionists throughout the United States and Great Britain, circulated and aggressively sought signatures on petitions that called for the abolition of slavery in the District of Columbia and federal territories, and organized a series of fairs in which they sold hand-made goods inscribed with antislavery mottoes. This last effort served a dual purpose by getting the abolition message out while raising funds for the AASS. After joining in 1835, the Grimké sisters became very active in the society, but they also brought with them conflict and tension.[4]

Angelina Grimké began to cause a stir throughout the nation with her *Appeal to the Christian Women of the South*, which was published by the AASS in 1836. This pamphlet urged women of the South to join women of the North in stepping beyond the domestic sphere and taking public action against human bondage. It urged civil disobedience by encouraging them to follow higher law and reject the perfectly legal but completely immoral labor system. At virtually the same time she wrote the pamphlet Grimké attended an AASS training session in New York, where she met an enthusiastic abolitionist minister named Theodore Dwight Weld, and the two fell in love. While at the session she also was appointed the first female lecturing agent for the society. She then went on a speaking tour that was sponsored by the PFASS.[5]

The AASS was quite eager to embrace the Grimké sisters. First of all, they were from a slaveholding elite Southern family and thus had first-hand knowledge of what slavery was like. Second, they were women and could reach out specifically to women and expand upon Child's gendered assessment of slavery. They had much to contribute to the cause.

To the chagrin of some abolitionists, it was soon clear that the plan had gone awry. They intended the sisters to speak to women only, but they quickly stirred controversy by speaking to mixed audiences. They had not set out to cause problems, but their fascinating stories and descriptions of slavery drew large crowds—crowds that included men and women alike. The backlash that resulted forced them to defend their right to speak publicly to mixed audiences, and it led them to produce a series of articles and pamphlets that collectively present what historian Phil Lapsansky has described as "the earliest systematic presentation of the case for women's rights."[6]

Perhaps the most famous rebuttal to the Grimkés came from another female reformer. Angelina Grimké's 1836–37 speaking tour included an address to the Massachusetts State Legislature that set off a newspaper debate between Grimké and Mott on the one side and Catharine Beecher on the other. Beecher, a colonizationist, took issue with female abolition societies and petition campaigns. Colonizationist women considered themselves antislavery reformers, but they were conservative and carefully remained within the domestic sphere of influence. They worked through the churches to raise money for the colonization society, bought and made clothing for Liberian immigrants, and held fairs to raise money for schools in the colony. They worked quietly behind the scenes in separate societies and allowed men to represent and speak for them at the annual meetings. Beecher believed that Grimké's combative attitude and defense of women's rights took her reform efforts into dangerous territory. In her *Essay on Slavery and Abolitionism* she argued that immediatists were doing more harm than good by alienating the South and increasing regional polarization. She predicted that the South might break away and create its own republic in an effort to permanently protect slavery.[7]

Mott likely issued the first rebuttal to Beecher in a series of articles in Lundy's *Enquirer*, which, by 1837, was one of the nation's leading abolitionist newspapers, providing a voice for gradualists and immediatists alike. Soon after Beecher's essay appeared, Lundy printed a series of letters signed "L" that took Beecher to task, defending immediatist tactics and arguing that Beecher and other colonizationists should not consider themselves abolitionists. Their reform of choice, the author argued, was "half-way" or "neutral" at best. Grimké soon weighed in, and the letters from "L" stopped. This exchange marked the first public debate among women over both abolitionist and feminist tactics. In addition to arguing over how to end slavery, the women were engaged in a debate that plagued the women's movement from that point forward. According to historian Carol Faulkner, the essence of the issue was this: "Should women use their traditional roles as the basis for expanding public conceptions of their rights?" or "Should women simply insist that they are entitled to full equality with men?"[8]

Sarah Douglass watched that summer as her friend Angelina Grimké made the case for the second option in her *Appeal to the Women of the Nominally Free States*, which she presented at the Antislavery Convention of American Women in New York. Grimké, Mott, Maria Weston Chapman, and other women abolitionists from throughout the North had organized this convention and scheduled it to meet at the same time as the annual AASS meeting. The women who attended the convention thought they had signed up for an abolition convention but, in light of the debate raging between the Grimkés and Beecher, the meeting was as much about women's rights as it was antislavery. Grimké's second *Appeal* set the tone, and resolutions passed included a call to women to keep up the petition work, a censure of churches that refused to acknowledge that slavery was a sin, an appeal for the racial integration of churches and schools, and an appeal to white women to associate with black women on equal terms.

Sarah Grimké dominated the proceedings. She began by offering a series of resolutions that would have put the South on the defensive right away and would have worried many more traditional abolitionists. Her first-hand familiarity with slavery left her impatient with the notion of gradually ending human bondage, and her close friendship with black women who resisted the idea of colonization left her determined to end slavery immediately and without the condition of deportation. She had also run out of patience with anti-abolitionists and their assault upon abolitionists' rights of free speech. She laid the blame for anti-abolition violence squarely at the feet of "the combination of interest which exists between the North and the South, in their political, commercial, and domestic relations," and she offered a resolution that essentially called for abolitionists to use civil disobedience against the return of fugitive slaves. Arguing that "the women of America are solemnly called upon by the spirit of the age and the signs of the times, fully to discuss the subject of slavery," Grimké challenged them to insist upon, and act upon, those rights. Her sister and their friend Lucretia Mott spoke in support of the resolution, and Angelina took the issue further by offering her own resolution that challenged religious authority while declaring gender equality. Mott supported this addition, but some delegates wanted amendments added. After heated debate, Angelina Grimké's resolution was adopted without changes, but twelve delegates opposed the resolution so strongly that they insisted their dissent be recorded in the minutes.

While historian Katherine Kish Sklar maintains that "not all women abolitionists were willing to be associated with the radical claim that women and men had equal rights," the debate was not that simple. Some who protested were offended by what they saw as a stab at the churches. More importantly, others believed that putting the women's issue at the forefront at that time would have detracted from the main issue they had gathered over—the abolition of slavery. Simply by being there and taking part they were asserting their rights as women. Many thought that was enough testament to their rights and chose to maintain their focus on the original goal for which they had been fighting. At any rate, the issue proved so divisive that resolutions of this nature did not appear at future meetings of the group. The Antislavery Convention of American Women was meant to meet annually, but its second meeting, at Pennsylvania Hall, would seal its fate. The group would meet one additional time in 1839 before calling it quits.[9]

In addition to dividing women in the movement, the Grimkés' stance brought them into conflict with the clergy. Congregational ministers issued a *Pastoral Letter of the General Association of Massachusetts* in June 1837 essentially forbidding affiliated clergymen from opening their churches for the women to speak. It also received a divided reaction from male abolitionists, many of whom had tolerated and even admired Mott's outspokenness in the AASS. Why? As biographer Carol Faulkner pointed out, Mott used her actions to fight for the same rights the Grimkés sought, but while the sisters publicly announced their goal of women's equality, Mott just acted. Instead of arguing for her right to speak, she simply exercised it.

Several male abolitionists, including John Greenleaf Whittier and Weld, urged the Grimkés to take a similar approach and remain focused on abolition. "As '*southerners,*'" Weld insisted, the women could "do more at convincing the North than twenty *northern* females," but they lost this advantage by pursuing "*another subject.*" He added that "the *great* reason why *you* should operate upon the public mind far and wide at the north rather than Mrs. Child, Mrs. Chapman, Lucretia

Mott, etc., is that you are *southern* women, *once* in *law* slaveholders, your friends all slaveholders, etc., hence your testimony; *testimony*, TESTIMONY is the great desideratum." In essence, Angelina's future husband wanted her to proceed as if her right to speak was self-evident and remain on target with her antislavery message.[10]

Whittier agreed. The sisters must have written to him seeking his opinion on war, church, government, and family matters because he responded that he would like to discuss these issues with them but that "the more I reflect on this subject, the more difficulty I find, and the more decidedly am I of the opinion that we ought to hold all these matters far aloof from the cause of abolition." He added that the sisters were "doing much and nobly to vindicate and assert the rights of woman" through their actions. "Your lectures to crowded and promiscuous audiences on a subject manifestly, in many of its aspects, *political*, interwoven with the framework of government, are practical and powerful assertions of the right and the duty of woman to labor side by side with her brother for the welfare and redemption of the world," he concluded.[11] Instead of following this advice, however, the Grimkés stopped to engage their detractors in debate.

Garrison and H. C. Wright, always spoiling for a good fight, urged the sisters onward even as others recommended caution. Wright became their strongest supporter, arousing the ire of Weld, who was likely jealous at the interference of another man in a disagreement he was having with a woman he was interested in romantically. As a result, Wright was transferred to Pennsylvania by the AASS in July 1837 just as construction was beginning on Pennsylvania Hall. After debate, the PFASS took Garrison and Wright's lead by siding with the Grimké sisters. This was a fateful decision for the abolition movement and the new hall.[12]

When the ministers issued their *Pastoral Letter* in 1837, they were not only concerned with the Grimkés. Besides their alarm at the notion of gender equality, they also believed abolitionists were forcing their agenda upon the church. They began the letter by insisting that "agitating subjects . . . *should not be forced on any church as matters for debate, at the hazard of alienation and division*" and that antislavery congregants had lost respect for their pastors and were forcing the issue. Essentially, pastors wanted to keep the agitation out of the church, a place "into which we flee from a troubled world for peace." Equally important, they resented the intrusion into their realm and the disregard for their authority.[13]

Garrison and Wright, the two men who called most loudly for women's rights, also led a charge against churches that fell short of their immediatist standards. By 1837 they had grown tired of ministers' refusal to declare slavery a sin and had started openly to question church authority. Interpreting scriptures for himself, Garrison developed two radical ideas that led to clerical outrage. First, he found no evidence in the New Testament that the Sabbath was different than any other day and he introduced his idea of "anti-sabbatarianism"— the belief that people should live holy lives every day instead of focusing on ceremony and observances. Second, he developed the concept of "non-resistance," arguing that all human government, church or state, immorally rested on force. Collectively these concepts challenged ministers' authority and threatened their role as intermediaries between the people and God.

Garrison and some of his followers had also started to question whether or not politics had a place in abolition. In the early years the movement remained small enough that members simply voted their consciences, supporting candidates who respected their goals and against those who supported slavery. As the antislavery ranks swelled, however, they realized the potential for collective political action, and some began to question what form such action would take. For example, some began to ask if perhaps they should form a third party dedicated to antislavery. Garrison's non-resistance stance led him to eschew politics altogether, while Whittier, the Tappans, Birney, and several others favored political action. The fault line over this issue began to develop in full force in 1837.[14]

Garrison took one final step that alienated some abolitionists, including some immediatists, when he announced his new motto of "universal emancipation" in the *Liberator*. He issued a manifesto explaining that he had set out with one goal—"the total abolition of American slavery, and, as a just consequence, the complete enfranchisement of our colored countrymen." The first step had been to "overthrow" the American Colonization Society (ACS). He would continue to fight for both of those goals, but he had come to realize that true freedom—"universal emancipation"—meant "the emancipation of our whole race from the dominion of man, from the thralldom of self, from the government of brute force, from the bondage of sin." Henceforth, women's rights would take a prominent role in the broader freedom struggle.[15]

The December before the Grimkés began to cause a stir in the antislavery movement, David Paul Brown responded with enthusiasm to a flattering request: the Pennsylvania Hall Association had asked him to deliver the first address in their new hall. Taking it as a request to dedicate the building, Brown replied that he had, as of late, "declined applications that might be calculated to take any portion of my time from my profession." This request from Philadelphia abolitionists, however, spoke to his heart. Because he had "*always* said" that he would "fight the battle of liberty as long as I have a shot in the locker," he promised his fellow PAS and Philadelphia Antislavery Society members that he would "of course . . . do what you require." Little did he know that his speech would set off a firestorm that would lead to one of the city's largest and most infamous "conflagrations."[16]

Brown had been a leading figure in Pennsylvania abolition for most of his adult life. He joined the PAS twenty years earlier, in 1818, and had served in a number of capacities in the gradualist movement, including as a delegate to the Abolition Convention on multiple occasions. As one of the city's best-known lawyers, he worked many cases on behalf of the PAS. When Philadelphia men followed the women of the PFASS's lead by forming their own group—the Philadelphia Antislavery Society—in April 1834, Brown and a number of his PAS colleagues played important roles. Edwin P. Atlee, a secretary of the PAS, chaired the meeting and James G. Gibbons, a likely member of a PAS-affiliated family though not a member himself, served as secretary. Given his long PAS and Abolition Convention history, as well as his standing as one of the city's top lawyers, Brown was the logical choice as the group's first president. The group formed a committee to prepare a constitution and explanation of the Society's "general principles." This committee included a number of PAS members and officers, as well as former officers of the American Convention of Abolition Societies.[17]

The report they presented made no great departures from PAS doctrine, but it included wording that sounded quite Garrisonian. For one matter, it may not have used the word "sin" but it did declare slaveholding "incompatible with the principles of Christianity" and "an exhaustless source of evil." Defending abolitionists from the charge of endangering the Union, it laid that blame on "Slavery itself." While Garrison may have preferred the blame go to slaveholders, the Philadelphia group fell short by focusing on the system. Still, the report made a clear statement about the immorality and dangers of slavery. In line with Garrisonian "moral suasion," the group admitted that they could not constitutionally interfere with slavery but instead called upon their "fellow countrymen of the South" to consider the dangers their system posed to themselves as well as their Northern counterparts. Granted, their calm and reasoned appeal would not influence slaveholders whose livelihoods and very society rested upon slavery, but their approach made sense to them, given that they generally admitted they could not constitutionally do away with slavery where it existed. Thus they had to rely upon convincing their fellow Americans to go along with the plan.

The Philadelphia Antislavery Society's constitution combined gradual and immediate abolition goals. It began by reiterating the importance of moral suasion and pledged to continue the traditional PAS emphasis on racial uplift. It also mentioned plans to push Congress to ban slavery in the District of Columbia, prevent the admission of additional slave states or territories into the Union, and suppress the internal slave trade.

The new group offered along with their constitution a "summary exposition" that they hoped would clarify their principles. They began by explaining that the renewed drive against slavery resulted from "a strong disposition in some, to suppress all inquiry in relation to it." At the same time, though, they refused to blame their "fellow-citizens of the South," claiming that Northerners perpetuated a system based on racism, and that system had to be corrected as well. They would fight both issues and appeal to citizens of both sections with "the force of truth," reaching out to all so that "all may labor without fear of raising into angry collision, factions and parties." They concluded by unequivocally stating their goal as "the entire abolition of slavery in the United States, without expatriation," the same goal stated by the AASS.[18]

The group met the following July 4 to hold the first annual meeting at the PAS's Clarkson Hall. This was an interesting choice of dates, since colonizationists typically used the occasion for their annual fund drives and appeals to the churches. Brown co-opted the revolutionary date a year earlier, using the occasion to plead the cause of the slave. Asking his listeners to "understand the liberty we *enjoy*" and to "consider the slavery they *suffer*," he contrasted American freedom to American slavery. By this point Arnold Buffum had relocated to Philadelphia from Boston, joining both groups. Brown was re-elected president and Joseph M. Truman and James Mott, both of the PAS, were elected vice presidents. Benjamin S. Jones, who would soon join the PAS, was made recording secretary. To the board of managers were added Buffum, Henry Grew, James Forten, Frederick A. Hinton, and Daniel Neall. Neall was a vice president of the PAS and Grew would soon join. Forten and Hinton, as African Americans, were not part of the PAS. Many of these men would also join the Pennsylvania Hall Association. The group reported that it had distributed 1,500 copies of an address explaining its principles during the year and had sent agents to neighboring communities to recruit, resulting in a growth in membership. They added that their show of force had proven that "mobocratic intimidation" would not stop them, so the resistance had subsided.[19]

Even so, detractors still lurked. The group recounted numerous debates where colonizationists accused immediatists of endangering the Union. They insisted the charge was nonsense not even believed by those who put it forth. Instead, they argued abolition would save the Union and make it stronger. Colonization, on the other hand, was an impractical solution that had actually stopped manumissions. Even so, unlike Garrison they handled colonizationists charitably by maintaining that "a large majority of the supporters of the colonization policy" operated by sincere motives and upon "a more full investigation of the subject" could be brought to "act with us, in promoting the cause of universal freedom."[20]

As evidenced by the number of people active in both the PAS and the new group, there was no clear distinction between "gradual" and "immediate." The new societies formed not to replace the PAS but to reinvigorate the movement in the face of apathy on the part of some reformers and to combat the assault upon Northern civil liberties that threatened to shut down dialogue over slavery altogether. Philadelphia abolitionists generally followed Woolman's example in being willing to consider multiple ways of ending slavery. They hoped to reach out to Southerners, colonizationists, and anyone else they could win over to the cause. Benjamin Lundy and David Paul Brown took the lead in creating this hybrid form of Pennsylvania immediatism.

Lundy used his *Enquirer* to support a variety of antislavery initiatives, even reprinting colonization society reports. Uninterested in dogmatic debates, he set out to awaken the public to the "*alarming crisis*" slavery posed to the nation and to call attention to "the principles of aggression and marauding violence" that were "spreading over the land." He began by reporting on a mob's attempt to suppress abolitionist James G. Birney's Cincinnati newspaper, the *Philanthropist*. A mob of fifteen to twenty men, apparently from the neighboring state of Kentucky, had attacked the paper late at night, destroyed pieces of the press, shredded paper, and wasted a keg of ink. In response, Birney and others with the Ohio Antislavery Society issued a statement claiming that "There is no longer any reason to doubt, that there exists among us a secret confederacy, whose bond of union is a covenant to put down the liberty of the press and the freedom of speech." In highlighting this violent act, Lundy hoped to appeal to a wide audience by showing readers that their own liberty was as much at stake as the slave's.[21]

Lundy showed equal concern for a traditionally gradualist issue—the spread of slavery across North America and the resulting shift in the sectional balance of power in Congress. He resisted Texas's annexation because he knew that adding another slave state to the Union would give pro-slavery forces more votes in both houses of Congress and could ultimately pave the way for permanent national protection of slavery. These issues offered common ground on which all antislavery advocates—gradualists, colonizationists, and immediatists—could agree, and Lundy sought action over tactical debate.

Like Lundy, Brown saw little reason to quibble over differences. In his July 4 address to the New York group he presented a definition of "immediate abolition" that fit well with Pennsylvania's antislavery legacy. Like New York abolitionists such as the Tappan brothers, he took "immediate" to mean that the process of freedom should begin right away, even if the end result took time. Slaveholders had put abolitionists off for years by promising to free the slaves when the time was right. Brown was tired of waiting and now said, "we answer, restore them to their natural rights, and *name your time*; but let it be *in time*, and not *in eternity*." He saw the work of the new group as

David Paul Brown.
Library Company of Philadelphia

a continuation of the efforts of PAS heroes from past generations, and he had little use for extreme stances that conjured "up these red rags, these bloody phantoms, and all the horrors of civil or servile war."

Unlike Garrison, who would eventually call for disunion over continued connection with slavery, Brown insisted that, even given how horrible slavery was, "if the only choices were between that evil and a total dismemberment of the Union, we should undoubtedly and promptly prefer the former." Hoping to avoid such a dire choice, he called upon his listeners to "alleviate the distress by assuasives, rather than increase it by irritation." He basically admitted that civil rights for blacks might have to wait and that abolitionists should first worry about securing an end to slavery. Sounding quite gradualist, he said that slaves were not ready for immediate freedom, but he added that abolitionists should push for the process of emancipation to be immediately put in place: "exchange the term *immediate* for *certain*; we

will not quarrel as to a month, or a year, or twenty years, if our antago-
nists will only concur with us in reducing the liberation of the slaves to
an actual *certainty.*"

After explaining his view of immediatism, Brown offered suggestions as to how it could be achieved. Still optimistic that slaveholders
could eventually be persuaded to cooperate, he suggested a system of
apprenticeship or compensated emancipation as had been used in the
West Indies. Though he had dismissed colonization as a dead issue, he
suggested a "national colony" where the U.S. government could send
free slaves. (Whether he knew it or not, this was exactly what many
ACS founders had hoped to create with Liberia, but the government
never took over the colony.) Borrowing from the PAS, he put forth an
"auxiliary project" to educate slaves in preparation for freedom, arguing that such an initiative would take away the "chief argument" against
freedom. He also made a strong point in insisting that state laws pro-
hibiting manumission be repealed, and he pointed to the hypocrisy of
such laws, passed by state legislators who "contend that the general
government has no right to interfere with the privilege of property."
Finally, he proposed that all children born after a given time be freed
upon a certain age and reiterated that "immediate means" must be
adopted to put this in place. He asserted the right of abolitionists
to speak out against slavery and concluded by calling upon his fellow
reformers to stop arguing among themselves and antagonizing Southerners and colonizationists.[22]

Though Garrison would not approve of Brown's version of immediate abolition, other immediatists agreed with him, and the AASS
wanted desperately to bring Pennsylvania into the fold. Primarily, they
wanted a state auxiliary there, and they sent two agents, James Miller
McKim and Charles C. Burleigh, to help secure this end. After tour-
ing the state for a couple of years and forming around 100 new societies there, they played instrumental roles in founding the Pennsylvania
Antislavery Society (PASS) in 1837.

Lundy issued the call for a state auxiliary convention through the
National Enquirer in October 1836. After 1,200 men signed the call,
the convention met in late January 1837 in Harrisburg. About 250 delegates attended, including Lundy, Burleigh, John Greenleaf Whittier,
Bartholomew Fussell, and Lewis Tappan. Despite some opposition to
his being a "foreign agent" since he was from Connecticut, Burleigh

took a leading speaking role. Fussell, who would become a vice president of the group, called the convention to order. Lundy spoke on a number of issues, including Northern states' rights to provide trial by jury to blacks accused of being runaway slaves and the need to protest Texas's admission to the Union. Tappan contributed by introducing discussion over the role of the churches in the abolition movement. Other topics addressed included the internal slave trade, kidnapping of free blacks, free produce, and the importance of women to the movement. They also discussed the need to bring more working-class people into the cause after Lewis C. Gunn pointed out that if they could be convinced of "the true bearing of slavery" upon their own interests, "it will evermore be impossible for the gentlemen, who have stood behind the curtain exciting riot, again to succeed in getting up a mob." Burleigh would later try to take this message to the workers of Pennsylvania, but he would not be able to work fast enough to prevent them from helping to destroy Pennsylvania Hall.[23]

Before adjourning, the group wrote an address for public distribution to explain their new society. Like Brown's previous talks, the document stressed the right of free expression and the duty to speak out against the evils of slavery. It also pointed out that some slaveholders were probably virtuous people but added that "this does not alter the moral character of the system itself." Like Brown, they hoped to avoid alienating the South in their campaign of moral suasion against bound labor. They reiterated a point made by the AASS that they would respect states' rights and focus on slavery in the District of Columbia and the internal slave trade, both of which fell under the legal domain of the federal government. They boldly declared slavery a sin and expressed optimism that slaveholders could be brought around "with the weapon of truth, wielded with talent and energy." As Brown had argued before, one way to reach them would be to offer a scheme of compensated emancipation and apprenticeship.[24]

Even with the relatively mild arguments presented at the convention, the founding of an immediate state auxiliary caused quite a stir. Within weeks meetings were held in several parts of the state to denounce abolition and a new newspaper, the *Anti-Abolitionist*, was being published in Philadelphia. Soon, anti-abolitionists began to call themselves "Friends of the Integrity of the Union" and to plan their own Harrisburg convention.

One response offered by abolitionists was to stress the continuities between the PAS and the PASS to assure Pennsylvanians that there was nothing too radical about the new group. In a series of letters to the *National Enquirer* J. Blanchard, an agent of the new group, explained that the main difference was the name—though, he pointed out, an "abolition" society was by definition "antislavery," so even that difference did not mean much. Both societies refused to let slaveholders participate, and both relied upon petitioning, organizing societies, holding talks, and publishing antislavery documents. In short, "the two Societies are one in NAME, OBJECT, PRINCIPLE and MEASURES." The PASS made a similar argument in their address and Lundy reprinted it in the *Enquirer*, likely to emphasize Blanchard's point. Perhaps history should have taught them that even the gradualists had fallen into disfavor with their neighbors.[25]

Even as they tried to explain their new society to outsiders, Pennsylvania immediatists, like others throughout the nation, continued to argue among themselves on a number of important issues. Some wanted to take a stronger stance toward the churches, which they argued were not doing their share to combat the immoral system of slavery. Others wanted to use political means to fight the system, campaigning for sympathetic politicians, while others wanted to keep abolition completely separate from politics. Many wanted to avoid being drawn into these secondary debates. As Lundy tried to explain in the *Enquirer*, divisions only served to hurt the movement: "we wish to raise our voice against the spirit of intolerance, which has of late intruded upon the threshold, and even the sanctuary, of the Antislavery Cause in this country" and "we desire that it may be understood, and borne in mind by our correspondents, that we protest against all acrimonious controversies among ourselves. *The ENEMY is not yet conquered.*" Despite his warnings, the infighting over secondary causes continued.[26]

CHAPTER 5

....

A "Temple of Liberty" or a "Temple of Amalgamation"?

John Greenleaf Whittier arrived in Philadelphia in the fall of 1837, just in time to watch as the hall went up a little more than a block away from the boarding house where he rented a room. Benjamin Lundy had asked the young abolitionist poet to come assist him at the *National Enquirer*. Having learned from past mistakes,

Pennsylvania Hall. From Pennsylvania Hall Association, *History of Pennsylvania Hall* (Philadelphia: Merrihew and Gunn, 1838).
Library Company of Philadelphia

Lundy decided to avoid William Lloyd Garrison's inflammatory rhetoric. The last thing he needed was another lawsuit—not to mention that violence seemed to follow Garrison like a shadow. Divisions plagued the movement nationally, but so far Philadelphia abolitionists had managed to maintain harmony in their city. Whittier would understand and would work to continue building bridges. Garrison would not.

Likely noting the progress of the hall as he ventured around town during the day, Whittier returned to the boarding house at night to rich conversation at the dinner table, even though he complained that the food left much to be desired. Joseph and Rachel Healy owned the home. A local publisher who handled most of the city's antislavery books and pamphlets, Joseph also served as the financial agent for the Pennsylvania Antislavery Society.

Benjamin Jones and Sarah Lewis also boarded in the home. Jones, the recording secretary of the Philadelphia Antislavery Society, operated an abolitionist bookstore on Arch Street, but he must have been particularly eager to see the hall completed since he had made plans to move his store into one of the ground-floor rooms. Lewis operated a girls' school on Cherry Street with Sarah Pugh, an officer of the Philadelphia Female Antislavery Society (PFASS). Both women were planning to attend the second annual Antislavery Convention of American Women in the hall in May.

Though from New England, Whittier had ties to the Pennsylvania antislavery community. He had cousins on South Sixth Street, and his former schoolmaster, Joshua Coffin, was in Philadelphia participating in activities with the Underground Railroad. Abijah Thayer, the editor who first published Whittier's work, was also in the city and helped him get settled when he arrived. Whittier also had attended the founding convention of the Pennsylvania Antislavery Society (PASS) and made important contacts there, including Governor Joseph Ritner, a strong opponent of Texas annexation. According to Whittier, Ritner "alone of all the governors of the Union in 1836 met the insulting demands and measures of the south in a matter becoming a freeman." Whittier would soon see how accurate his image of Ritner was.

By the time Whittier made his way to Philadelphia in 1837, he had already made a name for himself as one of the nation's top politically focused abolitionists. A bit of a dandy in his custom-tailored jackets, stove-pipe hat, and specially made boots, he stood out among his fellow Orthodox Quakers, who were known for their simplicity of dress, especially their flat broad-brimmed hats. Even if he did not look the part, he was a birthright member of the Society of Friends and shared the abolitionist sentiments of his fellow Quakers from a very early age. Whittier began his career in journalism editing the *Manufacturer*, a politically oriented paper that promoted American manufacturing, the tariff, and Henry Clay. From there he went to Hartford, Connecticut, to edit another pro-Clay newspaper, the *New England Review*. While at the *Review* Whittier began writing antislavery articles. By 1833 William Lloyd Garrison was on a personal crusade to convince Whittier to abandon politics and "creations of romance and fancy" and focus exclusively on abolition. Hoping to convince his friend to enlist in the cause wholeheartedly, Garrison traveled to Whittier's hometown of Haverhill, Massachusetts, where they reconnected. Garrison won and Whittier agreed to commit himself to the abolition cause.[1]

Even though Whittier admired Garrison, he developed his own brand of immediatism. Willing to try whatever it might take to end slavery, Whittier maintained friendships with colonizationists even though he did not agree with them or support their cause. He also supported Clay, a longtime president of the American Colonization Society (ACS). Known as the "Great Compromiser," Clay was the quintessential American politician and perhaps the leading figure in the Whig political party. While some Americans regarded Clay's propensity to compromise as a sign of his being disingenuous, Whittier admired his political skills. Instead of rejecting Clay altogether because of his belief in colonization, Whittier tried hard to convert him to the cause of immediatism. He ultimately failed in his endeavor and eventually gave up on Clay, but the patience and gentle determination he displayed in working to win over the elder statesman contrasted strongly with Garrison's absolutist approach. Like Clay, Whittier excelled at the art of compromise.

Whittier wanted slavery to end, but he certainly did not want to see the United States torn apart along sectional lines. He wrote to a colonizationist friend in 1833 that his poet soul could not handle the idea of war and disunion: "I have thrown the rough armor of rude and turbulent controversy over a keenly sensitive bosom—a heart of softer and gentler emotions than I dare expose." This tender side left him unwilling to entertain the idea that any war, even a war to end slavery, would be a just war. Likely defending himself from charges made by many colonizationists that immediatists courted the destruction of the nation, he responded that that was not the case: "For one, I thank God that He has given me a deep and invincible horror of human butchery—that I am not one of those who 'look on blood and carnage with composure.'" Apparently other abolitionists had realized this about Whittier, because he mentioned facing criticism for his squeamishness. Lundy, however, must have seen Whittier's ability to compromise much as Whittier saw Clay's—as strength rather than weakness.[2]

Instead of choosing between politics and abolition, Whittier blended his two passions and created a political brand of antislavery that fit well with the ideas of Benjamin Lundy and David Paul Brown. He laid out his doctrine in *Justice and Expediency or, Slavery Considered with a View to its Rightful and Effectual Remedy, ABOLITION* (1833). Setting the stage for the political abolition of the 1840s and 1850s, this work presented the argument that free labor was more efficient than slave labor. It also called out against colonization—the pet project of Whittier's friends and political associates in the Whig party.[3]

After coming under attack from a Virginia newspaper for the sentiments he expressed in the pamphlet, Whittier used the writings of Thomas Jefferson and other Virginians to show that the founding generation opposed the permanent perpetuation of slavery and assumed it would die out. While conceding that slaveholders had the constitutional right to their property, he called upon a higher law and insisted that slaveholding was immoral and against God's laws. Although he and his New England friends would respect the Constitution, they resented Southern expectations that they would participate in the immoral system by helping to hunt down and capture the human beings who managed to escape bondage. He also pointed out that abolitionists, contrary to popular belief, did not wish to encourage slaves to revolt and instead feared that prospect and hoped wholeheartedly to avoid it. Neither, he added, did they wish to interfere politically with slavery as it existed in the South.

Slavery was an immoral system based on sin, but neither he nor his associates intended to force Southerners to repent. Instead, they hoped to confine the sin of their Southern neighbors to the South. Just as Southerners argued that they had the right to keep slaves, Whittier pointed out that Northern states that had outlawed the system within their own borders had the right to erect a moral cordon and keep themselves free from this sin. This meant they should not be expected to chase fugitives or help slaveholders if slaves should indeed revolt. In this sense he and other political abolitionists turned the South's "State's Rights" argument on its head.

The arguments Whittier put forth make it obvious that he deserved to be known as the "Father of Political Abolition." He articulated free soil and free labor ideas that would later take center stage in the Republican Party's antislavery agenda. The differences between Whittier's antislavery and Garrison's version of immediatism lay in the pragmatic approach. Garrison had no time for such tepidness; Whittier, by contrast, had no stomach for the specter of civil war.

Though Whittier realized his support of abolition was costing him politically, he actively participated in the founding convention of the American Antislavery Society (AASS). Even though he was the youngest delegate, he served as a secretary and helped draft the AASS's Declaration of Sentiments. He also tried to enlist the support of his fellow Quakers but met with limited success. On the positive side, he met Lucretia Mott during his first trip to Philadelphia and they forged a lasting friendship. While some Quakers were avoiding the immediatists out of concern for their businesses, the Motts remained dedicated to abolition and free produce. They switched to wool in their textile business to avoid relying upon Southern cotton. After meeting such dedicated abolitionists, Whittier left the city in a positive frame of mind. Soon after he attended the founding convention of the Pennsylvania Antislavery Society, Lundy asked him to join him in Philadelphia and prepare to take over the *National Enquirer*. As he considered his options, he wrote "our friends in Boston are fully persuaded that the grand battle is now to be fought in Pennsylvania, between mobocracy (excited by the slaveholding influence of Virginia and Maryland . . .) and the friends of liberty."[4]

Before heading to Philadelphia, Whittier spent the summer in New York at the American Antislavery Society's office. There he worked with fellow abolitionists Henry B. Stanton, Theodore Dwight Weld, and James G. Birney to edit two antislavery newspapers, the

Emancipator and the *Antislavery Review*. They also managed petition drives, wrote pamphlets, arranged lectures, and sent letters, all in an effort to raise public awareness and to lobby Congress against the interstate slave trade and Texas annexation and for abolition in the District of Columbia. These were all traditional antislavery goals. During this time Whittier and Weld became particularly close and were known for chatting the night away.

At this point abolitionists began to divide. Politically minded abolitionists began to work together in 1837, right around the time the clergy issued the *Pastoral Letter* that fueled dissention among abolitionists over the "women question." The political group included Whittier, Birney, the Tappan brothers, and Gerrit Smith, among others. These men favored political action, even though Garrison argued that the Constitution was a corrupt pro-slavery document and refused to have anything to do with the political system it created.[5]

Facing disagreement and dissention within their ranks, abolitionists also continued to deal with resistance from without. Increasingly in 1837 they found themselves shut out of venues they once used to hold their meetings. Halls and churches throughout the North refused to allow abolitionists to use their facilities. Some did not agree with the "radical" turn abolition had taken. Others had no problem with the message but feared that negative public reaction could result in property damage or destruction. To preserve their investments they closed their doors to abolitionists. Even the Quakers refused to risk their property for public abolition meetings. As a result, Philadelphia abolitionists decided to build a place of their own.[6]

Somehow, despite the financial hard times brought on by the Panic of 1837 and the anti-abolition resentment, the city's reformers managed to raise funds for two major projects in 1837—a new Shelter for Colored Orphans and Pennsylvania Hall. The Association for the Care of Colored Orphans oversaw the first of these projects. The women who collected the funds for the orphanage included Quakers, many likely affiliated with Pennsylvania Abolition Society (PAS) members. One, Sarah E. Cresson, was the sister of Quaker colonizationist and former PAS member Elliott Cresson. By October they had raised enough money to appoint a building committee and enlist the aid of men to oversee the construction, which occurred roughly in tandem with that taking place on the corner of Sixth and Haines.[7]

Like the orphanage, Pennsylvania Hall was built with money raised primarily by women. All phases of the project, however, were overseen by the men of the Pennsylvania Hall Association, which met for the first time in March 1837. The group's specific purpose was to build their own hall, and contemporaries and historians alike have emphasized exclusion as the driving force behind their decision. There was, however, another factor at play. Gradualists worked behind the scenes and held closed meetings. Immediatists, on the other hand, were cultivating a much more open and public movement. Whereas the gradualists simply needed a room to accommodate those they had invited or elected into their ranks, the immediatists needed enough space to house large audiences. This meant that while the Pennsylvania Hall Association was pushed by exclusion to build the hall, it was also pulled by the need to build something grand enough to accommodate large crowds.[8]

To fulfill their mission, the association needed money, which they hoped would come from two main sources. They anticipated that once the structure was built it would pay for itself with rent revenue. The idea was obviously a sound one, because requests to rent rooms came in immediately from the Philadelphia Lyceum, the Temperance Society, and the PFASS. Meanwhile, however, they had to come up with the money to get the hall built. This they did by selling stock for twenty dollars per share. PFASS members played a central role in raising the forty thousand dollars needed. Some people who did not have money to purchase stock donated materials and labor in exchange for shares.[9]

The Board of Managers that oversaw the fundraising and construction included abolitionists affiliated with both the PAS and the Philadelphia Antislavery Society. Many were Quakers who were members of both groups. Daniel Neall, a Hicksite Quaker, dentist, and member of the executive committee of the PASS, served as president of the board. Samuel Webb served as treasurer, and William Dorsey, the secretary of the Northern Liberties Antislavery Society, was secretary of the board. Frederick A. Hinton, a free black barber and active member of the Philadelphia Antislavery Society, served on the business committee responsible for constructing the hall. Thomas Stewart drew the floor plans in exchange for two shares of stock.[10]

The PFASS and several members of the association made major financial contributions by purchasing stock. Managers also stressed the contributions of "mechanics, or working men." This claim appears dubious, given the class antagonism of the time, not to mention the dire straits many workers faced. Perhaps the claim was true. What is most likely is that workers contributed their labor in exchange for stock, hoping to make money once the hall was open and generating rent revenue. What is clear is that abolitionists in Pennsylvania had been trying to reach out to working-class whites since the AASS sent agents to the state in 1836.

By June 1837 the fundraising efforts yielded enough to buy a lot and begin construction. The managers acquired property at the corner of Sixth and Haines Streets, between Arch and Race, near Franklin Square. Just blocks from Independence Hall, the property was located in the heart of the abolition community on the north side of downtown. Construction crews began pulling down the old buildings on the lot in early July. Lundy reported in the *Enquirer* that several people and organizations had already applied to rent space in the building, leaving him certain of the profitability of the venture. "But what is of far more importance," he added, "is the effect which it must produce on the public mind, when it is seen that the friends of freedom, and liberty of speech, are numerous enough to require such as building." The new hall, he concluded, was expected to hold five hundred more people than Musical Fund Hall, the city's largest hall at the time.[11]

In late November the abolitionists held a party at Ellis and Longstreth's Carpenter Shop to celebrate the raising of the hall in a "Temperance Feast of articles produced by Free Labor." After dinner, Webb, in many aspects the driving force of the project, dedicated the building "to Freedom and the Rights of Man," promising that "its proximity to Franklin Square—its central situation—its massive walls, and solidity of construction, render it peculiarly suitable for the purposes intended." The "mechanics" who had helped raise the building attended the festivities and shared in the jubilation.

From all descriptions of the building, the association had good reason to celebrate. Their new building was sixty-two feet wide, one hundred feet deep, and forty-two feet high. It could seat three thousand people in total and included an elaborate and ornate roof ventilation system that allowed for fresh air to circulate even when the windows were closed. It was also one of the first buildings in Philadelphia to have gas lighting. The first story housed four stores, which would soon include Benjamin Jones's bookstore, a free produce store, and the offices of the *National Enquirer* (soon to be renamed the *Pennsylvania Freeman* by Whittier). The main entrance faced Sixth Street, but there were two more entrances and three rooms at the rear of the building. One of those rooms was to be a session room and the other was to be rented by the Philadelphia Lyceum. Under these rooms were a series of large dry cellars. Three large stairways between twenty and thirty feet wide led to what managers called the "Grand Saloon" that took up the entire second floor. It was surrounded by galleries on three sides and included a speaker's platform adorned with the state motto of "Virtue, Liberty, and Independence" engraved in gold. Several speakers at the hall-raising party reiterated that the hall was a venue for free discussion, not just an "abolition hall."[12]

Indeed, underneath the jubilation ran a defensive current of determination to fight for the right to speak freely. This is not surprising, considering those attending the party had just learned of the murder of abolitionist Elijah P. Lovejoy in Alton, Illinois. Throughout 1836 and 1837 mobs attacked antislavery presses in the Northern and Midwestern states, and Lovejoy had raised funds and rebuilt his press more than once before the fatal confrontation. Local officials, unable to protect the abolitionist or his property, had deputized and armed Lovejoy, who chose to fight back and defend his press. When all was said and done, Lovejoy was dead and abolitionists all over the country were debating what many saw as his violation of the principles of peaceful resistance.

One thing, however, was for certain. Abolitionists were not willing to be silenced, and they now had a martyr to rally around. Lovejoy had been more than an abolitionist; he had been a defender of white as well as black freedom. According to one abolitionist paper, "he spoke in defense of LIBERTY—he lifted up his voice like a trumpet in the advocacy of TRUTH—*and for this he fell!*" Unfortunately Pennsylvania abolitionists failed to see the implications for their own situation: "Let us thank God, however, that while such scenes are enacted in Illinois, there is in Pennsylvania a redeeming spirit, which, in the maintenance of truth, has erected a temple to 'VIRTUE, LIBERTY, AND INDEPENDENCE!'" Optimistically, one speaker at the raising celebration declared, "here shall Free Discussion find a refuge and a home!" Apparently no one present stopped to think that Pennsylvania Hall could be the next martyr to fall in defense of free speech.[13]

As construction crews put the final touches on the building, and as the Pennsylvania Hall Association began to prepare for the grand opening, Whittier dove into the Philadelphia abolition scene. He had arrived in the city just as an upsurge in the number of runaway slaves seeking refuge led some of the more radical abolitionists there to consider extra-legal means of relief as they came to realize that legal and moral boundaries did not always fall along the same lines. In 1834 a Committee of Twelve had met to consider the merits of helping known fugitives escape their masters. This group attracted more supporters, all of whom became active on the Underground Railroad. In 1837 a biracial group of Philadelphians, which included James Forten and Robert Purvis, created the Vigilant Association. The goal of this group was to help escaped slaves evade the slave hunters who chased them through the streets of Philadelphia. Black and white women, many of whom were affiliated with the PFASS, met in each other's homes to make clothing for the refugees. Together the men and women constructed an elaborate operation where barbers and dressmakers worked together to disguise the fugitives and send them along to New York, the next stop on their journey to freedom.[14]

Even though the Vigilant Association performed an important service, their work remained controversial because they were breaking the law. Even so, Whittier felt drawn to the cause. By the time he arrived in Philadelphia, his friend James G. Birney had found himself at odds with the law and on trial for aiding fugitives. Though Whittier and his closest friends had not taken Garrison's radical stance on the Constitution, they had taken a turn that was, in some ways, even more radical. They still hoped to work within the American political system to overturn slavery legally. Meanwhile, if they had to break a few laws to help secure black freedom, they would do what they had to do.

The Pennsylvania Freeman

In March 1838 Lundy retired from the *National Enquirer* and the Pennsylvania Antislavery Society officially adopted the paper.

Whittier took over and renamed it the *Pennsylvania Freeman*. In his valedictory editorial Lundy expressed appreciation for the years of support and explained that his health was deteriorating. He suffered from respiratory discomfort, and his friends were noticing that part of his face appeared paralyzed. Lundy explained that he wanted to go West, find the family he had long neglected, and reestablish the *Genius of Universal Emancipation*. He had helped revive antislavery in Philadelphia, and now he hoped to expel the "Fiend of Slavery" from the "unsubdued *forests*" of the newer territories. He trusted Whittier to further the cause in Philadelphia. Soon after writing his final editorial, Lundy packed all of his belongings into a trunk that he decided to store in the *Freeman*'s new office in Pennsylvania Hall.[15]

Whittier promised to proceed with the newspaper much as Lundy had. Like Lundy, he hoped to build a strong antislavery coalition, and he believed that by sticking to established antislavery principles, "we can all stand shoulder to shoulder, in the struggle for liberty—with one common interest—lending our united strength for the overthrow of slavery." Though a friend of Garrison, he would have none of Garrison's dogma and divisiveness.[16]

As Benjamin Lundy prepared for his westward journey and John Greenleaf Whittier settled into his office in Pennsylvania Hall, Robert T. Conrad looked on in anger. Abolitionists eagerly awaited the grand opening of their "temple of Liberty," but Conrad saw nothing but an ostentatious display of radicalism. Many other Philadelphians shared his hatred for what some would soon dub the "Temple of Amalgamation," and Conrad was shocked that the abolitionists had spent the time and money to build something that would surely draw the wrath of so many.

Given the tense racial climate, the presence of so many Southerners in this border city, and the popularity of the colonization movement, it did indeed take a certain sort of courage to build such a grand edifice. The economic tensions brought on by the Panic of 1837 only made matters worse. Of course, abolitionists knew what they faced and decided to take a calculated risk. Almost a year earlier, in June 1837, they appointed a special committee to decide the feasibility of building their hall "in the face of almost universal disapproval" of their cause. They consulted with Mayor John Swift, who promised that "the abolitionists should never be molested while he was mayor!" Perhaps with a false sense of security, they decided to go forward with their plans. They managed to raise the money they needed in just a few days and hoped their support would be as strong as the resistance they would face. Crowds attacked abolitionists in communities throughout the rest of the country, but this was Philadelphia, the birthplace of American antislavery.[17]

Of course, Robert Conrad's Philadelphia was about more than Quakers, abolition, and peace. It was also about trade, much of which was dependent upon friendly relations with the South—and Southern associates were asking questions. As immediatism began to take hold, Conrad's Southern friends grew concerned. Would Philadelphia abolitionists join their radical counterparts from New England in labeling slavery a sin and pushing for its immediate demise?

At first Conrad promised that the answer was no and that all was well in his city. Known mostly as a writer of tragedies and editor of the *Daily Commercial Intelligencer*, the name of which he later changed to the *Philadelphia Gazette*, Conrad had recently begun to practice law. Plagued by poor health, he would go back and forth between editing and serving in various legal capacities in the city. He would be a judge of criminal sessions for the city and county of Philadelphia beginning in 1838 and mayor of the city in 1854, and he would continue to write tragedies and poetry until his early death in 1858. On August 24, 1835, however, he was a young lawyer who led a group of the city's merchants in a town meeting at Musical Fund Hall. There they passed a series of resolutions they hoped would smooth things over. Southerners had "appealed to the non-slave-holding states, to manifest their disapprobation" of abolitionist radicalism, and the Philadelphia merchants responded by promising to help protect "the domestic institutions of the South." Assuring Southerners "that we are their brethren, and as such, sympathize in their dangers and wrongs," the merchants insisted that they viewed "with regret and indignation the incendiary measures which have disturbed their tranquility." They considered abolitionist actions "unwise, dangerous, and deserving the emphatic reprehension and zealous opposition of every friend of peace and of the country."

Not realizing how much they sounded like many Philadelphia abolitionists, they went on to insist that they held the Constitution sacred and they disclaimed any and all interference with slavery in the Southern states. Echoing David Paul Brown, they professed an abiding love for the Union and deep horror for "all that is calculated in the most remote degree to endanger or impair it." They agreed with their Southern associates that abolitionists posed a serious threat to the "peace and permanence of this Union" and that antislavery agitation only served to tighten the bonds of slavery. Promising that most Northerners "neither claim nor desire a right to interfere with the institutions of the south, and regard with decided and marked disapprobation, the principles and measures of the abolitionists," they assured Southerners that Pennsylvania was not afflicted by radicalism. "We have reason to believe, that there is no abolition press or publication in this city, and that no incendiary measures have been adopted or sanctioned by the friends of emancipation in this state."[18]

Conrad and his associates found the opportunity to prove their sincerity the very next day. Dockworkers accidentally broke open a box as they were unloading it from a New York steamboat. When abolitionist literature such as the *Liberator* and *The Slave's Friend* fell from the broken package, they sent for Conrad and his friends, who then tracked down the person to whom the box had been addressed. When he denied ownership of the box, the committee decided to destroy the contents by dumping the materials into the Delaware River. The *Pennsylvania Inquirer* described a solemn scene "conducted in a spirit which exhibited a fixed purpose to resist everything like the circulation of incendiarism of any description, and at the same time to avoid any improper excitement among ourselves." In exchange for the public display of solidarity, Southern merchants spent unprecedented amounts of money with these Philadelphia merchants. A year later the merchants celebrated record-breaking sales. To the delight of abolitionist Lewis C. Gunn, however, many of the goods were bought on credit and after financial panic set in in 1837, the merchants were left holding the bag.[19]

Conrad likely understood the nature of the market and forgave his Southern trade partners. He and his fellow merchants, many of whom had businesses on Market Street, remained dedicated to their pledge to resist radical abolition. By early 1838 their businesses were struggling, and the building at Sixth and Haines stood as a powerful symbol of their impotence and powerlessness. Not only was the building itself a tangible symbol of the "incendiary" movement, but the newspaper in the basement broke the promise that no abolition publication would emanate from this city—an antislavery hotspot placed precariously on the border between the North and the South.

Between the 1835 merchants' meeting and the completion of Pennsylvania Hall in 1838, abolitionists found themselves increasingly at odds with their neighbors. Merchants had commercial ties with the South and sought to protect their economic interests. Workers felt their livelihoods threatened as both freedmen and fugitives continued to augment the city's black population even as the economic panic made jobs increasingly hard to come by. This made for a tense atmosphere that often led to crowd violence in which local officials were indifferent at best and complicit at worst.

Abolitionists were not the only ones facing violence, however. Jacksonian society was notoriously rough. In addition to the race and abolition riots, cities saw fights break out between immigrants and American-born citizens, political rivals, and opposing street gangs, many of which were made up of volunteer firemen. Unorthodox religious groups, particularly the Mormons, were attacked for their beliefs, and laborers often rioted against the exploitation they faced in newly emerging factories. Americans amused themselves with prize fighting, animal fighting, and other violent games, and some settled their differences with duels. Lundy observed in 1837 that many Philadelphians were carrying concealed weapons, and he attributed it to the violence inherent in a nation that condoned slavery.[20] If slavery made American society violent, economic instability made it worse.

The Panic of 1837 exacerbated racial unrest. It began when the prosperity that had fueled speculation and overuse of credit in the early to middle 1830s came to a screeching halt after the international economy collapsed in 1837. For the working classes it meant job loss, starvation, and bread riots. Abolitionists, already resented by upper-class Northerners who blamed them for threatening commercial relations with the South, drew the wrath of working-class whites who faced job competition from free blacks. Of course, the workers reserved plenty of hatred for their black neighbors as well. Philadelphia mayor John Swift had to send forces to defend black neighborhoods twice that spring. One of the mobs included members of the Robert Morris Hose Company. One historian described the situation as "an ominous sign of a transition" of the fire departments "from defenders of the public order to sympathizers with the attackers—or attackers themselves—of the city's scapegoats." The truth of the matter, however, is that the city's fire departments had a history of such behavior and were notoriously connected to violent street gangs.[21]

Foreign immigration to the city throughout the 1830s intensified the job competition and lawlessness. Skilled workers arrived from Germany and Ireland and pushed black artisans downward into the ranks of the unskilled. At the bottom of the labor market, both skilled and unskilled blacks competed with unskilled immigrant workers for scarce jobs. This situation only heightened existing racial tensions.

In many minds abolitionist efforts only added to the problem by making Pennsylvania, especially Philadelphia, an attractive destination for free blacks and escaped slaves. As a result antislavery activists, especially those affiliated with the professedly immediatist PASS, found themselves under attack throughout the region. Traveling agents were often interrupted by loud crowds, impromptu fife-and-drum bands, and flying projectiles—including eggs, tomatoes, and stones. In one instance, a protester threw cayenne pepper on the stove in a meeting hall, forcing temporary evacuation. In these cases Southerners had to rely upon sympathetic friends in the North to harass those who challenged human bondage. Every now and then they found a way to exact their own vengeance.

In one instance that occurred just as the Pennsylvania Hall Association was beginning its work, the unsuspecting son of a well-known abolitionist made the fateful decision to travel South on business. Immediately upon his arrival in Savannah, Georgia, John Hopper was recognized as the son of PAS member Isaac Hopper. Word spread throughout the city, and a crowd gathered at the young Hopper's hotel room before he had a chance to realize the danger he faced. Aware of the mob's lethal intentions, the mayor and alderman of the city rescued the visitor from his attackers at the hotel and jailed him for his own protection. Determined to make a statement, the crowd surrounded the jail several times during the night, but city authorities managed to sneak Hopper onto a ship in the nearby harbor. The mob learned of this move and planned to attack the ship. The captain hid Hopper on a small boat and sent him to another ship, distracting the mob while the young traveler made his way upstream to safety. Incensed, the *National Enquirer* fumed that "an unsuspecting youth" could be "thus maltreated—*merely because he was known to be*

THE SON of a member of a society, of which FRANKLIN was President!!!" Calling for action against "so gross and palpable an infringement of the rights of our citizens," the editor asked, *"what is the Federal Union worth,* if things of this nature are to be tolerated?" He concluded, "There is not, probably, a set of cannibal savages on the globe, more devilish in heart, or murderous in design, than the infuriate rabble who do the bidding of the despotic slaveholders of our southern states."[22]

A Hunting Ground for Slave Catchers

The Hopper incident illustrates the growing sectional tensions on many levels. While the *Enquirer* described Isaac Hopper merely as a member of the PAS, he was actually much more dangerous to Southern interests than an average abolitionist. He had already gained a reputation as the Father of the Underground Railroad. A Hicksite Quaker who spent his adolescence watching slave catchers and kidnappers hunt their prey in the streets of Philadelphia, he tried to protect African Americans and help them evade capture. The PAS elected him to membership in 1796, and he worked with the group to devise clever legal maneuvers to help blacks win their freedom. By the mid-1830s he was known throughout the United States for aiding and sheltering fugitive slaves. To the Savannah mob, then, capturing John Hopper would have been an important victory in an ongoing war with someone who had thwarted their efforts and interfered with their business for decades. They called upon Northerners to rein in men like Isaac Hopper and respect Southern property rights. Of course, as the editorial in the *National Enquirer* revealed, much more than property rights were at stake. Though John Hopper was not in the South as an abolitionist, the attack revealed the extent to which anti-abolition mobs would go to suppress others' rights to free speech and freedom of conscience. Increasingly, abolitionists began to insist that their rights to speak freely be protected, just as slaveholders insisted on protection of their right to own human beings. Philadelphia's geographic location left the city at the center of this battle.

The fugitive slave issue surfaced as soon as the Pennsylvania State Legislature outlawed slavery in 1780, but it intensified with the founding of the PASS in 1837, when delegates at the founding convention formed a committee to investigate state and federal laws regarding fugitive slaves. They traced the history of fugitive slave laws in the state, arguing that abolitionists had made progress toward securing for fugitives the right to trial by jury. This progress, however, came to a screeching halt after 1829 in the face of Southern insistence that citizens of the North aid in the recovery of their human property. Disgusted, the PASS asked if their state's commercial success had transformed the general population "into a community of mercenary traders, and induced her to offer her philanthropy, once proverbial in the nation, as sacrifice upon the altar of avarice?" Even Governor Joseph Ritner had had enough and called upon Pennsylvanians to renew their efforts on behalf of the slave. "In rapid and startling succession," he contended, "all the principles of Pennsylvania policy, all the objects of state pride have been attacked," not just by Southerners but by Pennsylvanians themselves. "Worst of all," according to the governor, was "the base bowing of the knee to the dark spirit of slavery!" To the fury of slaveholding interests, and the delight of abolitionists like John Greenleaf Whittier, Ritner concluded by vowing to resist the spread of slavery into the Western territories. "While we admit and scrupulously respect the constitutional rights of other states, on this momentous subject, let us not, either by fear or interest, be driven from aught of that spirit of independence and veneration for freedom, which has ever characterized our beloved commonwealth." He warned that "the Union being a voluntary compact to continue together for certain specified purposes" could easily give way to a situation of subjection "the instant one portion of it succeeds in imposing terms and dictating conditions upon another." Clearly, concern for "states' rights" could go both ways.[23]

Slaveholding interests, however, remained determined to do whatever it took to silence the abolitionists. By 1837 Southern leaders were insisting that antislavery agitation left them no choice but to consider secession to protect their interests. Not only were more radical abolitionists like Isaac Hopper and members of the Vigilant Association not returning fugitive slaves, they were even helping them don disguises and escape. Whereas PAS members of the previous generation had fought patiently through the courts to help slaves gain their freedom, abolitionists of this generation were losing their patience with slave catchers and kidnappers who chased escaped slaves

into free territory and made Pennsylvania courts "tools in the matter."
According to AASS agent for Pennsylvania Henry C. Wright, by
complying with requests of slave catchers the state's courts were
"converting men into property!" As Wright argued, "southern men-
hunters" had turned Pennsylvania into "literally a HUNTING
GROUND for those who sport in the tears and blood of men."[24]

Despite abolitionists' appeals to conscience and reason, slave
owners wanted further assurances that Northern legislatures would
continue to prosecute those who interfered with Southern property
rights. Comments like Ritner's left them doubtful. Once again a group
of Pennsylvanians took the bait, deciding to pledge their loyalty to the
Union and their opposition to their abolitionist neighbors.

Friends of the Integrity of the Union

As soon as the PASS formed in Harrisburg, detractors proposed a convention of their own. Philadelphia colonizationists Joseph R. Ingersoll
and Job Tyson, along with Alderman Morton McMichael and a number
of other Pennsylvania lawyers, judges, editors, and businessmen, came
together in Harrisburg at the Friends of the Integrity of the Union
convention. They began planning the meeting and choosing delegates
in February 1837 and held the meeting that May. Abolitionists attributed the gathering mainly to the work of colonizationists, probably
because while the delegates admitted slavery was evil they censured
abolitionists for endangering the Union with their radical rhetoric and
actions. Delegates also endorsed the ACS and pledged financial aid to
the Pennsylvania Colonization Society. When all was said and done the
convention failed to make a strong stand against abolitionists, and very
few present seemed interested in speaking out in favor of slavery.
Indeed, several delegates were apparently at least loosely affiliated with
the abolitionists and were there to co-opt the meeting. The most interesting of these was Thaddeus Stevens, who turned the proceedings into
a comedy of errors. Reverend T. W. Hanes of Allegheny began to sus-
pect trouble and tried repeatedly to unmask the abolitionists among
them, only to find himself teased by Stevens in a playful and good-
natured manner that brought much laughter and distraction from his
point. In the end the convention was reduced to what the *Enquirer*
described as an "impotent display of political knavery."[25]

Even though their convention failed, anti-abolitionists decided to create their own newspaper, *The Anti-Abolitionist*, in June 1837. Editors Robert D. Powell and Hervey Lightner of Montgomery County issued a prospectus for the paper, promising to "keep prominently before the public mind the immense value of that Union" upon which "rest all the glory of the past and the hopes of the future." They vowed also to "watch with a vigilant eye the actings and doings of the abolitionists" and "take frequent opportunities of exposing the inevitable tendency of their doctrines to alienate one portion of the country from another." Excited by the challenge, the *Enquirer* printed the entire prospectus and waited with interest for the first edition of the new paper. Lundy reported with obvious disappointment two weeks later that he had the first issue in hand and it did not live up to the editors' grand promises. Like a man who had practiced for a debate only to have his opponent forfeit before the first question was asked, Lundy expressed disappointment that *The Anti-Abolitionist* appeared to be just another "bearer of the colonization *Mace*." By the paper's fifth number it had still failed to take the strong ground promised in the prospectus, going "no farther than the mid-way position of the famous 'Integrity Convention.'"[26]

Black Voting Rights and the State Constitutional Convention of 1837

While the Integrity Convention and *The Anti-Abolitionist* proved relatively insignificant, abolitionists and African Americans faced a much more serious challenge the same year. As the abolitionists collected money and built their hall, state representatives met in a constitutional convention where some tried to bar black immigration into the state. Failing in that endeavor, they did manage to take away black men's right to vote in the commonwealth. Up to that point the constitution had stipulated that men who owned enough property could vote, and delegates met to consider revising the property restriction. During the discussion a number of delegates suggested adding the word "white" to the revised constitution, leaving even the wealthiest black men ineligible to vote as the franchise opened to more white men. Abolitionists of both the PAS and PASS followed the proceedings in horror: not only were the delegates not dealing with slavery and the right to trial by jury for accused fugitives, they were revoking rights long held in theory if not in practice by free black property owners.

The PAS sprang into action. First they turned to Charles Gardner to help them conduct a census of the city's black population. Meanwhile, they issued an address to the state's black citizens, urging them to be "wise as serpents and harmless as doves" while they came up with a plan. They reminded the black community that they still had some allies in the convention who were trying to resist disenfranchisement, and they contended that the best way to help their supporters would be to "give to all around, clear practical evidence, in life and conversation, that you are the followers of the PRINCE OF PEACE." Rowdy whites would certainly try to provoke blacks to "excite resentment and revenge," but they must not take the bait. Once the census was complete, the abolitionists hoped to use it to defend the black community's honor by offering "an unprejudiced comparison" of whites and blacks of similar socioeconomic status.[27] Indeed, the census revealed that black citizens were, on the whole, industrious, hardworking, and well behaved. In the end, however, it did not matter: despite the efforts of the PAS and black leaders like Gardner and James Forten, black Pennsylvanians lost the right to vote in 1838, just as construction crews were putting the finishing touches on Pennsylvania Hall.

CHAPTER 6

······················

An Amalgamation Wedding

As she walked through the streets of Philadelphia in anticipation of attending the second Antislavery Convention of
American Women, Laura Lovell felt a sense of excitement
tempered with a hint of foreboding. The women planned to meet in
the new hall that had the national abolition community abuzz, and
Lovell arrived early to get settled in the city and do a little sightseeing.
Walking through the same streets that abolitionists had trod for
generations, she saw the famous Pennsylvania State House, which
some were beginning to call Independence Hall. On top perched the
Liberty Bell, keeping a vigilant watch over the city. A few blocks away
she found Pennsylvania Hall standing stately and ready for the week's
festivities.

After exploring the city, Lovell reported back to her sister abolitionists in Fall River, Massachusetts, describing a "beautiful, quiet city"
where "order, harmony, love and freedom prevail." A little too close
to the South for comfort, however, she added, "I am nearer than ever
to the wretched scenes of slavery, and doubtless many a wave from that
broad sea of pollution, reaches and washes over even the fair city of
'Brotherly Love.'" As she looked into the faces of African Americans
she encountered on her walk, she realized that most of them had likely
either been freed from slavery or were fugitives who had freed themselves and lived their lives on the run. These "hunted beings, who may
not look on their fellow men, or inhale the free air without fear"
worked hard to avoid the slave catchers who walked the same streets
looking for victims to either return or kidnap. She also noticed around

83

her "those who tread these streets with independent, and lofty bearing, the 'haughty southerner,' who cherishes within, a heart so hard, and a conscience so seared, that he not only holds his fellow beings in bondage, but dares to justify his sin."[1] Whether Lovell and the other abolitionists noticed or not, those same Southerners were also checking out the new hall.

Perhaps Lovell crossed paths with some of the more famous antislavery figures as she explored. The city teemed with abolitionists, most having traveled to Philadelphia after attending the fifth annual American Antislavery Society (AASS) convention in New York. Though they addressed serious issues such as the gag rules that left their petitions unread and the role of various church denominations in perpetuating human bondage, abolitionists left New York in high spirits. John Quincy Adams, the former President held in high regard by abolitionists for his efforts to fight the gag rule, continued to fight the good fight in Congress. The General Conference of Free Will Baptists and a few other religious groups had started to speak out against slavery. Some branches of the Methodist Episcopal and Presbyterian churches seemed to be coming around as well. Abolitionists had certainly caused a stir, and they remained confident that this was only the beginning.

During the convention abolitionists learned that 340 auxiliary chapters had formed during the previous year, bringing the total number to 1,346. Thirteen states had auxiliaries, and many of those had their own newspapers. The AASS had managed to raise $44,000 in 1837—$5,000 more than the previous year. Not counting newspapers like the *Liberator* and the *National Enquirer*, which John Greenleaf Whittier had recently renamed the *Pennsylvania Freeman*, abolitionists had distributed 646,502 copies of their publications. The group employed 38 traveling agents and had 75 local agents. Despite the gag rules, they had sent 414,571 signatures to the House of Representatives on petitions that called for abolition in the District of Columbia, protested the annexation of Texas or the admission of any new slave state into the Union, requested an end to the gag rules, and called for a ban on the interstate slave trade and slavery in the territories. All in all it had been a productive year.[2]

Returning to his assigned state after the convention, C. C. Burleigh, one of those AASS traveling agents, arrived in Philadelphia on May 6.

The AASS had sent him to the state to lecture, enroll members, and help create the Pennsylvania Antislavery Society (PASS). He had spent the last three or so years trying to stay one step ahead of the anti-abolitionists. He tried particularly hard to convince working-class Pennsylvanians to join the cause. L. C. Gunn, another abolitionist lecturer, traveled with him back from the convention. The voyage must have been particularly rough because both men suffered from serious seasickness.

William Lloyd Garrison, Henry C. Wright, and John Greenleaf Whittier left New York and arrived in Philadelphia together. Realizing that the city's most famous abolitionist couple, James and Lucretia Mott, "would be fully supplied with guests," Garrison and Wright went to the home of Edward Needles. A major figure in the Pennsylvania Abolition Society (PAS), Edward and his wife Mary welcomed the travelers "with unbounded cordiality." Garrison had by this point reached superstar status among abolitionists, and the Needles found themselves hosting a number of impromptu gatherings as "a considerable number of sterling male and female friends," including the Motts and the Grimkés, stopped by to visit. On Friday morning Garrison walked the few blocks to "see the noble edifice" that brought so many abolitionists to the city. He described Pennsylvania Hall as "the largest in this city, and one of the most commodious in the republic." After taking a peek at the hall, Garrison and Wright called on the Grimkés.

Angelina Grimké was particularly excited as her friends gathered in Philadelphia. She had arrived a week earlier so she could make the final plans for her wedding, which would take place Monday night at her sister's home just blocks away from the hall. Two years earlier the thirty-two-year old Quaker convert attended an AASS training seminar in New York where she met Theodore Dwight Weld, a dynamic abolitionist known for his passionate oratory. After his abolitionist zeal resulted in his dismissal from Lane Theological Seminary, Weld became an agent and trainer for the AASS. Once an itinerant Presbyterian minister, Weld approached abolition through his religious mindset, even at a time when Garrison and his strongest followers were rejecting organized religion as an oppressive force that inhibited true reform. In New York he led most of the sessions Grimké attended and they developed a special bond. He proposed to her in

February 1838, and they spent the next months like any engaged couple, debating the guest list, deciding what to wear on their wedding day, and planning the modest ceremony that coincided with the Pennsylvania Hall opening.[3]

Garrison and Wright had reservations about this union and stopped by the Grimké home to share with Angelina their concerns. Garrison worried that Grimké, the leading female figure in the antislavery movement, would embrace Weld's religious zeal, and he also worried that marriage would lead her to desert the antislavery cause. Grimké listened patiently to Garrison before making it clear that she did not need his guidance in this matter. Garrison let the matter rest and, despite their disagreement over religion, Garrison, Wright, and the Grimkés continued to enjoy each other's company. That evening the four of them walked to the home of Grace and Robert Douglass. There Grace and her daughter Sarah entertained their visitors with tea before the group walked a few blocks over to the Arch Street Meeting House. Garrison found the sermon less than satisfying. He did not record whether or not he was able to sit by his friends, but Sarah had complained previously about the segregation and racism she and other black Quakers faced at Arch Street, so odds are that they sat apart. The next morning Garrison and Wright went to see the English Quaker who preached the night before, Joseph John Gurney, and explain to him the error of his sermon, but Gurney learned of their visit and "chose to be absent."[4]

Meanwhile, more abolitionists arrived from New York. Hoping to share the antislavery doctrine with his fellow passengers, many of whom were slaveholders, Alvan Stewart narrowly missed being thrown overboard during his steamboat journey. Fortunately the captain intervened and the abolitionists found it prudent to continue their discussions privately. Garrison later recounted meeting an Alabama slaveholder who had been on that ship. Though the man shook Garrison's hand "with great courtesy," the sincerity of that greeting remains unclear. Perhaps Stewart had mentioned the ceremonies soon to be held in the hall, leaving Southerners on the lookout for Garrison. Maybe the slaveholder made sure to meet Garrison face to face so he would recognize him later. Perhaps he and his friends were already making plans of their own for Pennsylvania Hall. At any rate, Maria Weston Chapman and her group, including her sister-in-law

Anne Warren Weston, arrived that night. They planned to board with the Motts. Lucretia, who suffered from a digestive disorder referred to as dyspepsia, was ill that weekend as her guests began to arrive, but she cheerfully greeted them and made them feel at home.[5]

Those who came from out of town did not have to worry about finding lodging because the city's abolitionists eagerly made room in their homes for guests. Mary Grew, a key figure with the Philadelphia Female Antislavery Society (PFASS), sent out a circular on behalf of the women in the group inviting their sisters throughout the northern United States to stay with them during the Antislavery Convention of American Women. Daniel Neall, the president of the Pennsylvania Hall Association, volunteered early on to host as many guests as he had room for in his home. This added to the festive environment as abolitionists visited the various homes, staying up late into the night discussing the important causes for which they fought so hard.[6]

Many guests planned to attend both the wedding and the meetings at the hall. Quakers like the Motts, John Greenleaf Whittier, the Needles, and Sarah Grimké, however, knew that attending the wedding would lead to their excommunication since Angelina had chosen to marry Weld, who was not a member of the Society of Friends. Garrison, who planned to attend and speak at the ceremony despite his reservations about the marriage, found this ridiculous. Of course, Garrison had strong opinions about religion and politics and never hesitated to share them. Tellingly, Garrison was not asked to speak at the opening of Pennsylvania Hall.[7]

Preparing for the Grand Opening

In the months preceding Pennsylvania Hall's grand debut, members of the association oversaw the final touches on the building and planned the opening ceremonies. Although the board declined one contractor's offer to supply a set of fireproof doors for $120, payable in cash or trade, they did hire watchmen to protect the building. Perhaps they felt some degree of danger but did not anticipate the full scope of what was to come. If they did, then maybe they would not have decided to include gas lighting. This cutting-edge innovation made the hall one of the most modern buildings in the city, though, and Daniel Neall and Joseph Truman took the lead in choosing the gas fixtures. The board then purchased benches made of polished walnut and cherry at a dollar per foot. Remaining true to their free produce principles, they made sure that all of the furniture was built by free laborers. Finally, they purchased shutters and venetian blinds, which they chose to place on the inside of the windows. Whether an intentional safety precaution or not, this decision would save many people from injury during the opening ceremonies. They concluded their work by hiring a janitor and making arrangements to have a fire hydrant installed.[8]

Hall managers began planning the guest list and lining up speakers for the opening ceremonies in November. Stockholders and managers merited individual invitations, as did all public officeholders in the state and city, including judges on the Pennsylvania Supreme Court, the mayor, the sheriff, members of the state legislature, and members of select and common councils of Philadelphia. The Board issued a general invitation to Philadelphia citizens and sent specific invitations to church wardens and ministers who had allowed abolitionists to use their facilities in the past. Members of the different antislavery societies of Philadelphia and the surrounding county were also invited specifically. All public announcements of the opening focused on free discussion rather than abolition.[9]

The board invited a number of government officials and major figures in the local and national antislavery movement to speak during the ceremonies. John Quincy Adams, the former U.S. President who was now championing the right to free speech in Congress, and Thaddeus Stevens, a member of the Pennsylvania House of Representatives known for defending fugitive slaves, were probably the most famous political figures they reached out to, but neither could attend. Among the abolitionists, the board chose Gerrit Smith, a man who had spent much money and energy supporting the colonization movement for years but had recently joined the immediatist camp. He could not join them because of business obligations that kept him in New York, but he sent his best wishes to the "friends of the Freedom of Speech, and of cherished humanity." Optimistically, he added, "long may this hall stand to testify to the sacred regard for Human Rights in which it originated, and to furnish rich gratifications of the mind to the lovers of Free Discussion." They also invited Theodore Dwight Weld to speak. He would be in Philadelphia for his own wedding and would attend meetings at the hall, but he explained that he could not participate actively because "an affection of the throat" had left him unable to speak in public for the past year and a half. (He would never again regain his voice.) Similarly, William Jay, the son of Founding Father John Jay and an abolitionist in his own right, wrote that he was honored to be invited to speak and that he would try to make it to the ceremonies, though he was unsure if he could. The most obvious person missing from this list of abolitionists was William Lloyd Garrison. He was not asked to speak. The specific reason is unclear, but it likely had to do with his reputation for being radical and for introducing subjects that divided abolitionists and inflamed the public.[10]

As they finalized their opening week program, association members also agreed to a number of proposals for renting out various parts of the hall. Representing the board of managers of the Philadelphia County Antislavery Society, Edward M. Davis asked to rent one of the stores. The committee agreed to lease one of the other stores to a free produce grocer, and they rented out the other two stores as well. The Lyceum asked to rent one of the rooms, hoping to use it as a reading room, and to rent the lecture room one Saturday each month and one of the committee rooms one day each week. In February the PFASS asked if the facilities would be ready for them to use the main room, a room they had already been referring to as the "Grand Saloon," for their convention on May 15–17. They also made plans to rent rooms for use throughout the year, and the German Congregation of Evangelical Christians asked about using the main room for Sunday morning services. Clearly, the managers had a profitable venture on their hands. At this rate the hall would pay for itself in no time at all.[11]

Moving into the Hall

By February 1838 the doors of Pennsylvania Hall were open on a limited scale. The association began meeting periodically in the hall, even as contractors continued with the final touches, such as paving the sidewalks around the building. They also held a few public meetings in the hall. In one case they met to discuss a state-level gag rule. In another meeting at the hall they issued a series of resolutions condemning state legislators' ongoing attempts to repeal black suffrage. In March they met a couple of times with colonizationists to discuss and debate the merits of their respective movements. Interestingly, there is no clear evidence of any specific problems between the two groups at that point, other than clear disagreement about how best to end slavery.[12]

John Greenleaf Whittier ran the first notices to advertise opening-week activities in the *Pennsylvania Freeman* in mid-March. The PASS had split into an eastern and a western branch, and the PASS for the Eastern District planned to hold its annual meeting in the hall on May 16. The Requited Labor Convention, a free produce group, hoped to meet the next day. In between these meetings, the women's convention, and Lyceum programs, the managers planned to offer the public "a rich treat, an intellectual banquet . . . such as is seldom enjoyed in this or any other city."[13] Similar notices soon followed in Garrison's *Liberator*.

While most of the announcements served to invite the public to the various meetings, one had a more confrontational tone. A General Assembly of the Presbyterian Church was scheduled to meet just blocks away from the hall. This denomination had split into "Old School" and "New School" branches the year before, with the New School being more open to antislavery ideas and the Old School refusing to address the issue. The Old School's General Assembly was the one meeting in Philadelphia that week, led by slaveholder William S. Plummer of Virginia and attended by many other Southerners. In early May the *Liberator* ran a notice from "GB" challenging the "Preaching Slaveholders from the South, and their accomplices of the North" to a public debate in Pennsylvania Hall. The question? "Do the Holy Scriptures sanction involuntary and unlimited servitude?" In other words, was slavery really a sin? The notice challenged "Any Doctor, Rabbi, Master or Bachelor of Arts" brave enough to take the affirmative to contact the agent of the PASS at 223 Arch Street by April 19 so they could plan the debate. This notice ran in the *Liberator* after the deadline, so Garrison likely reprinted it from the *Freeman*. An equally provocative article ran in the *Liberator* on May 25. This announcement promised a "full discussion of the subject of COLONIZATION vs ABOLITION." Arnold Buffum would represent the abolitionists and W. W. Sleigh would speak for the colonizationists. The debate would occur on the 21st, a week after the opening ceremonies. "The Hall will be brilliantly lighted with gas," the *Liberator* promised, "and we anticipate a crowded house." Unfortunately for anyone eager to attend the meeting, the gas had already been used for much more sinister purposes by May 21.[14]

Monday, May 14, 1838: The Doors Open

As the early-morning sunshine started peeking in through his bedroom windows, Samuel Webb gave up trying to sleep. After a night made restless by excitement and eager anticipation, he got dressed and walked the short distance to Pennsylvania Hall. As treasurer and an executive board member of the Pennsylvania Hall Association, he had devoted much of his time during the past year to seeing the project to fruition. Today abolitionists and other reformers from throughout the nation would see his vision in all its glory.

Webb arrived before the others so he could take one last tour of the palace he would soon open to reformers from across the Northeast. He entered through a door that faced Haines Street and visited the new office of the PASS, Eastern District. Making sure the books and pamphlets were all in order, he progressed through the other rooms on the floor. He noted with pleasure the variety of goods displayed in the free produce store and the abolition bookstore. He must have felt a sense of pride as he thought about the work he and his friends in the Pennsylvania Hall Association had done. The antislavery office in Boston held plenty of books and pamphlets—as well as a few goods sold by the women to raise funds—but they could not rival what Pennsylvania abolitionists now had. Only in Pennsylvania Hall could someone attend an abolition convention, buy goods made exclusively by free laborers, and find almost any abolition tract all in one place.

The first floor of the hall contained four stores that opened onto Haines Street as well as a large lecture room that could comfortably hold two to three hundred attendees. For smaller gatherings, Webb and his associates had thought to include two committee rooms. One of these waited for delegates of the Antislavery Convention of American Women to assemble the next day.

As grand as the first floor was, the true beauty was upstairs. Webb chose one of the three seven-foot-wide stairways to take one last look at the room before guests began to arrive. The huge room, which could seat up to three thousand spectators, was surrounded on three sides by galleries. On the west end sat the forum. An Ionic column graced each side of this stage, and they supported a beautiful arch. Roses decorated the underside of the arch, and over it was painted the motto "VIRTUE, LIBERTY, AND INDEPENDENCE" in large gold letters. A dome divided into panels supported by Ionic pilasters lay beyond the arch. On the stage the managers had arranged a beautiful desk embellished with a silk panel of a rich blue shade. The president would sit behind the desk with the vice presidents on each side. All would sit in elegant chairs carved from Pennsylvania walnut and lined with plush blue silk. Sofas upholstered in blue damask moreen sat beside each vice president's chair, and in front of these sat tables for the secretary and treasurer, each with chairs that matched the others. To complete the elegant look, they had covered each table with a blue silk cloth. They had managed to do all of this while avoiding slave-produced materials. Not one piece of the beautiful cloth had been tainted by the blood, sweat, or tears of the oppressed. Perhaps the most beautiful part of the building was the ceiling. At the center of the single panel, a nine-foot-wide ventilator featured a sunflower with golden rays that reached across its circumference. A concave mirror served as the center of the flower, and light from the gas fixtures bounced off of it at night, causing it to sparkle like a diamond. From each corner a square ventilator complemented the centerpiece. Trap-doors above the ventilators allowed for a constant stream of fresh air to circulate even while the windows remained closed.[15]

Satisfied with his final inspection, Webb went back downstairs, where he could hear the crowd beginning to gather on the street. Daniel Neall, the president of the Pennsylvania Hall Association, and William Dorsey, the group's secretary, joined him in the entryway. They had promised opening ceremonies would begin promptly at 10 a.m., and it was nearly time.

Monday Morning

After leading the huge crowd upstairs, Daniel Neall took his seat in the center of the stage. As president of the association, he had the honor of presiding over the opening ceremonies. As he looked out over one of the largest crowds to ever assemble in Philadelphia, his friend William Dorsey welcomed their guests. Calling attention to the golden letters of the motto overhead, he told them the hall would "not be used for antislavery purposes alone" but for "any purpose not of an immoral character." Before introducing the keynote speaker, Dorsey read from letters of support sent by those who could not make it to the ceremonies. He finished by reading David Paul Brown's letter of acceptance. Immediately Brown stood and said, "I am here to redeem my pledge." "As priest of this day's sacrifices," he added, "I solemnly dedicate this temple to liberty."

In his speech Brown walked a tightrope between gradual and immediate abolition as he described the dangers of the Southern "slave power," discredited the colonization society, urged the less prudent in the immediatist ranks to consider the implications of their actions, and laid out his plan for ending slavery. His ideas had changed little since he helped establish the Philadelphia Antislavery Society in 1834, and many passages in the speech came directly from his July 4th address from 1835.

Boldly calling slavery an "unquestionable evil," Brown argued against two of the slaveholders' favorite claims—that the Bible sanctioned slavery and that they inherited the system from their ancestors. Brown expressed sincere irritation at such use of the Bible, and he argued that if slaveholders were really shackled by an inherited system, then they should free themselves by releasing the slaves as they had been promising for a generation to do "in their own time." Brown called upon them to restore slaves "to their *natural* rights, and name your time; but let it be in *time*, and not in *eternity*." He also called slaveholders and their apologists to task for their repeated threats at secession. They had used these "air-drawn daggers" to blackmail the free states long enough. By this point, the repeated threat to leave the Union had grown hollow: "Threats like these, . . . from being familiar, have long since ceased to be terrible." He had also had enough of the argument that abolitionists should shoulder the guilt for endangering the Union, and he repeated his promise that, as much as he abhorred slavery, he would never put the Union in jeopardy to end it.

Because Brown believed the free states lacked the power to emancipate the slaves in the South, he sought to convince Southerners of the merits of the cause. He argued that slavery cursed the entire nation and that its removal would benefit everyone. Abolition would save

Southerners from the negative influence their system exerted over whites and blacks alike. It would also take away the threat of slave retribution that endangered all whites. His attempts to build bridges with Southerners resembled colonizationist efforts to build a movement that transcended sectional lines, but Brown decried the work of "our sometime cousins" in the colonization societies. He did not agree with the notion of racial inferiority, but he argued that colonizationists did. He regretted the time and money wasted on the "sickly and misbegotten offspring of an illicit alliance between the North and the South—this child of forty fathers." Even so, he pointed out that many "valuable, though misguided men" supported the movement. In a passage that seems to deliberately describe Elliott Cresson, the city's most avid colonizationist, he contended that "their purposes are honest" and their "characters are ample vouchers for their sincerity." Even so, "holy zeal, when manifested in an unholy cause, is more pernicious than the most insidious, crafty, and destructive vice, as it enlists much of the might and majesty of virtue, beneath the banner of sacrilege and crime."

After calling men like Cresson to task, Brown took on the overzealous from the other side of the spectrum. In a passage that clearly described William Lloyd Garrison, he argued that some of his fellow immediatists, though "no doubt, also honest," were "too wild and visionary for reasonable reliance." He insisted that most who argued for immediate abolition were not the fanatics they had been made out to be by their detractors. As for himself, he would prefer that slaves be prepared for freedom and educated before their release, but he fought for immediate emancipation "because the system of delays is dangerous to this enterprise." Immediatism would "succeed better than those projects, that claim but little in the first place, and eventually relinquish *that*, for the purpose of conciliation." Reiterating his previous definition of immediatism, he added that "immediatism" merely meant "certain" emancipation at a specified and guaranteed point in the future.

How, then, could they end slavery? To begin with, they needed to convince slaveholders to allow slaves free time in which they could work and earn money to buy their freedom. The federal and state governments could contribute to this compensated emancipation endeavor by offering funds to augment the slaves' earnings. Meanwhile public schools should teach slaves to read and write, preparing them for freedom. He also suggested that the government might establish "a national colony" within the United States, perhaps in the western territories, to offer an asylum for blacks who wished to go. For any of this to work, he insisted, the laws that many states had adopted to prevent manumission had to be repealed. He also called for a law "rendering all colored children born after a given time, free, upon their arrival at a certain age." He concluded that "although no one of these methods might be calculated to counteract the evil complained of, in their *joint* and concentrated influence their success will be inevitable; and in less than half a century from this period, the groans and clanking chains, and heavy curses of slavery, shall be heard, and seen, and felt no more." Crucially, the whole process had to be set in motion immediately.

Brown concluded with a warning to the "individuals with us who carry their zeal to an improper extent." While they had the right to use every possible effort with the government, and with the free states, to abolish slavery, they must be "discreet" and prudent. They must consider how their words might affect the slaves and make sure "to abstain from every measure that may be calculated to excite in them a hostile or rebellious spirit." Rebellion could only lead to further repression. He exhorted his listeners to continue fighting for the slaves' freedom and their own right to speak out freely, but they must never allow "the indignation which you feel for the sufferings of your fellow men [to] betray you into intemperate measures that shall rather increase than allay those sufferings."[16]

As Brown concluded his speech and the meeting adjourned, Garrison and his closest friends likely complained about the browbeating they had just suffered at the hands of one of the city's leading abolitionists. They would have been eager to correct his misguided notions. But that would have to wait until the next day; for the time being, they had a wedding to attend.

Monday Afternoon

After a mid-day break for lunch, members of the Philadelphia Lyceum began to file into the "Grand Saloon." This organization had applied to use the facilities as soon as they heard about plans to construct the building. Indeed, one of the first tasks at the Pennsylvania Hall

Association's first meeting had been to consider the Lyceum's request to rent a room in the hall and use the room every Sunday afternoon. Webb had likely told his friends with the Lyceum about the association's plans because he was heavily involved with both groups, serving as president of the latter by May 1838.

Lyceum activities began at 3 p.m. First was a lecture by Victor Value. The principal of Mantua Academy, a school near Philadelphia, Value gained a reputation for his pedagogy when he published a mathematics text in 1823. For this occasion he had prepared a short talk on the Lyceum system of instruction. One of the nation's best-known meteorologists, James P. Espy, followed. He had recently discovered the cause of precipitation and was there to explain what caused winds, clouds, storms, and "other atmospheric phenomena." A Pennsylvania native and member of the American Philosophical Society, Espy came to Philadelphia during a wide lecture tour in which he shared and tested the theories he would soon publish in his book *Philosophy of Storms*.[17] After the two presentations, Lyceum leaders posed a number of questions for members to consider overnight and meet to discuss the next day. They concluded their activities for the day by discussing "Which has the greater influence, wealth or knowledge?" Two Lyceum members opened the debate and then invited the audience to participate.

Obviously the Lyceum discussions had nothing to do with the issue of slavery or abolition. Even so, the Philadelphia rumor mill was starting to churn. Perhaps locals read announcements in the newspapers that the hall would be opening on this day and had been preparing a counterattack. Maybe the Southern steamboat passengers who nearly threw Alvan Stewart overboard had spread the word about the abolitionist gathering. Whatever the source, rumors started flying on Monday. They spread like wildfire as soon as observers noticed the wedding taking place nearby.

Blocks away from the hall Angelina Grimké waited at her sister Ann R. Frost's home on Spruce Street. Surrounded by thirty to forty of the nation's top abolitionists, including Lewis Tappan, Henry B. Stanton, William Lloyd Garrison, Henry C. Wright, Maria Weston Chapman, James G. Birney, Abby Kelley, Sarah Douglass, and Sarah Grimké, she prepared to marry Theodore Dwight Weld. After meeting him at the New York training session, she found herself thinking about him all the time. Delighted when he confessed to her that

Theodore Dwight Weld and Angelina Grimké.
Library Company of Philadelphia

she occupied his mind constantly as well, she agreed to marry him despite their religious differences. As a Quaker she knew the decision would mean excommunication, but some things were more important than dogmatic religious affiliation. She had found a man who shared her antislavery convictions and appreciated her talents. Though he had asked her to focus on abolition rather than women's rights in her speeches, he believed fully in gender equality. After all, he had agreed wholeheartedly to remove the word "obey" from the ceremony. This was unheard of at the time, and she knew of few other men, besides perhaps Garrison or Wright, who would have taken their convictions this far. Weld had also taken an active role in helping Grimké plan the wedding. They helped each other decide what to wear, compiled the guest list together, and coordinated efforts as they sent out letters of invitation. They also worked together to find an African American baker who would make the cake out of free produce sugar.

As the guests began to assemble, many noticed that some of their favorite friends had not joined them. The Motts and John Greenleaf Whittier lived in Philadelphia but could not attend the ceremony. As Quakers they faced excommunication simply for attending a ceremony that united a Quaker with a non-Friend. Sarah Grimké and

Abby Kelley faced the same threat but attended anyway. Whittier escorted a young woman to the house and promised to join them "after the excommunicable offence." To make up for his absence, he wrote the couple a poem and presented it to them the next morning.[18]

Two ministers—one white and one black—attended the ceremony, but neither presided. The couple made up their own vows on the spot. According to Sarah Grimké, "Theodore addressed Angelina in a solemn and tender manner." Alluding to "the unrighteous power vested in a husband by the laws of the United States over the person and property of his wife," he "abjured all authority, all government, save the influence which love would give to them over each other as moral and immortal beings." Angelina responded with "a promise to honor him, to prefer him above herself, to love him with a pure heart fervently." Everyone in the room knelt and the couple each took a turn praying for blessings upon their union, and Weld included a wish for "increased sympathy for the slave." Each minister then offered a prayer and Sarah Grimké added a few words. William Lloyd Garrison read the certificate and passed it around for those present to sign it. The signatories included two former Grimké slaves, liberated by Ann Frost. According to Maria Weston Chapman it was indeed an "abolition wedding."[19]

As abolitionists gathered for the wedding, watchful eyes traced their moves. Because they could not follow the guests into the home, they simply recorded what they saw—and what they saw disturbed them very much. Blacks and whites were gathering in a private home, and those who listened heard them talking about a wedding. As they caught bits and pieces of the conversations and processed what they saw with their own eyes, they began to put the picture together. The "amalgamators" who called themselves "abolitionists" were meeting in town and now someone in their group was getting married. Blacks and whites were coming together for this event. At some point someone put two and two together and determined that they were witnessing one of their greatest fears—a biracial wedding. The abolitionists had clearly crossed the line this time.

Monday Night

As the abolitionists celebrated at Frosts' house, temperance advocates made their way to the hall for the night's meetings. Arnold Buffum spoke for about an hour beginning at 8 p.m. Though he was a long-time abolitionist, he did not address that subject. Instead he exhorted moderate drinkers and silent objectors to join the temperance cause and support complete abstinence from liquor. He then introduced Thomas P. Hunt, a colonizationist from North Carolina, who spoke at great length about the need to outlaw drinking altogether. Though both of these men expressed ideas that were unpopular with some people, neither addressed slavery.

By this point, however, what actually happened in the hall mattered less than what the people outside *thought* went on inside. Word had started to spread about David Paul Brown's morning speech. While immediatists like Garrison went away unhappy at Brown's timidity, moderation, and, some were saying, "gradualism," opponents of abolition fumed over what they saw as his radical, anti-Southern stance. Even more importantly, throughout Philadelphia people were sharing and embellishing the story of a wedding that threatened to altogether destroy the racial order of the country.

At some point that night someone threw a brick through one of the hall's windows. As the glass shattered, some of the men in the gathering crowd began inspecting the gas pipes. Coincidentally or not, the Democratic Young Men of the City and County of Philadelphia had just met nearby at the county courthouse. They had resolved that Governor Joseph Ritner, a man derisively referred to as an "abolition governor" by the state's Democrats, owed his position "to an unhappy division in the democratic ranks." They then denounced his rule as insincere, inconsistent, and extravagant. Before they left they chose delegates for their Fourth of July Convention. One of these delegates, Alderman Morton McMichael, had participated in the Friends of the Integrity of the Union Convention the year before. Perhaps as he and his friends left their own meeting they heard the rumblings about the abolitionist agitators and their "temple of amalgamation" at Sixth and Haines. He had already pledged his loyalty to the Union. Maybe this was his chance to prove himself.[20] Unaware of the attention their gas pipes had attracted, the managers of the hall counted their losses at just one shattered window. They deemed day one a success and went home to prepare for the next day's exercises.

CHAPTER 7

....

This "Tabernacle of Mischief and Fanaticism"

As William Lloyd Garrison awakened the next morning at Edward and Mary Needles' home on Arch Street, he thought about the day ahead. According to the itinerary published earlier that month in newspapers throughout the country, including his own *Liberator*, he could look forward to a number of interesting talks during the second day of opening ceremonies at Pennsylvania Hall. That morning Pittsburgh Congressman Walter Forward and U.S. Senator Thomas Morris, a Democrat from Ohio, were to deliver addresses on the importance of free discussion and the right of Americans to petition their representatives. Forward was in the process of defeating an effort to disenfranchise the state's African American voters, and Morris had taken a brave stand against the gag rule. Garrison did not place much faith in political means of ending slavery, but he hoped that these men would at least outdo the tepid effort David Paul Brown had displayed the previous morning. The *U.S. Gazette* and other local papers reported favorably on Brown's speech that morning, but once Garrison returned to his own press in Boston he would not be so kind. The hybrid address that combined gradualism, colonization, and immediatism may have gained Brown favor with the press and adherents to the old abolition and colonization societies, but it fell far short of Garrison's vision.

Tuesday, May 15, 1838: A Garrisonian Rededication

Activities in the "Grand Saloon" began at 10 a.m. Neither Forward nor Morris could be found among the crowd, so the managers read letters in which Forward had pledged to be there "if it be possible, without great inconvenience" and Morris had made a similar commitment "if life and health permit." Fortunately John Greenleaf Whittier and C. C. Burleigh rose to fill part of the void the managers faced in the absence of their scheduled speakers. Whittier brought a poem he wrote for the occasion, but given his penchant to shy away from public speaking he relied on Burleigh to read it for him. As Burleigh read Whittier's poem the women began to file into the room. Their order of business that morning, choosing officers, had not taken long at all, and they were eager to join the main meeting. Most of these women admired Garrison, and those from Boston were particularly determined that he should address the crowd.

Local abolitionist Lewis C. Gunn rose as Burleigh finished reading Whittier's poem, however, and began to speak extemporaneously on the right of free discussion. It remains unclear how much time he had to prepare the talk, but he obviously came to the hall prepared to speak at some point. Maybe managers had taken note of the non-committal nature of Forward's and Morris's letters and asked local speakers like Gunn to be ready to speak if needed. If not, Gunn's months on the traveling lecture circuit had left him well prepared to address a crowd without prior notice. Either way, he incorporated a number of immediatists' favorite themes and tailored them for the occasion. He began by pointing out that Americans had a constitutional right to speak freely and that most were generally allowed to do so, except when it came to slavery. Those who tried to discuss the evils of slavery found their rights, and often their bodies, under attack. He then discussed many instances in which mobs used violent measures to silence abolitionists. He told of Elijah Lovejoy's murder in Alton, Illinois, Amos Dresser's public beating with a slave whip in Nashville, Tennessee, and Garrison's narrow escape from a tar and feathering in Boston.

Ironically, he pointed out, such violent measurers only led to more support for abolitionists—if not in their opposition to slavery, at least in their right to speak freely against it. More and more Northerners had come to realize that silencing any group, even abolitionists, would set a dangerous precedent. According to Gunn, "They have seen the right of free discussion assailed and trampled underfoot; and they have discernment enough to perceive that, although silence is now required only on *one* subject, the *right*, in all its length and breadth, is thereby completely destroyed." At the same time, he added, "*Free discussion elicits truth*," and by exposing the evils of slavery abolitionists were slowly but surely awakening their neighbors to their cause. Southern leaders fought so hard to suppress abolition speech and keep their tracts and newspapers out of the South because they realized that a truthful discussion of slavery might also change the minds of Southerners, including many slaveholders. They also feared that abolitionist rhetoric would spark slave rebellion.

Gunn concluded by addressing a topic that occupied the minds of many abolitionists in the room—David Paul Brown's brand of abolition. Speaking for immediatists throughout the United States, he tried to set the record straight. Even though Brown called himself an immediatist, Gunn insisted that he had laid out a gradualist plan the morning before. True immediatists "go for no gradual emancipation" and "believe that slavery is a heinous *sin*, and that being sinful, it ought to be immediately repented of, and immediately abandoned." Arguing against Brown's definition, he insisted that "immediate abolition does not consist in merely beginning to act immediately, or in fixing a *certain* date at which slavery shall die." Further, he argued, "we hold that no preparatory education is necessary before emancipation" and that laws "to *ameliorate* slavery we have no more fellowship with than with laws to ameliorate highway robbery or murder." Finally, he spoke strongly against any and all schemes of colonization.

Burleigh followed Gunn on the podium with an extemporaneous speech on Indian removal and the fate of the Cherokee. Apparently Cherokee civil rights leader John Ross had been invited to participate in the opening ceremonies but he and his fellow Cherokee faced removal from Georgia to the "Indian Territory" of present-day Oklahoma on May 23, a day that was just a little over a week away. Burleigh read from a letter in which Ross expressed gratitude for the invitation but declined, given the dire situation he and his people faced at the moment.

Managers had hoped to end the morning's meeting at this point, but the Garrisonians had other plans. Alvan Stewart rose and asked to speak about another Native American group, the Seminoles. He described the group and told listeners about their fate. Under attack by Americans since 1817, they also faced removal to the Indian Territory. They had angered Americans by siding with the British in the War of 1812, but, even more importantly, they had drawn the wrath of slaveholders by harboring fugitive slaves. Thus, their persecution stemmed not only from their native heritage but also from their abolitionist convictions. With that, Stewart brought the topic of discussion back around to antislavery.

While Stewart spoke, someone in the audience sounded the call for Garrison to speak. At that point Garrison left his place at the back of the gallery and made his way to the front, where "in a modest and respectful manner" he "requested to be excused from speaking on account of the state of his health." With a little prodding from the audience, especially the women, however, he consented to say a few words from where he stood at the front of the gallery. According to Laura Lovell, "he declined taking the platform, as he had but few words to offer, but the audience were not to be denied seeing freedom's champion occupying the highest place in freedom's hall." He gave in and "amidst loud expressions of approbation, he came to the platform waving his hand towards the audience, saying 'it is too much, I beg you to desist.'"[1]

Biographer Henry Mayer describes Garrison, who had not been invited to speak in Philadelphia since 1835, as "half embarrassed, half vindicated." Perhaps, but given the widespread disappointment with Brown's speech, Garrison's likely unhappiness over not being asked to participate officially in the first place, and his close relationship with many of the women calling for him from the audience, it would be hard not to question the sincerity of his reluctance and embarrassment. Even Mayer admits that "it is possible—though no evidence exists—that the entire episode was a neat bit of 'wire-working' on the immediatists' part that exploited Garrison's celebrity and his ability to take control of a meeting."[2]

At any rate, once Garrison had the floor he began to call local abolitionists to task on a number of matters. To begin with, he pointed out, "not a single colored brother" had occupied the platform since the hall opened, due either to "a wicked prejudice, or to a fear of giving public offence." He also pointed out that he and his friends had noticed "a squeamishness with regard to coming out boldly in favor of the doctrine of *immediate* emancipation, and letting the public understand, distinctly, the object of our assembling together." He pointed to the managers' reluctance to state clearly in the press releases their main concern, and he added that someone named Orange Scott was listed as a speaker for that evening but that they had neglected to state the topic of his discourse. Scott then rose and said that he thought the managers knew his topic was "American slavery" and he did not know why they had not announced the subject. Garrison then placed Burleigh's Indian removal speech in the context of abolition by showing that the whole scheme was undertaken so that more land would be made available for slaveholders to profit from.

Garrison then took it upon himself to rededicate the hall. He claimed that Brown had started out admirably "but just as every eye was kindling with a radiant flame, and every heart was leaping exultingly, and every knee bent in homage," he had "seized the dagger of expediency, and plunged it" into the Goddess of Liberty's heart. Garrison added that "all that the slave-holders require to enable them to hold their slaves in interminable bondage, was to be found in that speech." He called upon listeners to help re-baptize the hall during the remaining meetings and to "wash out this stain of reproach."

The main problem with Brown's speech, according to Garrison, was that it was "adapted to please all parties." He described men like Brown as "men of 'caution,' and 'prudence,' and 'judiciousness,'" and he added that he had "learned to hate those words." And then, prophetically, he added "slavery will not be overthrown without excitement, a most tremendous excitement!" He went on to say "there is too much quietude in this city," adding that the cause "will not prosper here . . . until it excites popular tumult, and brings down upon it a shower of brickbats and rotten eggs, and is threatened with a coat of tar and feathers."

In his parting shot he took on the colonizationists. "There is too much colonizationism here," he said. Commenting on handbills he had seen advertising a debate on the merits of colonization that was to take place in the hall the next week, he asked, "can it be possible that any man at this day will have the audacity to come forward, publicly, as an advocate of that wicked scheme?" He may have been trying to stir Elliott Cresson, his nemesis and the city's top colonizationist, into a debate, but Cresson was out of town. Instead, W. W. Sleigh responded from the audience, "I am that man." In response an unidentified African

American man called out, "He is not an American," and Garrison chastised this "foreign adventurer" who had come from England to "join a ban of haughty and tyrannical conspirators, in banishing one-sixth part of our own fellow citizens to an uncivilized and pestilential coast." Sleigh felt compelled to defend himself. He argued that he supported colonization as a friend, rather than an enemy, of African Americans, and he pointed out that Garrison had traveled to England to seek support for his cause and "his having been a foreigner was not thrown in his face." But, he asked, what should he expect from a man who had just shown such disrespect for Brown, one of the city's most dedicated abolitionists? Garrison responded by saying that, had Sleigh come to the United States for more noble purposes, he would have made no mention of his being a foreigner.

Burleigh then took a turn criticizing the inconsistency between the beginning and end of Brown's speech. He went on to criticize gradual emancipation. Stewart followed with a thorough critique of colonization. With no end to the debate in sight and the Lyceum members waiting to use the room, Samuel Webb rose and said that the managers had conferred and agreed to host a debate the following morning. "All who chose to participate" were welcomed to come and explain their views, "whether in favor or against *immediate* or *gradual* abolition, *colonization,* or *even slavery itself!*"[3]

Tuesday Afternoon

That afternoon the Lyceum used the hall to consider "the history, present condition, and future prospects of the human mind," the "physical education of children," and whether wealth or knowledge held greater influence. They concluded by posing a new question for members to ponder—whether opposition or approbation from others provided greater proof of a man's merit. Even with such fascinating topics, however, the greater excitement remained outside the hall.

Trouble had started to brew the night before, and when word began to spread about the morning's events and the newly scheduled debate, crowds began to gather. Rumors of "amalgamation" spread like wildfire. According to some accounts blacks and whites were sitting side by side in the hall and walking arm in arm in the streets. Curious onlookers gathered to catch a glimpse.

Many grew furious as they watched a white man step out of a carriage and extend his hand to help a black woman out behind him. In this act they found concrete proof that black and white were indeed mixing in intimate ways. Anyone familiar with Philadelphia's abolition and African American community would have known that the mixing had occurred generations before and in the slave South rather than the free North. The "white" man was Robert Purvis, the son of a wealthy white slaveholder from South Carolina and an enslaved mother of mixed ancestry. He looked white, but American racial standards said anyone with as much as "one drop" of "African blood" was black. Purvis probably could have crossed racial lines and spent his life "passing" for white, but he chose to be true to himself and honest about his ancestry. Identifying himself as African American, he had become an important part of Philadelphia's free black community. He had also chosen a wife who, although of mixed ethnic ancestry herself, looked black. Her name was Harriet Forten Purvis, and she and her family had played a major role in raising the funds needed to build Pennsylvania Hall. Her father was the city's wealthiest and most famous black abolitionist, and she, her mother, and her siblings had all contributed to the Philadelphia abolition community in various ways.

In a second case of mistaken racial identity, the crowd began to shout at a black man who was walking with two "pretty white girls." What they did not realize was that those women, like Robert Purvis, had the requisite drop of "black blood" and were thus African American. One of the women was the wife of a leading black Philadelphia businessman and the other was her sister-in-law.[4]

Harriet Forten Purvis and the other women were likely on their way back to the hall to attend the 4 p.m. session of the Antislavery Convention of American Women. Meeting once again in the session room, the women put together a committee and charged the members with preparing the business agenda for the convention. They then adjourned to meet the next morning at 10 a.m. at Temperance Hall.

At some point during the day, while most of the mob lingered outside the hall trying to intimidate the abolitionists, others went about the city placing placards on trees, poles, and awnings. The placards warned Philadelphians that "a convention for the avowed purpose of effecting the immediate abolition of slavery in the Union is now in session in this city." They called upon "all citizens, who entertain a proper respect for the right of property, and the preservation of the

Robert Purvis.
Library Company of Philadelphia

Constitution of the United States" to meet at the hall at 11 a.m. the next morning and "interfere, *forcibly* if they *must*, and prevent the violation of these pledges, heretofore held sacred." Although the Pennsylvania Antislavery Society (PASS)'s Eastern District convention would not convene until the next day, the speeches made by Garrison, Burleigh, and Stewart made it clear that immediatists had taken charge of the hall. The debate now scheduled for the next day only confirmed to many that Pennsylvania Hall would be used primarily to spread the word of immediate abolitionism.

Tuesday Evening

George Ford Jr., of Lancaster, Pennsylvania, opened the evening's ceremonies. Echoing many of the points Gunn had made that morning, he discussed the importance of unfettered speech. As Gunn had, Ford began by describing cases of mob rule and vigilante justice. He agreed with Gunn that anti-abolition violence only strengthened the antislavery cause. "Persecution," he insisted, "might serve as a stimulant to build up rather than allay or counteract" abolitionist exertions. In the face of such repression it became "the bounded duty of all men, to support each other in the exercise of their natural and constitutional rights; for if a violation of them is sanctioned one day in one man, it may become the fortune of the individual inflicting the injury, to become himself the victim upon whom the vengeance of the mob may be wreaked tomorrow."

Stewart followed with remarks concerning the right of petition. He lamented Congress's passage of the gag rule and expounded upon another recurring theme—the argument that slaveholders knew they were wrong and sought to silence abolitionists to hide their own shame. The gag rule, he insisted, was born of Southern guilt: "Fear, *fear*, shame, *shame* yes, burning SHAME, laid those resolutions on the table."

Alanson St. Clair wrapped up the evening. He began by addressing lukewarm abolitionists, presumably men like Brown, who opposed slavery but remained reluctant to fully embrace immediatist tactics. Clearly unaware that he was asking them to do what Brown probably believed he had done the day before, St. Clair called upon those who shared immediatist principles but did not like their tactics to "come in and do better." Ignoring, or simply unaware of, the reality of the Pennsylvania situation, where gradualists and immediatists had been working together for years, he claimed that "had the prudent and cautious taken hold of the work at the first, and given us their sympathies, counsel, and influence, instead of shunning, frowning upon, and jeering us, we should probably have been saved from all the evils of which they now complain." While St. Clair's call for cooperation may have seemed moot in a place where gradual and immediate abolitionists had just come together to build the very hall in which he stood, he offered a second point that made more sense. Like others who spoke before him, he insisted that slaveholders knew they were in the wrong and that they knew the abolition cause was gaining ground. "These men are not fools, whatever may be said of their morality," he argued, "if they considered our measures either ill-suited to the end they are designed to attain, or impotent in themselves, instead of putting themselves thus on the defensive, they would bid us go onward, and laugh at our folly." He concluded by arguing that the use of the ballot box and the petition would work in time. He offered his state of Massachusetts as evidence. According to St. Clair, politicians there had come around and learned to respect the power of their constituents. He predicted that legislators from other states would soon follow.[5]

As the abolitionists concluded their meeting, people who had noticed the placards throughout the city made plans to go to the hall the next morning. Some were just curious onlookers who wanted to see what would happen next. Others were the sons of Southern planters, in the city to study medicine at the University of Pennsylvania and the College of Physicians. Still others were men who wanted above all else to stop the abolitionists from endangering the Union. And finally, some were workers who resented the growth in the city's black population and blamed antislavery agitation for the job competition they faced every day. The emotions of all of these people ranged from curiosity to outright hatred. And they would be back at Pennsylvania Hall the next day. The question was, would the authorities be there as well? If so, how would they react if matters escalated?

Wednesday, May 16, 1838

The Wednesday morning sun peeked through the clouds as W. W. Sleigh addressed a letter to the Pennsylvania Hall managers. Though just blocks away on Race Street, Sleigh would not attend the debate that morning at the hall. In the heat of the moment the day before, he had spoken out against Garrison's accusations and was initially enthusiastic when the managers offered to host this morning's debate. Having calmed down and thought about the situation, however, he realized that he was not prepared to extemporaneously defend the colonization cause. The main figure in the Pennsylvania Colonization Society, Philadelphia's own Elliott Cresson, had offered to give him plenty of documentary evidence in support of the cause, but Cresson was out of town and not expected back until next week. Realizing that people expected him at the hall in the morning, he stayed up late Tuesday night and wrote to register his protest against any colonizationist "sanctioning, by their voice, any such *hasty, cursory, partial,* and indefinite investigation as this proposes to be, on a subject of such *importance*." Afraid that he would harm rather than help his cause should he "enter upon its discussion, without *order*—without *regulations*—without system—without admitted evidence, and without knowing whom I would have the honor of debating with," he respectfully declined the opportunity. Cresson would return next week and furnish him "with such *documentary* evidence as is indispensably necessary for a *full, free, just* and *impartial* discussion." Then he would happily debate seasoned abolitionist Arnold Buffum in the debate advertised by the flyers that had upset Garrison and led to the current challenge. For now, though, he wanted to make it "distinctly understood" that he was not an official agent of the colonization society, presumably in case he had said something in the heat of the moment that abolitionists could use against the cause.[6]

The messenger who delivered Sleigh's letter would have noticed the fifty or sixty people gathered outside, prowling around the hall, and making occasional threats against those who began to arrive for the day's activities. This group would continue to grow throughout the day as more and more people read the placards scattered about the city and heard about "the parade of black and white amalgamation in the fashionable promenades of the city." Speaking loudly and taking every opportunity to drown out the discussions inside, the crowd used increasingly abusive language as the day wore on. In the absence of the authorities, managers hired two watchmen to keep the peace at the hall.[7]

Wednesday Morning

Many of the managers and their associates with the PASS for the Eastern District first encountered the mob as they gathered for their 8 a.m. meeting. Vice President Abraham Pennock called the meeting to order and they chose three secretaries, one of them Lewis Gunn. Other major Pennsylvania abolitionists present included Dr. Isaac Parrish and Benjamin S. Jones, the owner of the bookstore in the hall. The group conducted business and adjourned to meet again at 2 p.m.

After the men concluded their morning session in the "Grand Saloon," others began to join them in anticipation of the debate announced the morning before. As spectators began to file in to the room, "a person from the country who was not even a stockholder" invited three black men to sit on the forum. When the managers arrived they asked the men to sit in the audience instead because they had reserved seats on the forum for managers, speakers, and invited guests "from a distance." There is no evidence that the men, one of whom "was well known . . . as an intelligent, worthy man," resented the move, but given Garrison's comments from the previous day this likely did not sit well with him. According to the managers, however, "we could not vary our regulations in their favor, especially while a number of our stockholders were then standing below unable to procure seats."[8]

Without Sleigh, the colonizationists had no representative, but the abolitionists still planned to discuss "Slavery and Its Remedy." Alvan Stewart, William H. Burleigh, Alanson St. Clair, Edward C. Pritchett, and Elder Frederick Plummer each spoke, but only Pritchett and Plummer kept notes from their talks. Before they began, however, managers read a letter from another colonizationist, Pennsylvania Assemblyman Walter Forward. They had invited him to speak but he could not make it. Instead, he sent his best wishes and voiced unqualified support of their efforts to speak out and to petition their leaders. "However partial I may be to the scheme of Colonization," he wrote, "I am none the less inflexible in the resolution, never to submit to any attempt, under whatever plausible pretext, to subdue the spirit of free discussion, or to render the servants of the people inaccessible to their complaints."[9]

Pritchett then rose to speak. He began by praising Brown's speech of the day before but then added that he was disappointed at the ending. He then offered a number of reasons for opposing colonization. For one thing, he pointed out that Africans and African American colonists would not necessarily get along. He also insisted that colonizationist efforts tended to increase the prejudice that held African Americans down to begin with. Finally, he called colonizationists out on a paradox they had created. They argued that American blacks had to go to Liberia because of "a natural repugnance between the races" at the same time that they insisted that if blacks remained in the United States, "they will amalgamate." He then added that amalgamation occurred under Southern slavery, not in the free North.

Unlike most speakers at the hall, Plummer had never been part of either an abolition or a colonization society, and he opened his remarks by introducing himself to the crowd. Professing to be "antislavery in sentiment," he said that he came to the debate "to hear the master-spirits on both sides of this very important subject." So far, however, he felt disappointment because, with Sleigh refusing to debate and Cresson out of town, "the discussion has been all on one side." As far as those who had spoken, Plummer felt unsatisfied because "they have said much relating to the evils and horrors of slavery, which we do not question; but the grand difficulty is, in my opinion, that it is legalized by our national compact, and the slave is claimed as legal property." So, he asked, "how far [do] we have a right, legally and morally, to deprive the slaveholder of what he has honestly inherited?" He then asked if a program of compensated emancipation might be fair to both master and slave. Whether his suggestion would work or not, he called upon both abolitionists and colonizationists to work together and stop "leveling their artillery against each other." Sounding like many members of the Philadelphia abolition movement had all along, he called for measures "in which the slaveholder and the whole nation can combine their will and ability to liberate the slave, and thus accomplish this very desirable object, and preserve the national union."[10]

As the men listened to these speakers, the Antislavery Convention of American Women reconvened at 10 a.m. in Temperance Hall, engaging in a number of serious debates of their own. First, Juliana Tappan of New York offered a resolution that seemed to support the behavior of martyred abolitionist Elijah P. Lovejoy. Since Lovejoy had died while engaging in armed self-defense, this led the women to debate the role of self-defense and violence in the movement. The women also engaged in heated discussion over the church issue. Philadelphian Mary Grew resolved that they should "keep ourselves separate from those churches which receive to their pulpits and their communion tables, those who buy, or sell, or hold as property, the image of the living God." Those who opposed this resolution insisted that they could do more good work through the churches than they could if they withdrew from them. Though the resolution ultimately carried, the dissenters asked that their opinions and reason for disagreeing be included in the report of the meeting. Finally, the women split over whether or not it was acceptable for women to speak in front of audiences composed of members of both sexes—"promiscuous audiences." Some members wanted to include both sexes in their meeting that night at Pennsylvania Hall, but others objected. Ultimately they concluded that the meeting would include both men and women but that it would not be an official meeting of the Antislavery Convention of American Women. After solving this last problem they adjourned to meet the next morning at 10 a.m. at Pennsylvania Hall. Those who chose to would go to the hall that night for the unofficial meeting.[11]

Wednesday Afternoon

The PASS met in the saloon at 2 p.m. for another short meeting. Among other issues, John Greenleaf Whittier offered a resolution that further illustrated yet another difference between Garrisonians and Pennsylvania immediatists. He resolved that abolitionists should use the right of suffrage to elect legislators who supported abolition. The meeting concluded with little controversy, and they adjourned to meet at the hall Friday at 7:30 a.m.

At some point either during or after the PASS meeting, a man identifying himself as part of the committee of arrangements approached the managers and asked them about using the main room that night for what he called "a public meeting addressed by Angelina E. G. Weld, Maria W. Chapman, and others." Thinking he wanted to use the hall for an official meeting of the Antislavery Convention of American Women, the managers agreed. Almost immediately, word of this meeting circulated among the crowd outside, and they became enraged that the white woman who had allegedly married a black man was to speak that night.

Meanwhile, as the PASS adjourned, the hall managers began the final session of their dedication ceremonies. It began with a rambling discourse in which Alvan Stewart traced the history of slavery and spoke about the importance of living up to the nation's revolutionary promise of freedom for all. He then pointed out that much of the rest of the world had ended slavery, and the thirteen slaveholding states in the southern United States made the whole nation look evil. He concluded by saying, "Let this Hall be like a moral furnace, in which the fires of free discussion shall burn night and day, and purify public opinion of the base alloy of expediency."

After Stewart finished, a number of speakers offered brief remarks. The very last speaker, William H. Burleigh, offered a final thought in hope that something might be done to save the Cherokee and prevent the forced removal they faced in less than a week. As the meeting concluded, Whittier prepared an article for the *Freeman* in which he outlined the day's events and expressed the hope that "long may that Hall stand the pride and ornament of the city of Penn."[12] Of course, for that to happen it would have to survive the night, and that was looking less likely as the day wore on.

Wednesday Evening

Laura Lovell made her way to Pennsylvania Hall after the women's convention adjourned for the day. Like many of the women, she had decided to attend the night's meeting even if the convention refused to officially sanction it. When she arrived she found a noisy throng around the door, but she managed to make her way through and find a good seat near the platform. She sat in amazement looking at "the most eminent abolitionists of both sexes" on the platform before her and prepared for "entertainment of the highest order." Soon the room filled with about three thousand people and hundreds had to be turned away by the managers for lack of room. The crowd included mostly women, but some men as well, making up the "promiscuous audience" dreaded by so many. Perhaps even more importantly, the group was mixed in one other way—whites and blacks sat side by side as they waited for the speakers to begin.

When Garrison rose to start the meeting, the crowd erupted in applause. Perhaps his host, Edward Needles, or one of his other more "moderate" friends such as Lucretia Mott had approached him about his critique of David Paul Brown's speech the day before, because he spent his time on the platform arguing that his treatment of both Brown and Sleigh was justified. He went into great detail about why Brown's speech reeked of gradualism, and he went point by point through Brown's comments to show that *"he is no abolitionist."* Admitting that he knew full well of Brown's reputation for gratuitously defending those arrested in Philadelphia as runaway slaves, he added that "such conduct is worthy of the highest encomiums; but, while it should ever be gratefully appreciated, it ought not to furnish a cover for the dissemination of sentiments which are hostile to the liberty and equality of the human race." He also pointed out that "true humanity is not local, but universal in its sympathy; it is concerned not only for the safety of the slave who has emancipated himself by flight, but also for him who is actually wearing the galling fetters of slavery."

After finishing with Brown, he once again took on Sleigh and Cresson, though neither man was there. He argued that Sleigh, an Englishman, had come to the United States "to help the white birds drive away the black ones, that they may have all the strawberries and cherries, insects and worms, to themselves." But, thanks to "a Southern amalgamating process" it would not be that easy because "the land is swarming with *white black-birds!*"[13]

Some members of the audience left during Garrison's remarks to find Sleigh. They arrived at his home and found his son, who informed them that his father was at church. Telling the younger Sleigh that his father was being "abused . . . before a crowded assembly in Pennsylvania Hall," they had him get his father and bring him to the hall. Sleigh arrived around 8:30, where he found several of his friends who told him Garrison had been talking about him and Elliott Cresson. Sleigh called out to the chair to demand a hearing but nobody on the platform could hear him over the noise in the hall. When he tried to make his way to the front to ask privately for a chance to speak, he could not penetrate the crowd. He gave up and left the building.[14]

Sleigh could not be heard because at this point the crowd outside, which had grown to around three thousand, surrounded the hall and began to throw rocks and bricks through the windows. Fortunately the managers had directed the carpenters to include strong blinds that went inside the building rather than shutters on the outside, so the rocks and bricks were not able to reach the people inside. Determined not to be silenced, the abolitionists continued their meeting despite the attack. At one point a small part of the mob broke into the lobby, but those seated in the back of the room managed to bar the doors to the saloon so that Garrison could finish his speech. He then introduced his close friend Maria Weston Chapman, a thirty-two-year-old abolitionist who had helped to found the Boston Female Antislavery

Society, served as editor and main contributor of the group's annual reports, wrote abolition books of her own, and helped to edit the *Liberator* and the *National Antislavery Standard*. She was there to make her first appearance in front of a mixed audience. As Garrison sat down, the crowd outside produced what Lovell called a "deafening shout" and threw a fresh volley of projectiles at the windows. At the same moment a small number of troublemakers who had managed to enter and station themselves among the audience tried to scare the abolitionists and break up the meeting.[15]

Despite the chaos and violence, Chapman rose and offered a few short remarks. She only spoke about ten minutes but was repeatedly interrupted by the uproar of the mob outside and the detractors inside. The crowd outside continued to try to push their way inside, but those inside continued to fend them off.

At some point the managers sent for police protection and were told that the only four men available had already been sent to the hall. The mayor was out of town that evening and had left the city solicitor in charge. The solicitor told the police not to make arrests because they would have to leave the scene to take the suspects to the jail and thus leave even less authority at the hall. Strangely, he insisted that since no trouble had been anticipated he had not brought in extra help and was thus shorthanded.

When Daniel Neall learned of the police presence he stepped forward on the platform and told everyone to keep calm. He said that police officers had arrived and "on the least overt act the boys around the house will be secured, and we shall be protected." Lovell, who had never experienced a mob before, "saw the propriety" of listening to his advice, "having previously concluded that it would be safest to keep our seats, unless we saw the house actually falling or burning over our heads." Even so, she doubted the usefulness of a police force that had not managed to stop the attack already.[16]

As Chapman sat down, Angelina M. Grimké Weld, the main object of the mob's wrath, rose to speak. She was a woman speaking to a group that included men, was rumored to have married a black man two days before, and was seen by Southerners as a traitor since she had left South Carolina to move North and speak out against the Southern way of life. Though the abolitionists in the room saw her as one of the main heroes of their movement, anti-abolitionists hated her deeply.

Noting the size of the crowd, she started by asking if they were there out of sympathy for the cause or out of curiosity. Instantly the yells outside intensified, and she replied that "these voices without . . . know not what they do." By joining in sympathy with the slave interests and trying so hard to silence people like herself who were exercising their constitutional right to free speech, "they are undermining their own rights and their own happiness, temporal and eternal." She went on to call to task both Southern slaveholders and Northern mobs who did their bidding for them by attacking abolitionists. She spoke for over an hour despite the shouts both outside and inside, and the breaking of glass.

After Grimké Weld concluded her remarks, Abby Kelley of Lynn, Massachusetts, and a local Quaker named Ester Moore each made a few remarks. Before adjourning, Lucretia Mott rose to announce that the meeting had not been officially sanctioned by the women's convention because not all had agreed on the issue of speaking to gender-mixed audiences. Hoping "that such false notions of delicacy and propriety would not long obtain in this enlightened county," she adjourned and calmly led the women out of the building at 10 p.m., as scheduled.

Lovell and one of her friends managed to avoid the mob entirely by going down an alley. Some of the white women walked out arm in arm with their black friends to protect them from the mob. The mob chose not to attack the women, but they did assault a black man in one of the alleys. Given the city's record with race riots, the black community remained on high alert throughout the night.[17]

As they dispersed, members of the crowd talked about burning the hall down, but the abolitionists had trouble believing it would go that far. Despite it all, they had "confidence in the peaceable disposition of the inhabitants" of Philadelphia, and their respect for the reputation of their city." Apparently so did a Southerner who was visiting the city that week. After writing to the editor of the *Augusta Georgia Chronicle and Sentinel* about the outrageous abolitionist behavior he had witnessed, he lamented that Philadelphians would put up with such behavior: "'Tis true, they profess to be *offended* at these things. But then, they do not think the peace of the city should be disturbed in its repose, or violated in its regularity." Whether they liked the hall and what it stood for or not, "They think that the temple of these *audacious meddlers* may still rear its gorgon crest *before the eye of the Southron—that those from whose hands they receive their daily bread, and whose substance clothes their merchant cities in beauty and affluence*, may still bear their insults." Angered at their "lethargic indifference to the conduct of *these mad zealots*," he looked forward to the day when these Northern traitors "shall no longer enjoy the aid and support of the productive South."[18] He would soon be writing another letter to tell the editor that he had spoken too soon.

CHAPTER 8

....

Free Speech "Consumed
in a Blue Blaze"

With the images of the angry faces and memories of the hateful words spewed at her the night before still fresh in her mind, Lucretia Mott prepared herself for whatever Thursday might bring. She still sheltered a houseful of guests, and she had a number of important meetings to attend at Pennsylvania Hall that day. And she refused to let fear keep her at home. After searching her soul overnight and praying for strength, she determined to "suffer whatever the cause required," so she headed to the hall for the early meeting of the Requited Labor Convention. She and her husband James had worked long for the cause of free produce and there was no way she would miss the chance to help build a new national free produce association. Perhaps she and her neighbor Mary Needles walked to the meeting together because they both went on the record as delegates. If so, they would have discussed not only what they thought might happen if the violence were to escalate at the hall but also what might happen to their own homes if the mob went uncontrolled. Even so, both women remained steadfast.

When she arrived at the meeting, Mott found many of her friends, including Pennsylvania Hall Association president Daniel Neall. A member of Mott's Hicksite Quaker community, Neall served on the executive committee of the Pennsylvania Antislavery Society (PASS) and had been chosen as president of the hall association at the group's first meeting. He had earned respect throughout the Philadelphia abolition community, and when they needed dental treatment, many of the city's Quakers and reformers headed straight for 325 Arch Street, where they knew they could find him or his son Daniel Neall Jr. Neall was a good man with the best of intentions, but that morning he offered Mott advice she had no desire to take. He asked her and the other antislavery women at the convention to encourage their black friends to avoid the evening meetings at the hall. He feared the crowd would attack blacks, and he knew that even though most white men would stop short of physical violence against white women, they would not extend the courtesy to black women. Mott listened politely and promised to pass his warning along to the women at their meeting later that day. Even so, she would not endorse his suggestion.[1]

Thursday, May 17, 1838

The Requited Labor Convention convened at 8 a.m. in the session room of the hall. They met long enough to elect officers, enroll the nearly three hundred delegates from assorted antislavery and free produce associations, and form a National Requited Labor Association. They then appointed a committee to draft a constitution for the national association, a committee to prepare the convention business, a committee to prepare and publish an address on the "*duty* of abstaining from the produce of slave labor," and a committee to "inquire into the best mode of supplying the market with articles produced by remunerated labor." After that they adjourned to meet at the same location at 2 p.m. About half of the delegates were women, and most of them had other business to attend in the meantime at the Antislavery Convention of American Women meeting in the main room of the hall.[2]

As the free produce advocates met, the crowd began to return and surround the hall. Fearing what might happen next, some of the hall association managers formed a committee and went to Samuel Webb's house to discuss the situation and come up with a plan of action. They decided to write letters to the sheriff and mayor asking for protection. They also made plans to have the authorities appraise the damages from the previous night so they could seek restitution under an 1836 city act stipulating that the city would pay damages to the victims of mob action.[3]

Acting as the group's attorney, David Paul Brown took charge of the legal matter while Daniel Neall, Peter Wright, and Samuel Webb went to tell Mayor John Swift what was happening. They showed him a copy of the placard the anti-abolitionists had posted on Tuesday, and they offered to give him the name of one of the "ringleaders of the mob." They also gave him the letter that provided a written account of the situation, laying out what had happened the night before and what activities were scheduled to take place in the hall on Thursday and Friday.

The mayor replied that he needed to consult with the attorney general to clarify if the county was responsible for the damages. Dismayed, the committee replied that they "had not called to claim *damages*, but to ask for *protection*." They believed the matter of damages was a less pressing issue that could be resolved later. For now they wanted the authorities to "protect us and our property in the exercise of our constitutional right, peaceably to assemble and discuss any subject of general interest."[4]

The mayor gave little indication that he wanted to intervene. His first concern remained whether the city or the county would be responsible for damages. As for protecting the building, he replied "There are always two sides to a question—it is public opinion makes mobs—and ninety-nine out of a hundred of those with whom I converse are against you." He concluded he would go to the hall in the evening and address the crowd but that he could do nothing beyond that.

As the managers appealed to the mayor for protection, the crowd around the hall grew. Even so, the women gathered there to continue their convention. They remained nervous over the previous night's attack but Mott urged them to stay "steadfast and solemn in the prosecution of the business for which they were assembled." As the mob filled the doors of the hall and threatened to enter the room, the women remained remarkably calm and went about their business, passing a series of resolutions that defended women's right to participate in the antislavery cause and criticized churches whose actions helped perpetuate slavery. They also made plans for a new fundraising initiative, planning to form cent-a-week societies. After concluding their business they adjourned with plans to reconvene at 4 p.m.[5]

At some point that morning Sheriff John G. Watmough went to the hall to check out the commotion. He reported that the crowd of mostly well-dressed people appeared more curious than violent. While most of these "respectable citizens" remained across the street, some noisy young people ran around, in and out of the building. By several accounts the mob included about two hundred people who looked on threateningly as workers arrived to replace the broken windows.

Between 10:30 and 11, PASS member Bartholomew Fussell finished the committee work he had been assigned and left the hall through the Haines Street entrance. There he found Henry C. Wright, who had been lecturing the crowd about slavery. He asked Wright to join him, and they walked casually up Race Street "not thinking of danger." They soon found themselves followed by two men who called out to them "making use of heavy threats and foul profanity." One of their pursuers swore he came from a Quaker family and was a Quaker himself, but he threatened Wright that "if he ever again uttered such sentiments that all slave-holders were robbers, he would knock his brains out there in the street, for that would make George Washington a robber." He "would not hear" such an accusation "and let a man live." Wright replied, "As to my life, you may take it. I make no resistance, but was George Washington a slaveholder? If he was, I assert he was a robber." Enraged, "the bully then declared that the hall should come down before 10:00 that night, and swore still more boldly that he would kill Henry." At that point a man ran up and urged the abolitionists to go or "we would be destroyed," for the mob was "greatly enraged" and out for blood. Wright stood still "unmoved as he was confident,—undaunted as he was peaceful" while the mob closed in yelling "Kill him! Kill him!" Right at that moment someone—either an opportunist out to take advantage of a chaotic situation or an abolitionist sympathizer with perfect timing—stole the pocketbook of someone in the crowd and took off running across Sixth Street. While the "whole rabble" turned and pursued the thief, Wright and Fussell "walked off in peace and rested at the house of a friend without any alarm."[6]

Thursday Afternoon

That afternoon delegates of the Requited Labor Convention met at 2 p.m. in the main room. Alanson St. Clair presented a resolution in favor of boycotting slave-produced goods when free labor goods could be had. Several people spoke in support of the resolution, and the group adjourned to meet again in the same room at 10 a.m. the next morning. Meanwhile, realizing "that no efficient steps would be taken by the Mayor" to prevent the hall being "offered a sacrifice to propitiate the Demon of Slavery," the managers appealed to the sheriff. They wrote him a letter similar to the one they gave Swift and went to his office around 2 p.m. to apprise him of the situation. During the meeting, which lasted about an hour, the sheriff told the managers that their situation fell under the mayor's jurisdiction. He added, however, that if he had the one hundred sixty men the mayor had available, he "would have suppressed the mob the first night." The sheriff's force, however, consisted of himself and three men, and he asked the managers what they expected four men to do. It would take time and money to put together a sufficient force and by now it was 3 p.m., so the sheriff argued that he had little time to find the men he needed. He added that the money would have to come out of his own pocket. The committee offered to furnish the money, but Watmough said he would much rather they furnish "a determined force to stand by me at all hazards."

What happened next remains controversial. According to Sheriff Watmough and City Council member and lawyer Henry J. Williams, the sheriff's friend and legal advisor, they warned the managers that while the sheriff had the power to "call on any man in executing his duty" to protect "persons or property," in this case it would be difficult because "the feelings of the people" would not be on his side. Williams warned that the sheriff would not "find the citizens generally disposed to aid him, in consequence of the excitement which appeared to exist against the Abolition Society." Thus, both men suggested the managers close the hall that evening. Williams further pointed out that matters would escalate after dark, but one of the managers replied that "the street was lighted with gas, and every individual could be distinctly seen." Williams claimed that the managers also "expressed a confident belief that not one in ten of the community were opposed to their proceedings." Even so, he reiterated his concerns and asked if the managers did not fear that by holding their meeting that night they might jeopardize any claims they might hope to make on the county for any damages they might suffer. The managers, however, appeared to "have no doubt on that head."

One particular point of contention involved the matter of gathering the force of men to protect the building. Watmough insisted that the managers agreed to bring him five hundred young men "with no problem." In fact, he argued, one member of the committee boasted that he could get fifteen hundred men. Watmough replied that five hundred would be sufficient but that he needed them quickly.

He added that he had "requested them to select their own place, near their hall, for the young men to meet me—told them I would be on the ground early, and expressed confidence that all would yet be well." According to Watmough they then arose "with every expression of confidence and hope." At the close of the meeting he felt "highly pleased at the confidence and firmness of their manner, and the zeal with which they set out to rally a sufficient force for me."

Williams also claimed that the managers promised to raise sufficient money and five hundred men "who would stand by the sheriff in every extremity." He added that the managers initially suggested their friends be sworn in as special constables, but he convinced them that for the sake of expediency they should dispense with that ceremony and allow the sheriff to call upon the men as his "posse comitatus." Finally, he pointed out that "the more secret the presence of such a body of men was kept, the more effectual would be their action upon an emergency." Like Watmough, Williams believed that when the managers left around 3 p.m. they were on a mission to "prepare their friends to be in readiness for that evening." "From the determination they expressed, to hold their meetings according to their previous public notice," he added, "I thought them less apprehensive on the subject that I expected they would have been."

Nevertheless, when Watmough arrived at the hall at 4 p.m., he found no assistance. He later claimed that he waited until 7:30, at which time "a young gentleman" approached him with a letter that said the managers "cannot undertake to defend the hall by force." "As law-abiding and peaceful citizens," the managers had decided to "throw ourselves upon the justice of our cause, the laws of our country, and the right guaranteed to us by the Constitution, peaceably to assemble and to discuss any matter of general interest." They concluded that they would not have "any 'immediate or active participation in any mob or riot' which may occur."[7]

What had happened? Given the wording of the note the managers sent Watmough, it is likely that one of their legal advisors, perhaps David Paul Brown, had alerted them to the law under which they would need to appeal to claim restitution for damages, should the hall be destroyed. That law, which appeared in the *Liberator* a week later, said that "in case any dwelling house or other building or property" shall be "injured or destroyed" in the city "in consequence of any mob or riot therein," the owner of the property could apply to the mayor for compensation. But there was one catch: the property owner would have to prove that he had no "immediate or active participation in said mob or riot." This explains the unattributed quote in the manager's notice: "we will not have any 'immediate or active participation in any mob or riot' which may occur."

In their account of the meeting with Watmough, the managers stressed this written communication and added that "any *conversation*" they may have had with him was "considered by the Board as informal." Clearly someone had warned the committee that their promise to help gather men to actively fight against the rioters jeopardized their ability to claim damages under the riot law. Thus, they later insisted that they did not furnish the men because "we did not intend to do anything that would injure our claim for indemnity."[8]

As Watmough stood outside the hall reading the managers' letter, the Antislavery Convention of American Women reconvened inside. Mott shared Neall's suggestion that black women avoid the evening meeting for their own safety, but she urged them to ignore the request. Instead she suggested that they not allow a "little appearance of danger" to deter them.

Of course, the women realized the danger they faced. Rumors of racial mixing continued to fuel the angry wails of the mob, and they knew that Neall's warning made sense. Everyone realized that even if the mob might hesitate to physically attack middle-class white women, black women could expect no such respect. Indeed, many African American women had not waited for a warning to stay home that night. They had instead decided to skip the afternoon meeting as well. Most of the women at the afternoon meeting vowed to attend the gathering that night, both in support of the Wesleyan Antislavery Society that was hosting the meeting and in defiance of anyone who would dare try to scare them into staying away. One African American delegate from New York argued that it would be "both selfish and cowardly for her people to shrink in the hour of danger."

During the meeting three of the women went outside to address the crowd. Two of them, Harriet Burleigh and Mary Grew, lived in Philadelphia. Bartholomew Fussell listed the third as "Mrs. Grier" from New York, but he probably misheard Margaret Prior's name since there was no Grier on the list of delegates and Prior had taken an active role in the proceedings to that point. At any rate, each of these women went to a different side of the building to ask the mob to let them have their meeting in peace. Unimpressed by their pleas, the mob continued to harass the women in an effort to break up the meeting. Even so, the women continued with their business. Managers who passed through the "Grand Saloon" while the convention met noted the dignity and calmness the women showed even as the crowd grew louder and more threatening. One manager noted that they stayed composed even as the mob tried to force its way into the room.

As the meeting came to a close, some of the managers tried to convince the women to leave through the back door because the crowd out front was so thick that it formed almost a solid wall. The women decided not to take that advice, but the white women protected the black women by taking them by the arm and walking out in pairs. According to Laura Lovell, "We passed out through a mob of two or three thousand, fierce, vile looking men, and large boys. They allowed us just room to walk, two abreast. We heard the worst language, and saw the most hideous countenances, but I believe none were seriously molested."[9]

This scene concluded the last meeting in Pennsylvania Hall. The Wesleyan Antislavery Society of the Methodist Episcopal Church of Philadelphia was to meet there that night, and as they left, most of the women planned to return and attend that gathering. But that would never happen: the next time most of them saw the hall it would be on fire.

Blocks away, Colonel Augustus Pleasanton of the Pennsylvania Militia was returning home after a long day of drilling his regiment at the arsenal. One of his neighbors walked over to tell him about the Wednesday night attack at the "Abolition Hall." Familiar with the climate of his city and the widespread disgust toward abolitionists' "inflammatory proceedings" and "indiscriminate intercourse between the whites and the blacks so repugnant to all the prejudice of our education," he started to wonder if his men would be called to form just the type of posse comitatus the managers had failed to supply. Fearing "some terrible outbreak of popular indignation, not only against the abolitionists, but also against the colored people," he prayed "may Heaven preserve us from any such calamity!" Oddly, he made no effort to reassemble his men and head to the hall to help the sheriff or the mayor.[10]

Thursday Evening

Just after 6 p.m. Mayor Swift returned to the hall. When he arrived he noticed one man stirring the crowd, so he sent him away. By some accounts the abolitionists pointed out the ringleaders to him, but instead of arresting them he seized a harmless drunk and dragged him two blocks way, scolding him as they went. After that he went into the hall to meet with the managers. Those inside were quite alarmed by the activity outside. The mayor asked them again to cancel the night's events and to give him the keys. He told them that by this point there was certainly an organized plan to attack the hall if it was used that night. This time they agreed.[11]

Laura Lovell was blocks away at a friend's house having dinner when she received word that the night's events had been cancelled. As she had left the hall that afternoon she dreaded the prospect of returning but also began to question her dedication to the cause if she chose not to. "It appeared very rational to conclude, and very evident too from appearances, that the mob was now ripe for some violent outrage," she later recorded. She added that she had heard many threats echoing through the streets, and she thought the crowd, having been emboldened by being allowed to get away with Wednesday night's attack, had no reason not to escalate the violence. Though many of the women had remained determined to return, she had concluded that the mob was "not to be reasoned with, or treated like rational beings." When word arrived that the hall had been closed, she no longer had to worry about whether or not skipping the night's session would make her look cowardly.

Arnold Buffum, one of the twelve pioneers in the immediate movement, sat nearby and shared a story of his adventurous journey to the dinner party. Along the way he had stopped on the sidewalk to visit with a friend. Finding himself "surrounded by about forty savage looking men," he tried to move along. At that point, one of the crowd shouted "Down with the Quaker, down with the nigger's friend." Buffum replied that he was in search of family members who were out and wished to pass by, but they repeated the threat. One member of the mob suggested they "cut him in pieces and throw him into the Delaware." At that point, "a giant-like, fierce looking fellow" made his way through the crowd to confront Buffum, asking him if his wife was black. The abolitionist answered in the negative. The man then asked,

"Would you have married her if she had been?," to which Buffum also replied "no." He then asked if Buffum had daughters and if so, if any of them had married black men. Buffum said that he had daughters but that none of them had married blacks. Finally, he asked Buffum, "Are you for amalgamation?" After Buffum responded that he was not, the man said, "You are a good fellow, you may go along."[12] As other guests chimed in with similar stories, Lovell began to relax a little and enjoy dinner with her abolitionist friends.

Meanwhile, back at the hall, Mayor Swift left the building to address the crowd while the sheriff helped the managers bolt the doors from the inside. After the building was emptied, the mayor stood at the front door and addressed the crowd. He told them the hall was now officially closed and there would be no further meetings that night. "I must hope that nothing will be transacted contrary to order and peace," he told the crowd. "Our city has long held the enviable position of a peaceful city—a city of order. It must not lose its position." He added, "I truly hope that no one will do anything of a disorderly nature; anything of the kind would be followed by regret ever after." He then added that the managers had a right to hold their meeting, "but as good citizens they have, at my request, suspended their meeting for this evening."[13]

By one account, an abolitionist called out "Get the militia" as the mayor was concluding his remarks, and the mayor replied "We never call out the military here. We do not need such measures." He then called upon his "fellow citizens" in the mob to serve as his police. "I trust you will abide by the laws, and keep order," he told them. Then he bid them "farewell for the night" and walked away as cheers and applause echoed in the street. The Pennsylvania Hall managers, who recorded the details of the event, did not mention an abolitionist calling out for the militia, but that would explain the mayor's remarks. If nobody did indeed ask for troops, then the mayor's assertion that there would be no militia brought in would have been a random comment that would have essentially welcomed the mob to attack. Either way, the mayor did not disperse the crowd and he did not stay, though he did station a few men near the hall and told them to get him if any trouble erupted. As he walked away he heard the mob yelling "three cheers for the mayor!" Swift believed that the crowd of about three hundred "very young men, chiefly boys and striplings, and some respectable persons attracted there by curiosity" left after he spoke, but he did leave his friend Captain Thomas Hayes and the city solicitor Edward Olmsted there to monitor the situation.[14]

Within a half hour of the mayor's departure, between ten and fifteen thousand people had assembled at the corner of Sixth and Haines. Abolitionists who had not received word of the canceled meeting arrived to find locked doors. Curious onlookers gathered to see what would happen next.

Sheriff Watmough noticed part of the crowd moving around to the side of the building just before 8 p.m. He prepared for the chaos to break loose as he heard the sounds of breaking glass. The crowd began to cheer as a number of young men attacked the north side of the building by throwing rocks and bricks through the windows, many of which had just been replaced that morning. While the mob extinguished the gas lights on the street and, under cover of darkness, began to attack with fury, Watmough called for volunteers from the crowd to help him. Only one person, a man named Thomas Connell, responded. Connell called out that the sheriff was there, apparently thinking that would make the crowd disperse. Matters were escalating quickly at this point. The sheriff gathered about a dozen of the troublemakers but could not keep custody of them because the crowd intervened and forced him to release them. In the melee the sheriff was physically attacked and suffered head injuries before he and Connell both gave up.[15]

Once the sheriff was out of the picture, the mob started trying to push its way into the hall. The mayor's watchmen sent messengers to his office to alert him that the violence had commenced. The crowds made it hard for Swift as he tried to make his way up Cherry Street to the hall, but he eventually made it. Upon his arrival for the second time, Swift sounded his watchman's rattle and one of the deputies shouted for the crowd to "support the Mayor!" and then tried to reason with the crowd, to no avail. During this time period private citizens were often called upon to help enforce the law when extra forces were needed, but no one responded in this case. Even though most of the people in the crowd did not participate in the attack, it was quickly obvious that they did not intend to intervene, even at the request of authorities. Instead, some members of the crowd began to assail the policemen. Realizing that he was hopelessly outnumbered, and less than keen to help from the beginning, the mayor gave up.

Shipwrights from nearby Front Street brought in axes, crowbars, and wooden beams to help the mob break down the doors. Using the beams as battering rams, they eventually forced their way inside. Once the doors gave way, the mob rushed the building and Samuel Yeager, a local hatter from a respected family, ran to the top of the stairs and rallied the mob to break the furniture into kindling. Pilfering the anti-slavery offices and bookstore, they gathered the abolition literature that so many from both North and South had denounced as "incendiary" and "inflammatory." One participant later wrote that they went straight for "the abolition sanctuary (the book store)," throwing "many hundred volumes into the street" before piling the others up on the third floor and setting them ablaze. Perhaps others shared his targeted anger, or maybe they merely sought the most flammable materials.

Benjamin Lundy had just moved all of his belongings into the building in preparation for a final move to join his family in Illinois. His papers were among the first casualties. It was ironic that his life's work helped to start the blaze in the hall, just as it had helped to ignite the metaphorical flame that fueled the angry mob. He lost almost everything that night. Jones had recently moved merchandise from his Arch Street bookstore into one of the hall's first-floor rooms. The owner of a free produce store had made a similar move. Plundering these rooms, the mob gathered what they could easily carry and added it all to a pile they were making on the platform in the "Grand Saloon." Then they went into the cellar and gathered wood shavings left by the builders, adding these to the mix. They tore down the freshly painted Venetian blinds and threw them on for good measure. The shipwrights offered tar and turpentine to get the fire going, and someone pulled the gas pipes loose, aiming them at the pile.[16]

As the mob tried to set fire to the building, Captain Hayes and an Officer Miller with the police force went in and tried to put out three fires that had been set on the second floor. Men in the building addressed Hayes by name and asked him to leave. When he refused, they forced him and Miller out. Hayes later reported that though the men knew his name he did not know who they were.

Daniel Neall, president of the Pennsylvania Hall Association, stood amidst the chaos in the grand structure as the glass from the windows shattered above him. Perhaps he regretted the decision to include the innovation of gas lighting in the building plans. Another abolitionist made a mental note of Samuel Yeager's role in the destruction and even tried to convince the young man to leave the hall.[17]

A block away, John Greenleaf Whittier heard the commotion and ran out to see what was happening. Along the way he saw women shouting applause and waving their handkerchiefs from their raised windows. The mob was destroying the hall and the crowd was showing universal approval. His heart skipped a beat as he realized that everything Lundy owned was in that hall. So, for that matter, were the plates for his newspaper. As he approached the hall someone shouted out his name. Realizing the severity of the situation and the threat to his personal safety, he detoured to the nearby home of a doctor and fellow abolitionist, where he borrowed a wig and a lab coat. Safe in his disguise and determined not to let the mob silence his press, he pretended to participate in the destruction as he rescued the plates for the next day's edition.[18] Other Philadelphia abolitionists took the risk of entering the hall as they scrambled to salvage what they could.

Visiting with friends in another part of city and in "unusually high spirits," Lundy was discussing his plans to move to Illinois when someone came in to tell them about the fire. Rising from his chair in shocked silence, he went outside and stood quietly on the sidewalk. After a few moments he calmly told one of his associates, "everything I have in the world is there." He went back inside and told his friends "we must learn to bear these things." Realizing he could not save his possessions, he told a friend that he was overwhelmed but "not disheartened." He did not realize it, but at that very moment some of his friends were at the hall trying to salvage what they could for him. Someone managed to save a few of his belongings, including a small trunk that contained some of his papers and one of his journals.

Others took mental notes, identifying assailants. Lovell was still at the dinner party nearby when the conversation was interrupted by reports from friends that the hall was ablaze. She now stood outside watching in horror, disgusted by the work of the mob and the absence of the authorities. Down the block a Quaker man looked on tranquilly until a member of the mob asked him, "What the hell are *you* doing here with your sanctified face? You had better be off!" Taking the hint, he left, not to return to the scene.

Those who did not make their way to the scene went to the Mott home to sit with James and Lucretia. There the adults visited calmly while the younger members of the family came and went, bringing updates from the hall. By 9 p.m. they learned the hall was on fire.

By that point fire completely engulfed the building. Flames leapt from every window and the neighborhood glowed bright red and orange. As the attackers backed away to watch Pennsylvania Hall burn, the red and orange hues gave way to a bright blue flame caused by the combustion of the zinc in the building's roof. This blue haze created an eerie glow that blanketed Philadelphia. From atop Independence Hall, just down the street, the Liberty Bell rang out.

When the fire companies arrived at the hall, their first challenge was to push through the wall of people who had come from all parts of the city to investigate. Sixth and Arch Streets were crowded not only with those who had assembled to watch the mob but also with theatergoers attracted by the eerie glow as they left the Arch Street theaters. The blue haze attracted people from throughout the city. Witnesses estimated the crowd between ten and fifteen thousand, even though only two to three hundred participated in the attack. Once the firemen neared the building, however, the crowd refused to allow them to interfere. Most of the firemen were easily put off, though some witnesses did report one company's more forceful attempt to save the building. The other fire companies thwarted that effort quickly, however, by turning their hoses on the would-be rescuers. Instead of saving the hall, the firemen worked together to save nearby buildings.

Though complicit in Pennsylvania Hall's destruction, the crowd showed mercy for a widow whose home adjoined the offending building. While the firemen soaked her home and other nearby structures, onlookers took up a collection to cover the cost of the widow's repairs. Between the direct acts of destruction and the more orderly but equally damaging interference of the crowd, the fine line between mob participant and spectator blurred. This role confusion greatly impeded efforts to provide accurate accounts of the incident.

Near 10 p.m. someone with the *Colonization Herald* arrived on the scene in time to see the roof of the hall cave in, to the delight of the cheering crowd. Sparks flew over Sixth and Haines Streets while flames still lashed out from the hollow windows. Like other witnesses, the reporter noted how orderly the whole scene was, writing that "we do not remember ever to have seen such entire absence of confusion and turmoil at any fire, as there was on that occasion."

By midnight only the blackened granite walls remained. As the fire burned down, the onlookers quietly dispersed in a passive and orderly fashion while detachments of the mob prowled the streets the rest of the night and into the morning singing "triumphant choruses" and threatening abolitionists and African Americans. Lovell reported that it appeared "as if their appetite for destruction was rather sharpened, than satiated."[19]

After the building succumbed to the flames, abolitionists braced for attack. They knew they were in danger, especially the ones who had come to Philadelphia from out of town to participate in the various meetings held in Pennsylvania Hall. Most of them were boarding with local Quakers, who now had to protect their guests while adhering to their own nonviolent principles. Blocks away from the scene Sarah and Angelina Grimké waited at their sister's home, likely waiting for the mob to target them next. It would be thirty years before Angelina Grimké would speak publicly again.

Meanwhile, knowing the mob would soon head their way, the abolitionists at the Motts' new home at 136 North Ninth Street began to prepare. James and Lucretia Mott and their eleven guests were particularly vulnerable, given the family's reputation for lodging abolitionists, both white and black. This particular weekend their guests included Anne Warren Weston and Maria Weston Chapman. The day before, for the first time in her career, Chapman had dared to defy convention by speaking at Pennsylvania Hall in front of a "promiscuous" audience that included men and women of both races. Before all was said and done, she would pay heavily for the transgression. After a hasty escape from the Motts', she made it as far as Stonington, Connecticut, before suffering a "brain fever" that reportedly left her "a raving maniac."[20]

Nearby, the Edward and Mary Needles family harbored William Lloyd Garrison, the prime "agitator" who had spoken at Pennsylvania Hall. Perhaps they heard the crowd cheer as the roof crashed to the ground and realized that the hunt for Garrison was on. Unrecognized, Garrison had actually stood face to face with a man who taunted and threatened the abolitionists as they looked on in horror at the burning hall. If the man had known who he was jeering at and dismissing as an "enthusiast," Garrison would likely have found himself hanging from a nearby lamppost or, like the slaves he defended, bound and on his way to Georgia, where a $5,000 reward awaited anyone who produced this public enemy of the South. Always spoiling for a dramatic fight but aware of the danger he faced, Garrison acquiesced as his Philadelphia friends argued that this was not the time for him to take a stand. Fearing for the safety of their guest, William Needles, a mere boy at the time, piloted Garrison through the alleyways of the city to the inconspicuous home of John Oliver, an African American who offered temporary refuge along what the young guide later described as "the underground rail-way." Meanwhile, young men from other abolitionist families appealed to James Forten and Robert Purvis, two of the city's top black leaders, to help them get the Bostonian out of town. Both men and various members of their extended family had attended the hall's opening ceremonies but had returned home earlier in the day, likely bracing for imminent attack on their neighborhood. Given the history of race riots in Philadelphia, they knew full well who was most in danger—their friends and families. The whites seeking protection for Garrison either did not take that into account or simply assumed the black community was so accustomed to the violence that they automatically would know what to do. Apparently they did.

Purvis later recalled that the group of Garrison's rescuers included the son of Dr. Joseph Parrish. Perhaps local abolitionists realized that children and adolescents would more likely be allowed to pass through the streets unmolested. In such case, the Parrish in this group would have been sixteen-year-old Edward. At any rate, Forten and Purvis, whose work with the city's Underground Railroad made them accustomed to dramatic escapes, enlisted the help of another young man, James Forten's son Robert, to rush their friend to safety. Garrison protested but ultimately listened to reason. Even so, he could not resist a chance to return the taunts of the crowd. As the Forten carriage headed out of town, they passed a crowd that, unable to nab Garrison himself, was busy listening to a man assailing Garrison's character. Leaning out of the carriage, the abolitionist editor asked the speaker, "Do you know Mr. Garrison?" In reply to the man's reply, "No, I never met the . . .," Garrison quickly countered with, "Well, are you not ashamed to abuse so much a man you don't know?"

According to one account, as Garrison laughed at getting the final word, the carriage driver pushed on so quickly that they overtook the New York stagecoach, flying by so fast that the driver thought they were ghosts, and arrived in New Jersey by 1 a.m. A likely more accurate account is Robert Purvis's assertion that they arrived at his Bucks County estate near Bristol, twenty miles from the city, and rested a few hours before eating a rushed breakfast and venturing on to New York. What mattered was that, with the help of Pennsylvania's biracial antislavery community, Garrison had escaped his second mobbing. Years later, from the safety of his own printing office, he would describe the destruction of Pennsylvania Hall, and the lack of justice that followed, as a "legal lynching."[21]

CHAPTER 9

....

Aftershocks

As the Friday morning sun tried to cut through the hazy gloom that lingered in Philadelphia, John Greenleaf Whittier printed the May 17 edition of the *Pennsylvania Freeman*. Relieved that the press itself had remained behind at Arch Street, he rushed the plates over while the mob was preoccupied with their mayhem at Sixth and Haines. Earlier in the day he had finished writing his account of the week's festivities and had filled the paper with detailed accounts of the speeches made and the meetings held at Pennsylvania Hall, along with the usual news and interesting tidbits mined from corresponding newspapers. But now he had to find something to cut so that he could include one of the most urgent articles he would ever write. On the last column of page three, under the brief announcement of the Grimké—Weld wedding, he inserted, "POSTCRIPT! *Atrocious outrage! Burning of Pennsylvania Hall!*"

Under a dateline of 7:30 a.m. May 18 he reported that Pennsylvania Hall was in ashes. Setting the tone for other abolitionist accounts to come later, Whittier described the destruction in terms that evoked images of sacrifice and martyrdom. He informed his readers that "the beautiful temple consecrated to Liberty, has been offered a smoking sacrifice to the Demon of Slavery. In the heart of this city a flame has gone up to Heaven." This flame would not only alert God to the transgression, it would also "be seen from Maine to Georgia." Like all martyrs, Pennsylvania Hall would awaken the world to the important cause for which it had perished: "In its red and lurid light, men will see more clearly than ever the black abominations of the fiend at whose instigation it was kindled." After giving a hasty account of the attack, Whittier concluded, "We have no time for comment. Let the abhorrent deed speak for itself. Let all men see by what a frail tenure they hold property and life in a land overshadowed by the curse of Slavery."

Friday, May 18

After printing the *Freeman*, Whittier made his way to the scene of the carnage. When he arrived at the ruins he discovered that other abolitionists shared his determination to finish their meeting. The Pennsylvania Antislavery Society (PASS) met amidst the smoking walls with a mob lingering nearby and young boys pilfering the ruins for souvenirs. Lundy spoke and "drew tears from the eyes of men" according to Bartholomew Fussell, who added that Lundy "stated that he had now lost everything—everything but a clear conscience and a heart to feel for the slave."[1]

Though the crowd did not attack, many of the spectators continued to grumble and spread the rumors that had fueled the destruction of the hall. In addition to the rumors about "amalgamation" that had stemmed from the Grimké—Weld wedding and the appearance of the Purvises, people were grumbling that someone—in some versions David Paul Brown, in other versions William Lloyd Garrison—had called George Washington a thief and a "man stealer." The alleged attack upon Washington was just as fictitious as the wild stories of cross-racial intimacy; neither Brown nor Garrison made any such comment. What had really happened was that five years earlier, a writer at the *Vermont Chronicle* had taken comments Garrison had made about slaveholders in general and applied this to Washington in a way that made it look as if Garrison had personally assailed the former President's character. Readers of that article, and all reprinted forms, had taken for granted that the story was true. By 1838 the notion that abolitionists portrayed Washington as a "man stealer" commonly served as anti-abolition fodder, and many waited eagerly to hear abolitionists make such a comment so they could justify retaliating against them. Indeed, the only comment made to this effect during the week was when the group outside the hall pressed H. C. Wright on the issue Thursday morning.

Rather than risk their lives by stopping to reason with an irrational crowd and challenge these rumors head on, the abolitionists decided to move to Sandiford Hall, where they soon adjourned *sine die*—without determining when or where they would reconvene. Fussell offered his Philadelphia home, as did several local abolitionists, but the group determined that any home used might be torn down or burned. Despite Fussell's objection that it was "better half the city be destroyed than we seem to abandon our good work," the group decided to halt further meetings for the time being.

Meanwhile the Antislavery Convention of American Women met to wrap up their convention business in the schoolroom where Sarah Lewis and Sarah Pugh taught. They had tried to meet at Temperance Hall as planned but found the doors locked. Fearing their hall would meet the same fate as the abolitionists' hall, the managers asked the women to find another venue. One of the women apparently tried to convene the meeting outside the hall, but the police intervened. As president of the Philadelphia Female Antislavery Society, Pugh suggested they meet in her schoolroom. Jacob Pierce, owner of the building, fully expected its destruction, but he allowed the women to use it anyway. Fortunately, though the mob searched for the women, it never found them.

During the long walk from Temperance Hall to the school the women did face harassment. Lovell described "several low-looking women, who . . . came out of their huts to jeer at us; pointing the finger of scorn, distorting their faces to express contempt, and saying among other things which I could not understand, 'you had better stay at home, and mind your own business, than to come here making such a fuss.'"

Once settled in the schoolroom, the women shared a spirit of solemn defiance. Many fought tears and some actually cried while others offered prayers and read scriptures. Ultimately they defiantly adopted a resolution proposed by Sarah Grimké that said abolitionists had a duty to show unity by fighting race prejudice in solidarity with blacks and "by sitting with them in places of worship, by appearing with them in our streets, by giving them countenance in steamboats and stages, by visiting them at their homes and encouraging them to visit us, receiving them as we do our white fellow citizens." A minority of the delegates opposed the resolution, citing the inflamed state of public opinion, but it passed. Just as the women concluded their meeting they learned that the mob planned to attack the Mott home that night. Having spent the previous night in nervous anticipation of attack, Lucretia Mott once again began to prepare herself for the worst. She told the women that Thursday night had been "a searching time" but by the end of the night she had summoned the courage "to suffer whatever the cause required" and even managed to sleep "a few hours in tranquility and peace." She would need that strength to help her endure this second threat.

Around noon H. C. Wright made a pilgrimage of his own to the ruins. Bartholomew Fussell had tried in vain to convince his friend to lay low and stay off the streets. When Wright refused, Fussell trailed him at enough distance to give him privacy but close enough to help him should trouble occur. As he neared the rubble, someone recognized him as the white-haired man who had called George Washington a robber and rushed at him. Wright said, "Here I am—I offer no resistance . . . I am willing to die. Make a sacrifice." According to Fussell, Wright's response melted the "stoutest hearts" and "so far from injuring him, they turned and fought with those who were out of hearing of his voice and still wished to offer violence, and thus he walked on in peace." Fussell caught up to Wright and found him "quite composed." Wright said "he believed a few Christians could tranquilize the city."

Meanwhile, Samuel Webb gathered his family and hurried them to safety at the home of friends. With his wife and children out of harm's way Webb convened a special meeting of the Pennsylvania Hall Association at his home, where they prepared an address to the citizens of Philadelphia meant to explain to the public what exactly had happened and to defend the association from any charges of complicity in the melee. The board adopted the address and made arrangements to print and distribute it. Finally, they turned their attention to another pressing matter. Terrified for the lives of the city's African Americans, they wrote to Governor Joseph Ritner apprising him of the night's events. Pleading for help, they described their "exposed situation" and warned that "the entire colored population of this city [is] in danger of being murdered" by "an infuriated mob now raging in this city."

As the board met, that angry mob prowled the streets threatening not only African Americans but abolitionists and temperance advocates as well. The mob had first threatened Thomas Hunt the night before as the crowd began to gather around Pennsylvania Hall. An editor who had heard, and resented, Hunt's temperance speech at the hall earlier that week circulated a handbill urging the mob to take its fury to Hunt's home and Temperance Hall as well. Now that the abolition hall was out of the way, the mob set out to answer this call. Friends encouraged Hunt to evacuate his home, but he "did not feel so inclined." He was "determined to stand fast" with the help, ironically, of some of his young Southern friends attending medical school in the city. Some of Hunt's friends did manage to "carry away" Mrs. Hunt and the couple's young daughters, leaving a note to inform him that "they would be taken care of and restored in due time." With his family safely removed, Hunt "fortified" his house and took steps to protect Temperance Hall. He had tried to reason with the "few butcher boys" who had burned Pennsylvania Hall, but, he argued, "the mob understood that no resistance would be made against them at Pennsylvania Hall" because "the Quakers were non-resistants." Hunt would not make the same mistake his abolitionist friends had made. When the mob came for his home and his hall, Hunt made it clear that he did not share nonresistance principles. "When they came to the Temperance Hall we invited them to send in a committee and see what was inside," he said, adding that "when our preparations for defense both in arms and legal authority were known, the mob departed, hurrahing for Temperance."[2]

Unlike Hunt, many abolitionists and Quakers chose to take an inventory of their belongings and leave the city. They hoped that if they lost property they would be able to get help based on the law that made cities responsible for damages done by mobs. Fussell took his family to their Chester County home, where they were soon joined by some of their Philadelphia friends.

Others chose to do as Hunt had and ride out the turmoil. After sending his family away, Webb decided to stay in the city himself and face the mob if they threatened his home. The mob was more interested in wreaking vengeance upon David Paul Brown, and they showed up at his home threatening to tar and feather him, though they ultimately decided against it.

Realizing that the violence would only escalate with the return of night, Mayor Swift tried to find reinforcements. He sent word to Colonel Pleasanton that more rioting was imminent, but Pleasanton responded that he would only help if called upon in an official capacity. Pleasanton told the mayor he would "gladly offer any assistance to the legal authorities if regularly called upon—but that I would not act with a municipal mob, or unorganized mass of police officers against another mob—for I had no confidence in such a force." Rather than issue the official call for the militia, Swift "went away evidently disappointed" and organized the largest force he could muster to stave off violence that evening.

As darkness closed in, the Motts prepared for the mob. They sent their two youngest daughters and Mrs. Mott's mother, Anna Coffin, to the nearby home of their oldest daughter, Maria Davis and her husband Edward. C. C. Burleigh helped them move a few personal items, some furniture, and some of the family's clothing to safety as well. J. Miller McKim sat with the group at the Davis house since Mr. Davis was away. The Motts, the Needles, and their friends then set out a feast for the approaching mob and sat quietly in their parlors waiting for the guests who never came. At about 8 p.m. Thomas Grew, the son of another Quaker abolitionist family from the neighborhood, came running into the Mott house saying, "They're coming!" Guests in the home listened to the buzz of the mob approaching up Race Street. They heard the shouts growing louder as the crowd drew closer, but the mob never showed up. When it drew near the street a young man, likely Grew, posed as a member of the crowd and yelled, "On to the Motts!" and turned the wrong direction on Ninth Street. The crowd followed him into the distance. The Motts and their friends sat waiting calmly for a few more hours until they learned that the mob "seemed broken and scattered" and "concluded we were to escape that night at least, and retired to rest."

The Motts were spared because after Grew distracted the mob it decided to turn its fury upon the black community. First they targeted a black school on Cherry Street but were thwarted by Swift and his men. Then they set their sights on the new Colored Orphans Asylum. They set the building on fire but after a *"pell mell* battle" between the mob and members of the Good Will Fire Company, the firemen managed to douse the blaze with the help of Alderman Morton McMichael and the Spring Garden police. McMichael did not recognize any members of the mob as local to the neighborhood, and he worried that they would return to finish the job, so he made sure to keep a large force out the next night. He may not have approved of abolitionist agitation, but he apparently had his limits and felt compelled to defend the children's home. Fortunately the children had not yet moved into their new home, so they were spared the trauma of facing the angry mob. One black family on Sassafras Alley was not so lucky. After being chased away from the orphanage, part of the mob went on a rampage against African Americans and found themselves at the Sassafras home, where they broke in the doors and windows and dragged the family's furniture into the street. Nobody was hurt, but the family had to run and wait for the mob to finish scattering their belongings before they could return home.[3]

Authorities managed to stave off further attempts at violence on Friday night. Pleasanton heard the alarms go off as the crowd attacked the orphanage. Before he went to bed he expressed concern in his journal that more violence loomed on the horizon. "And if it begins now," he wrote, "there is no knowing what may be its termination."

Saturday, May 19

On Saturday morning the *Philadelphia Inquirer* reported that the "excitement has now subsided" and expressed hope that "the peace of the city will not be further disturbed." But Colonel Pleasanton quickly learned that this would not be the case. He went to the arsenal to work for a while, and on his way back he met High Constable Willis H. Blaney, who showed him that day's edition of the *Public Ledger*, the city's daily penny paper. Approximately two years old in 1838, the paper operated under the motto "Virtue, Liberty, and Independence." It was not an abolition paper, but Editor William H. Swain often exercised independence of opinion, taking on subjects that more conservative readers sometimes took issue with. In this edition he had criticized city officials for their inadequate action the night before in what Pleasanton described as "a highly abusive article." The *Ledger* write-up also called upon Philadelphians to assemble that afternoon in a town meeting to censure the authorities.

The *Public Ledger* also included a call for firemen to meet that afternoon at Independence Square. When the firemen arrived they tried to figure out who had called them to assemble because such an informal meeting violated fire department regulations. When nobody claimed responsibility for calling the meeting, the firemen present issued a series of resolutions "deprecating all interference in the regulations of the Fire Department by unauthorized persons" and adjourned to meet back there that night after investigating further the source of the call. When they met that evening they learned that the editor of the *Ledger* had printed the announcement at the request of "a number of citizens." *Ledger* officials apologized for having broken department protocol, which they had known nothing about, and the firemen adopted a resolution that they "would continue their customary exertions to prevent the destruction of property at *all* fires, whether the flames were kindled by the torch of the *incendiary* or otherwise." They concluded by appointing a committee of one fireman from each hose company to meet back there Monday evening to further discuss the matter.

By taking a stand against the lawlessness, the *Ledger* had stirred a hornet's nest. Later that afternoon a *Ledger* employee went to Pleasanton to ask where he could get a dozen muskets. The mob had threatened the paper and Sheriff Watmough had suggested employees arm themselves and help him in his efforts to defend the property. As predicted, the mob assembled at the *Ledger* office early that evening, but it found Mayor Swift and a large force of constables waiting. Swift appealed to them as property holders. He told them to stop destroying the property of others because such behavior encouraged others to retaliate and they just might find their own property destroyed in return. As Swift and the crowd faced off, a messenger arrived with news that a riot had broken out at a black church on Lombard Street. Both the crowd and the police left for that scene.[4]

The church at Sixth and Lombard, Richard Allen's Mother Bethel, had long served as a symbol of African American independence in Philadelphia. Anti-abolitionists and racists had long resented what it stood for, so the surprise was not that the mob targeted it but that they took so long to do so. Unlike at Pennsylvania Hall, however, the mayor and deputies put forth a sustained and determined effort, defending the church from multiple attacks between 8 p.m. and midnight. They eventually arrested about a dozen rioters, confiscated a number of pistols, razors, and other weapons, and managed to restore order before serious damage occurred.

Also unlike at the hall, officials enjoyed more support in their efforts to save the church. At some point during the evening a man trying to defend the church from inside fired a pistol and nearly hit an officer, but the bullet missed and the would-be defender was arrested along with the rioters. Outside the building, city officials rallied to help law enforcement. Before the police arrived, Samuel Rush, recently elected City Recorder, boldly addressed the mob and told them that, even though new to his office, he would maintain law and order "at the peril of his life." He called upon onlookers for assistance and "hundreds flocked to his support." Outnumbered, the mob "shrank back and slunk off."[5] After the mob met sufficient resistance at the *Ledger* and the church, it gave up for the night.

Sunday, May 20

By Sunday, May 20, the city was finally starting to settle down. That morning William Henry Furness, the pastor of the First Congregational Unitarian Church, addressed his flock. Furness, an acquaintance of the Motts, had contemplated abolition for several years but had not embraced immediatism. Impressed with George Thompson, whom he met in 1835, he found Garrison's strong language a bit much. Despite Garrison's efforts to bring him into the fold he remained reluctant to "go the whole."

That Sunday Furness remained unwilling to come out in favor of radical abolition, but he felt compelled to address his congregation about free speech. "Whether the Abolitionists are right or wrong, is, comparatively speaking, a small question now," he said. The mob action of the past three days had a much larger relevance—one that affected everyone regardless of his or her stance on slavery. If such lawlessness were to continue, "all personal freedom of thought and speech will be given to the winds." Everyone shared a responsibility to stop this from happening. He encouraged them to organize into associations to defend the law and work to defend "the acknowledged rights of thought and speech, even when in the exercise of these rights, individuals have been led to form and express opinions most repugnant to our own." Furness also pointed out something Whittier had hinted at in the *Freeman*—mob action makes martyrs. By attacking someone because of his principles "you animate the soul that is in him; and from the injustice and oppression around him, he turns to the great and good of the past, and associates himself in imagination with them, and joins himself to the noble company of the apostles and martyrs." Thus, every attack upon abolitionists strengthened their conviction and gave them yet another rallying point. While this sermon fell short of endorsing abolition, Furness did eventually join the immediatists. He, like many others, would come to see the cause as more than just antislavery. As this sermon showed, he would come to equate his own freedom with that of the slave, thanks to the mob's actions.

On Sunday night Colonel Pleasanton once again recorded his thoughts in his journal, and this time his musings took on an ominous tone. Referring to the incident at Mother Bethel on Saturday, he mistakenly reported that two black men had become confused and fired pistols at policemen who were trying to protect them. Frustrated and misplacing his irritation, Pleasanton wrote that "the result of all this abolition agitation will be the expulsion ... of all the blacks from the state." The actions of "a few foreign fanatics" had caused irreparable damage to race relations in the city. Philadelphians "will petition the Legislature to remove them from the state, in order that the public tranquility may no longer be at the mercy of a few misguided zealots—and I much mistake the people of Pennsylvania if they will not support Philadelphia in such an application." Pleasanton, who to this point had not recorded any colonizationist sentiments in his journal, was now contemplating forced expulsion of the state's African American population. Likely referring to Ohio's Black Codes, he wrote that the neighboring state had "some time since expelled from her territory the blacks." Why not Pennsylvania? Pleasanton's journal contains additional commentary in favor of expulsion of blacks after this entry, but none before it. Clearly the events surrounding the mobbing led him to contemplate the merits of something more sinister even than most colonizationists embraced—forced removal.

The general sense of unrest lasted through mid-June. On June 8 a black man killed a watchman, prompting fears of more rioting. However, in this case the sheriff took the formal steps to call in the militia, so no riot ensued. This prompted a series of entries in Pleasanton's journal in which he sought to justify his lack of intervention during the Pennsylvania Hall riot. Perhaps to convince himself of the correctness of his actions, he wrote in several entries about the right of the sheriff to call in the militia as a *"posse comitatus,"* but he repeatedly stressed the importance of going through proper and official channels to do so. Determined to vindicate his position, he even submitted statements to the *National Gazette* and the *Pennsylvanian*. Perhaps he faced criticism for his failure to act—or perhaps his argument was with his own conscience. Given the level of detail in which he recorded the attack in his journal, he likely stood and watched as the mob broke into the hall. Whether on the sidewalk or at home, he certainly failed to intervene.

The firemen had also failed to save the building, and their representatives showed little remorse. The committee put together on Saturday met on Monday evening to simply restate their previous position. Refusing to admit dereliction of duty, they reiterated their "fixed and unalterable determination to rescue, (as we have ever shown it our disposition to do,) the property of our fellow citizens from destruction." They then discharged themselves from "all further consideration of the subject." They offered no explanation as to their conduct at Pennsylvania Hall.[6]

Rumors continued to fly throughout Philadelphia in the weeks following the attack. Both "witnesses" and the press continued to rile the public with stories of the amalgamation wedding and the insults hurled at the nation's most revered founding father. To that they added detailed stories of black and white men and women walking arm in arm in the city's streets prior to the mobbing. One newspaper attributed the mobbing to "ridiculous and ostentatious amalgamation of colours in Chestnut Street during the hours of fashionable promenading." According to other accounts, "whites and blacks, arm in arm, were thronging the streets by scores, whereas the populace became greatly excited."

A correspondent for the London *Morning Chronicle* reported back that while he "certainly did not see any practical instances" of "racial mingling," the "report alone tended greatly to increase excitement in the public mind" and provided many with plenty of justification for what the mob had done. The *Salem Gazette* shared this reporter's skepticism regarding "nonsensical, and we believe fabulous stories, that are told by way of apology." Shocked and disappointed at "the general tone" of the press, this reporter blamed "the Reign of Terror, Proscription, and Club and Pistol Law" that had overtaken the nation since Andrew Jackson's election to the presidency. Thanks to Jackson's example, "the moral sense of the country has been tending

"Abolition Hall. The evening before the conflagration," by Zip Coon.
Unidentified origin.
Library Company of Philadelphia

downward at headlong pace" while "obedience to law, and the preservation of order, have lost their former high place in the scale of civil virtues." The *Massachusetts Spy* agreed but added that the people could overcome the spirit of lawlessness by voicing collective outrage and holding officials accountable.

Reporters closer to home often displayed less objectivity. Some newspapers shared the *Salem Gazette's* disgust with the lawlessness and mob violence and protested the attack upon free speech and citizens' rights to assemble. Most, however, stopped short of defending the abolitionists. Instead they generally blamed the abolitionists as well as the mob, sometimes stating and sometimes just implying that the radical agitators had gotten what they deserved even if mob law was not the answer. Most newspapers agreed that interracial mingling of one sort or another had caused the problems.[7]

Investigating the Police

Some newspapers followed the lead of the *Public Ledger* in blaming inadequate law enforcement. After the attack Mayor John Swift offered a $2,000 reward to anyone who could provide information and help to capture the chief culprits. Governor Joseph Ritner also offered $500 to be paid "on the due conviction" of "each and every" person involved in the burning of the hall or the attack on the orphanage. Of course, rewards after the fact could not make up for the losses sustained, and the question remained as to whether authorities could have done more to prevent the destruction.

On the one hand, it is true that nineteenth-century law enforcement was not yet centralized or professionalized in most cities. In addition to problems over jurisdiction, policing was generally inadequate in Philadelphia, a city that had no full-time trained police force. In the late 1830s, the law enforcement system included day police, made up of the mayor, high constables, and ward officers. At night there was a system of watchmen. The watch was divided into four sections, each of which had a captain. Each of the four divisions had about thirty-five watchmen. Their duty was to trim, light, and extinguish the public lamps and gas lights. They were also expected to walk rounds and announce the hours and "to secure the peace and quiet of the city." In addition to these, each division had eight silent watchmen to see that the watchmen performed their duties and to fill in where needed. Traveling in pairs between the regular watchmen's rounds, they were to walk quietly through their division and make sure that all was in order. In addition to these regular forces, the mayor had the authority to call in the militia and to swear in additional constables, and Mayor Swift had used this authority before.

Both the *Pennsylvania Freeman* and the *Public Ledger* pointed out that the mayor had acted decisively to prevent a riot a year earlier when a local political group had decided to meet at Independence Square to denounce the banks. Expecting a riot, Swift took a number of precautions. First, he posted bulletins at every street corner notifying Philadelphians of the intended violence and asking them to help him prevent it. He also gathered all available police and reinforced their ranks by adding 1,000 deputies. He then called up every company of volunteers and stationed them throughout the city. Finally, he brought in all of the Marines from the Navy Yard who could be spared to assist him. Measures like these would likely have saved Pennsylvania Hall. Indeed, when authorities finally did actively seek to regain control and save the orphanage and other buildings in the aftermath of the hall fire, their efforts met with success.

Even the city's colonizationists argued that officials should have done more. When the managers agreed to suspend further meetings and surrendered the keys to the mayor, "the assent of the parties to this recommendation threw both impliedly and in fact on the city authorities the full responsibility of taking all preventive and conservative measures, both for the safety of the hall and for the public peace," argued the *Colonization Herald*. This newspaper strongly took abolitionists to task for their behavior, but even so, the editor clearly saw dereliction of duty in the behavior of the city officials.

Given the number of questions raised about police conduct, the Select and Common Councils of Philadelphia asked the local Committee on Police to investigate the behavior of the police and the mayor. The resulting report exonerated the officials and blamed the abolitionists. It argued the reformers brought the attack upon themselves by offending public sensibilities. The abolitionists had blurred racial lines by inviting both whites and blacks and then seating them together throughout the hall. Perhaps most importantly, managers had invited outsiders known for deliberately agitating the public and trying to cause trouble. After clearly describing Garrison in this capacity, the report then took care to remind readers that the Grimkés were also outsiders. Perhaps in part because the managers refused to appear in front of the committee and give their side of the story, the report took for granted the truth of accusations that blacks and whites had walked together arm in arm. Clearly referring to Garrison and Grimké, it added that some of the out-of-town speakers had used "very indiscrete and intemperate language, greatly calculated to increase the irritation."

Judged in light of historian Paul Gilje's study of New York mobs in the 1830s, Philadelphia police and city officials acted as could have been expected initially. Mayors and sheriffs believed that if they acted firmly yet fairly, rioters would respect their authority and disperse. Officials hesitated to call in the military for a couple of reasons. First, Americans maintained the fear that a standing army used against the people would result in "despotism and arbitrary government." Second, militia troops were notoriously unreliable. Since all adult males in the state were expected to serve in the militia, calling up these troops could mean arming some of the rioters. According to Gilje, "no magistrate relished the thought of arming any part of the mob; and, if the object of the riot was odious to the entire community, there was always the possibility that the militia might disobey orders and join forces with the mob."

To avoid relying on the militia, authorities could turn to the community in general for help, as Swift had done during previous race riots and tried to do at the hall. In theory, anyone called upon in such a capacity, officially referred to as a "posse comitatus," was expected to help. Swift and Watmough probably thought they could rely on the public when they called out for assistance. After all, the community had assisted Swift in the 1834 race riot and had intervened on their own to stop the city from burning down during the 1835 riot. The catch, however, was that citizens often ignored such calls because they preferred not to risk their own lives or property without good reason. Perhaps it is significant that the 1834 and 1835 mobs targeted local blacks, many of whom were known as hardworking leaders of the community and were familiar to their neighbors. In 1838 the mob destroyed a local hall, but that hall was associated in the minds of many not just with Philadelphia abolitionists but more strongly with immediatists like Garrison who were seen as outside agitators there to create confrontation. As Gilje pointed out, "If the riot acted for the community, then it was difficult, if not impossible, to summon the community to oppose the riot."

Pleasanton's reaction illustrates this point. He knew the mayor could call such a posse, and if Swift had done so Pleasanton would have fulfilled his duty, but he certainly was not about to volunteer. A month later he was still preoccupied with the incident. Even news of a steamboat explosion in mid-June drew his thoughts to the riot. In clear exasperation he recorded in his journal that "the truth is, and we might as well admit it at once, there is no discipline or regulation anywhere in our country." While this thought may have applied to the lax regulations that led to the steamship accident, his next comment clearly referred to Pennsylvania Hall. "Fanatics provoke mobs," he wrote, "riots are the consequence, public sympathy is excited, in favor of the rioters, because nearly all the world condemn the fanatics—no one can be had to put down the riot, and when the mob have satiated their appetites for violence and outrage, order is restored by the exhaustion of the rioters." Due to lack of order and regulations, whether on steamboats or city streets, "numberless people are destroyed, property that is invaluable is lost forever, and yet all the world say 'nobody is to blame'—when will this state of things cease?"

As for volunteer militia troops, Pleasanton deemed them useless for riot suppression. They were, according to his assessment, too cowardly to fire upon a mob. They were also "tender-hearted" and "the most insubordinate, and intractable men in the whole regiment." Would the men have tried to repel the mob had they been assembled? Perhaps not, but nobody tested them in this case. Other entries in Pleasanton's journal take on a defensive tone as he seemed to be trying to convince himself that he was not to blame. Besides writing about the uselessness of the volunteer troops, he reiterated multiple times that it was up to Swift to ask for assistance through proper channels and he had failed to do so.

What remains puzzling is why neither Swift nor Watmough anticipated the level of resistance they would meet, given the city's history of race riots and the unpopularity of the abolition cause with the general public. When questioned about their lack of vigor in defending the hall, both Swift and Watmough continued to insist that the owners and occupants had caused the riot with their offensive behavior. They never adequately explained why they could not have prepared for the violence or intervened early on. Instead they held firmly to the assertion that it was simply impossible to defend the hall because the public detested the abolitionists and the abolitionists pushed public opinion over the brink with their radical behavior. "I failed in my endeavors," Watmough later explained, "because I placed more reliance upon the principle of appeal to the free citizen than upon the clubs and badges of an organized police." When the mob came back the next night to attack the orphanage he was better prepared because he had been "taught a melancholy lesson" that he could not count on citizens to help him. Thus, he spent his own money to hire additional forces.[8]

Assessing Blame

In addition to the mayor and sheriff, abolitionists blamed a number of other culprits. In most sympathetic accounts some small group—whether Southern medical students, merchants trying to gain Southern business, or simply nameless and faceless "strangers in the city"—planned the riot and then directed the ignorant masses as they destroyed the hall. Although some eyewitnesses commented on the "well dressed" "gentlemen of property and standing" in the crowd, most agreed that the poor and working classes did the dirty work. Shipwrights broke the doors down and workers, described as "recent immigrants" or even "Irish," went into the hall to destroy the furniture and set the fires.

This last assertion is interesting given the great pains abolitionists took to emphasize the role of "workingmen" in funding and building the hall. Indeed, C. C. Burleigh and other abolitionists in the state had tried to reach out to the working class since the 1837 founding of the PASS. Despite their claims to the contrary, either their efforts had gone completely awry or the role of the poor and working classes has been overstated. Tellingly, almost a year later the *Liberator* was still trying to convince workers to join abolitionists in the fight against slaveholding "bullies" who, along with bloodthirsty Northern capitalists, would eagerly take the freedom of all workers to maintain their position at the top of society's political and economic hierarchies.

So, then, who was at the top of this conspiracy? The Pennsylvania Hall Association claimed from the beginning that outsiders wrote the placards calling the mob to action. According to their theory, since the authors of the placards wrote "in this city" instead of "in Philadelphia," they were clearly not residents. Philadelphia did contain Southerners at any given time, and newspaper accounts indicate that Southerners in the city rejoiced in this anti-abolitionist display. Though some participated, it appears that they left it to their Philadelphia friends to initiate the attack and offer the hall as a sacrifice to cross-sectional unity.

H. C. Wright, an immediatist from New York and one of Garrison's closest friends, blamed Southerners, but he also blamed Presbyterians and colonizationists. Writing about the attack at 2 p.m. on Friday, soon after his encounter with the mob at the ruins, he insisted that he had seen "man stealers, women-robbers and kidnappers from the South" in the crowd urging the mob on in its destruction of the hall. He also pointed out that "the old school General Assembly of the Presbyterian Church" met nearby under the leadership of Virginia slaveholder William S. Plummer, and he accused them not necessarily of participating in the destruction but at least of countenancing the mob "by their silence." Wright reserved his harshest criticism for the colonizationists. He argued that the "same slang, and low vulgar abuse" he heard bandied about by the mob had also been spouted before by leading colonizationists such as Elliott Cresson to "excite hatred in our hearts toward our brethren." Each of these accusations, however, was speculative and calculated to stir his readers against people he had long seen as the enemy.

One problem with taking Wright's accusations seriously was that throughout his career he had made a number of inflammatory but baseless claims, presumably for attention. Years after the Garrison mobbing in 1835 he produced a narrative seriously at odds with other eyewitness accounts in an effort to prove the negligence of the Boston authorities. He also altered his account of a Connecticut Antislavery Society meeting two years after the Pennsylvania Hall attack in a way that, according to one witness, severely distorted remarks made by other participants. In this case, as in many others, Wright used innuendo and inflammatory rhetoric to stir his readers.

Despite Wright's exaggerations, it is likely that some members of the mob expressed colonizationist sentiments during the attack. During the race riot of 1834 some of the assailants mentioned that they were targeting black community leaders who had spoken out against colonization. Perhaps these same people helped destroy Pennsylvania Hall. After all, Garrison and others had spoken out against colonization during the meetings. Shouting out in favor of the cause does not necessarily equate to actively participating in the American or Pennsylvania Colonization Society, though. The fact remains that there is no evidence that Elliott Cresson or any other serious colonizationist participated in the destruction. In fact, Cresson was out of town.

Even if colonizationists were not directly involved in the mobbing, Wright had a valid point about their rhetoric. Colonizationists firmly believed that black Americans could never achieve equality in the United States, and they often talked and wrote about the "degraded condition" of free blacks. While Cresson and his friends insisted that they were trying to solve rather than perpetuate the problem, the truth of the matter is that their rhetoric did not help matters. To begin with, colonization made it acceptable for many whites to give up trying to reform American society. If free blacks could simply be sent away and racism dealt with that way, then why pursue the harder course of fighting racism at home? Second, if blacks were indeed "degraded," for whatever reason, then why should white Americans even want to create a place for them in society? These questions illustrate the problem colonizationists faced even as many of them insisted they were just trying to help.

Another possibility was that merchants played a role in the mobbing. In a letter giving a day-by-day account of the events at the hall, Bartholomew Fussell explained to his nephew that Tuesday's unplanned speeches by more radical abolitionists like Garrison and Alvan Stewart had attracted a great deal of attention, much to the chagrin of local businessmen. The hall was expected to hold nearly three thousand people, and he explained that the size of the audience "gave offense to the 'Integrity of the Union' men" who worried that the audience would believe the abolitionists and cause the businessmen to "lose our good name with the slave holder." Though he specified that the merchants associated with the Integrity of the Union meeting were the ones showing concern and directly quoted them in his letter, he never explained how he knew who they were or what they said. Even so, others shared his assessment. The *Emancipator* newspaper blamed a number of factors for the mobbing, including colonizationist sentiment, the presence of Southern medical students, the eagerness of Northern churches "to gain the good will of those of the South," and "above all, the eagerness of the merchants of Philadelphia just at this time to win the trade of the South away from New York."

Three months later, a Philadelphia abolitionist noticed a disturbing display at a local hotel. Under the heading "SOUTHERN AND WESTERN BUSINESS CARD" was a poster of Pennsylvania Hall in flames. "No one can mistake the object of this picture and inscription," the observer reported in the *Pennsylvania Freeman*. "It is manifestly intended to convince the Southern slave-holder that the 'merchant-princes' of Philadelphia, are willing to sacrifice principle and humanity, law, order, and decency, for the sake of Southern trade." The writer concluded that "The Pennsylvania Hall was destroyed for the benefit of the Southern trade . . . if this course of conduct is to be followed up . . . the rights and property of such free-born Philadelphians as believe in the Declaration of Independence are to be offered up on the altar of Southern Slavery, for the benefit of commerce and manufactures."

Any assessment of blame in this case would be incomplete without looking at the choices made by the Pennsylvania Hall Association and managers. First is the question of why they waited so long to seek help. Perhaps they assumed authorities had realized the danger and expected them to act accordingly. This would have been a logical assumption. Despite their assertions to the contrary, authorities had to have realized the magnitude of the storm that was brewing. Also, the mayor had promised months earlier to ensure the hall's safety, so they had every right to take him at his word.

In addition to acting slowly in seeking help, the managers did little to defend their hall in the heat of the attack, even after initially promising to help find men to fight off the crowd. This might seem a result of the nonresistance principles shared by most of the abolitionists, many of whom were Quakers. However, the initial promise to supply the sheriff with a posse complicated this matter. Had the men who promised to bring in reinforcements faced chastisement from their nonresistant friends? Perhaps they had. After all, many of their associates had recently denounced Elijah P. Lovejoy's attempts at self-defense. More likely, however, was that someone reminded them of the wording in the law and warned them that any participation—even self-defense—could provide groundwork for the courts to deny any claims they may need to make for damages. The wording of the note they sent to the sheriff as he waited outside the hall, as well as the passage in their report and history that stressed the supremacy of that written communication over any oral promises, supports this theory. What likely happened was that the managers realized any action on their part could constitute participation in the riot and thus result in denial of their claims for damages.

Finally, when the Committee on Police tried to investigate the affair, the managers refused to participate in the inquiry. Maybe if they had, the committee would have produced a more balanced assessment of the situation. So why did the managers refuse to give their side of the story? On the one hand, they probably realized the futility of it. On the other hand, they believed the case was simple: "We erected a Hall for lawful objects, and used it only in the exercise of rights guaranteed by the Constitution to all American citizens." They "built it under the protection of the law, and trusted it to the protection of the law." After being threatened they had "surrendered it" to the mayor at his request. It was then burned down under his watch.[9]

Abolitionist Reactions

While his neighbors debated the particulars of the mobbing, David Paul Brown tried to set the record straight about his own role. The one person assailed from both sides, he had to vindicate himself as an abolitionist while also addressing those who continued to spread baseless rumors about him. A week after the fire he wrote an open letter to the public and sent it to local newspapers. It began with the assertion that he was and would remain "an advocate of the Abolition Society" in spite of the mobs. Undeterred, he insisted, "I am a firm friend of Rational Liberty, and am not to be awed into its abandonment by licentiousness or vice." As for the more radical abolitionists, he would not quarrel with them. He insisted that "they may *freely* enjoy their opinion—I shall *boldly* maintain mine." He then reiterated many of the points he had made during his speech at the opening of the hall and directly addressed the rumors. Anyone who heard his speech knew full well that he had never supported amalgamation. Further, anyone who knew anything about him at all would know that he had always opposed racial mingling. As for the rumor that he had called Washington a thief, it was "perfectly preposterous!" He had mentioned Washington in his speech but only to say that he had "released all his slaves upon his death bed." Rather than calling him a man stealer, he had praised him as an abolitionist of sorts. Finally, assertions that he supported dissolution of the Union were directly at odds with what he had said at the hall or in any speech. In this open letter Brown remained firm in his support for abolition and consistent in his gradualist approach.

Unlike Brown, most who did not agree wholeheartedly with Garrisonian "radicalism," including gradualists and Quakers, worked hard to entirely distance themselves from the incident. Others tried to distance themselves from the more inflammatory aspects of the immediatist agenda, especially interracial mingling of any sort. Dr. Joseph Parrish, a longtime member of Philadelphia's antislavery community, tried in vain to convince the women to expunge Sarah Grimké's resolution that abolitionists should directly challenge segregation by sitting with blacks in churches, steamboats, and other public facilities, appearing with them in public streets, and encouraging blacks and whites to visit in each others' homes. Similarly, a Quaker signing off simply as "B" sent a letter to the *U.S. Gazette* to explain that the Society of Friends had never supported amalgamation. The Society of Orthodox friends sent a letter to the *Pennsylvania Freeman* denying any connection to the events at the hall and insisting that few of their members had been there. Temperance advocates and Lyceum members also scrambled to deny any connection to immediate abolition or amalgamation.

While some members of the Pennsylvania Abolition Society had joined the immediatists and held firm to that decision, others wanted to keep their distance from the radical abolitionists. Even so, they realized that lines between the two groups were never clear and had blurred even further in the eyes of the general public. Whether they agreed with the immediatists or not, most people saw them as one and the same. With that in mind, they took precautions to protect their own records and papers by purchasing a fireproof safe.

The attack on Pennsylvania Hall had a decided effect upon the African American community. Of course, African Americans could hardly deny their connections to the antislavery movement and, by extension, the hall. The families of James Forten, Robert Purvis, Charles W. Gardner, Frederick A. Hinton, and Robert Douglass knew all too well that the incident would somehow fall on their shoulders. Racial violence was not something they could simply escape from as they had helped Garrison do. While the Fortens and Purvises do not seem to have harbored any ill will toward Garrison for his assumption of the spotlight, his taunting of the mob, or his escape to safety, Hinton held him at least partially accountable for the riot and the burning of the hall. He argued that Garrisonians had provoked the violence, and he resented that the black community had to suffer the consequences. He also expressed irritation at Garrison specifically for bringing his radical views on women's rights into the mix. Like many of Philadelphia's abolitionists, Hinton wanted the antislavery cause to remain first and foremost about freeing the slaves. Garrison's auxiliary causes and inflammatory behavior could only hurt the cause, and when it did, blacks suffered.

The main African American newspaper to cover the story, the *Colored American*, also pointed to the impact on the black community, albeit more subtly. Reserving blame, the paper simply recopied a notice that appeared first in the *Rochester Democrat* and then in the *Liberator*.

The original piece reported that forty "*colored persons*" had been arrested and asked why. "Did *they* destroy the Pennsylvania Hall— mob their own Charity School—threaten and stone their own dwellings—or attempt to destroy their own church?" the Rochester editor asked. Disgusted with the situation, the editor said his only regret was "that when these colored persons were assailed and abused by the white mob . . . they had not maimed a score or two of them." Under this original story, the *Colored American* added a statement by the *Liberator* that although "the arrest of these colored persons is a mockery of law," it did not justify violence in return. According to the *Liberator*, "Christianity enjoins a different course of conduct."

The *Colored American* made no comment about violence or retaliation, but the Pennsylvania Hall attack did lead more people, black and white, to question nonresistance. By late 1838 black leaders were increasingly considering the merits of fighting back. They had also come to question the traditional moral reform goals so long pushed by Forten, Purvis, and other elite black leaders. In the next decade black leaders would focus on more direct action, including harboring and rescuing fugitive slaves.

Besides black leaders, a few other diehard reformers refused to shrink in the face of attack. Several groups connected in one way or another to the hall became even more determined to stay the course and push forward. The Antislavery Convention of American Women, for example, decided to meet again the next month in Philadelphia. Though traumatized, they reconvened in June to conclude their business. Lucretia Mott led the meeting and reminded the women of their commitment to fight against both slavery and racism. Her resolve strengthened the others and they made plans to hold future meetings, including a third annual Antislavery Convention of American Women, in Philadelphia. Though they would meet with the usual resistance when looking for a venue, they did hold their final convention in the city the next year.

The free produce advocates reacted similarly. They met at 10 a.m. at the ruins of the hall the morning after the attack and put together a committee to make arrangements to meet at a later time and finish their business. That committee made arrangements for the group to reassemble that September in Sandiford Hall. There they wrote a constitution for a new national group, the American Free Produce

Association. They then assembled a committee to look into the feasibility of establishing and supporting free produce stores. They also made plans to reach out to British abolitionists and seek their aid in convincing English manufacturers to use free labor cotton. Despite the attack, the free produce movement lasted for many years to come.

Like the women and the free produce advocates, the Pennsylvania Hall Association adopted a defiant stance, determined not to let the mob have the final word. Even though they faced a mountain of unpaid bills, Webb and the other managers announced right away their plans to rebuild the hall. Expecting reimbursement from the county to cover the losses, they announced before the end of the month their intention to start a new subscription for shares and erect a new hall "as soon as the sum of fifty thousand dollars is subscribed and paid." The new hall would be "larger, and if possible, more beautiful than the former."[10] Little did Webb, Neall, and the other managers realize, however, that they had a long hard fight ahead. They would lose much along the way as their case spent years winding through the courts.

CHAPTER 10

A "Legal Lynching" and the Martyrdom of Pennsylvania Hall

Benjamin Lundy had remained calm and collected during the destruction of Pennsylvania Hall. Some of his friends had managed to liberate a few of his letters and other manuscripts from the pillaging mob. An anonymous person had even saved one small trunk which contained "notes and memorandums" from his travels through the southern United States and Mexico. Though he did not know who saved these belongings, he offered his "kindest thanks" in an open letter he sent to Philadelphia newspapers. In the same letter he explained that

From Pennsylvania Hall Association, *History of Pennsylvania Hall* (Philadelphia: Merrihew and Gunn, 1838).
Library Company of Philadelphia

the remainder of his possessions had either been destroyed in the flames or scattered among the crowd that night. "Should any friend obtain possession of other articles, belonging to me," he wrote, "I shall esteem it as a particular favor to receive information thereof."

While he waited for information, he filed a claim with the county for $2,000 in damages and resumed his plans to join his family out west. On July 24, 1838, he left the city of Pennsylvania Hall's destruction to start a newspaper in the state of Elijah Lovejoy's martyrdom. A year later, in June 1839, the county of Philadelphia finally agreed to pay him $900 for his lost belongings. After deducting $100 for expenses, they gave him $800 worth of "county stock."

Two months later, while working in his printing office, Lundy took a break to write his children a letter. He had been feeling ill but, he wrote, he was much better. Perhaps things were starting to look up. That afternoon, however, severe pain set in. The next night he died. Lundy had received some compensation and a small degree of justice, but by the time he died the case of Pennsylvania Hall was far from closed. The owners of the hall would spend many years trying to recover their losses.[1]

Arrests and Criminal Cases

Authorities arrested several young men for participating in the riot. Sheriff Watmough seized approximately ten rioters in the early stages of the attack, but the mob intervened and freed them. Other officials arrested more rioters at the orphanage. About forty of those were black men presumably trying to defend themselves. The Police Committee reported "many arrests" but refused to give the names of the suspects or list the charges against them.

Newspaper reports and court records give some details about five men investigated at various times for their actions at the hall. The first two reported arrests involved Samuel Yeager and "a young man named Fulton." Newspapers reported Fulton being held on $1,000 bail on May 24, but then he disappeared from the record. Compared to the others, his bail was low, and reporters seemed uninterested in finding details about him, including his first name, so he was likely a lower-class member of the "rabble" and thus uninteresting to many readers. He also could have been innocent and able to prove it right away.

Yeager's case garnered much more attention. A twenty-seven-year-old hatter and father of five children, Yeager took an active role inside the hall. A man identified by newspapers as "Shotwell" (likely Isaac Shotwell of the Young Men's Antislavery Society of Philadelphia) saw him tear down some of the blinds near the upstairs landing and heard him call out "Hurra, boys, pull them down!" Shotwell had known Yeager for about a decade, and he tried to get him to stop and leave the building "for the sake of his relatives." After promising to follow the advice, Yeager "went downstairs," but it remains uncertain whether he left the building or continued the destruction beyond Shotwell's sight. What is clear is that Yeager was one of the first inside the building because when Shotwell found him, there were "not more than a dozen" people inside and the lights had not yet been turned off by the breaking of the gas pipes. The court initially set Yeager's bail at $3,000 but soon reduced it to $2,500. It is uncertain what ultimately happened in Yeager's case, but given the general climate of the time and his social standing as a respected artisan, this "young gentleman" who looked "like anything but a rioter" was likely acquitted.

The third and fourth cases might be connected. A "young man" named Edgar Kimmey appeared next, and the alderman set his bail at $2,000. After that a man named John Hosea accused a man named Jeremiah F. Kinney of helping set the hall on fire. Kinney responded by suing Hosea for slander in Delaware in the spring of 1840. The slander case ended in dismissal for lack of sufficient evidence, and Kinney's fate is unclear. Given the similarity of "Kimmey" and "Kinney," however, the cases may be related.

The final case for criminal liability occurred years later, in 1844. At that time another round of riots—this time involving anti-Catholic nativists and Irish Catholic immigrants—broke out in the city, and during the course of the unrest a man named Abraham E. Freymire (sometimes reported as Atram E. Frimer) bragged that he had participated in the destruction of Pennsylvania Hall six years earlier. Presumably trying to impress a woman named Martha Addis, he told her and her mother that he was the person who had broken the gas pipe to accelerate the fire. Acquitted in April 1845, he was still made to pay the court costs. After Freymire's acquittal, the *Hampshire Herald* expressed frustration at the lack of prosecutorial rigor: "The leaders of that gang of incendiaries were arrested, indicted, and bound over in light bonds for trial; but they have mostly disappeared, their bonds forfeited, though probably never paid." The editor added that the "villains" had managed to escape punishment "as it was generally supposed at the time would be the case, and doubtless through the connivance of those who should have been among the first to bring them to justice." The Freymire case simply provided "a show of justice" at a time in which most witnesses were "beyond the jurisdiction of the courts." Although the jury found Freymire not guilty, the editor argued that their forcing him to pay court costs showed they knew better. "We suppose they regarded the crime as the mass of people did—rather as a meritorious act." By that point, none of the "well known villains" of the mobbing had been convicted, according to the editor; neither had one dollar been paid in compensation to the owners. It was 1845 and justice seemed "as far removed as ever!"[2]

The Grand Jury

The process of keeping justice at bay began soon after the attack on the hall with the appointment of grand juries to oversee the case. As word began to spread that the managers planned to rebuild the hall, city officials claimed to receive petitions from citizens demanding that they prohibit such action. To deal with these petitions and the various arrests, grand juries were convened to inquire into the matter. Questions for consideration included whether or not to indict those arrested and whether the hall should be rebuilt.

The first jury initially met in May to consider the fate of Pennsylvania Hall's remains, and the second grand jury was to consider the fate of those arrested for participating in the destruction. Judge John Bouvier began his address to the second jury by explaining his philosophy on punishment. He said that those who had participated in the recent riots had "trampled the law under foot, and rendered our most valuable rights worthless." Even if abolitionists had offended public sensibilities, they had not broken the law. Any efforts of the mob to punish them for the transgression of offending public sentiment were illegal and set a dangerous precedent. If the mob was allowed to act as "accuser, judge, jury, witness, and executioner" in this incident, innocence would "be sacrificed upon the altar of passion and prejudice."

Initial reports, appearing on June 12, 1838, stated that the jurors ignored the bills presented to them against Yeager. Corrections soon appeared, however. Apparently Yeager's and Kimmey's cases were passed along to the next Court of Oyer and Terminer, which would meet in September. Kimmey could not produce the bail and was put in jail, despite the objections of his lawyer, C. J. Jack. Yeager was given time to "communicate with his bail." Basically it appears that the criminal case was merged into the case being considered by Judge James Todd's jury.

The foreman of Todd's grand jury was, of all people, Elliott Cresson—the city's most active colonizationist. On September 27, 1838, he read a report to the Court of Oyer and Terminer that instantly enraged the national abolitionist community. The man who had once called William Lloyd Garrison a "Bedlamite" and had spent the last decade trying to convince black and white Philadelphians to support colonization had the final say over the fate of Pennsylvania Hall. He may not have been there for the attack, but he was about to perform what some would call a "Legal Lynching."

The grand jury returned bills against "individuals charged with a violation of the law" in the Pennsylvania Hall case. They did so, however, only because they "felt that they were discharging a necessary duty." Even so, Cresson said, the jury agreed the abolitionists had caused the riot. They had exhibited controversy "in almost every shape" and formed associations "which would naturally tend to offend the nicer feelings of the public." Given their behavior, "it is certainly more the subject of regret than of surprise that violence should have ensued." In answer to the petitions protesting the hall's rebuilding, the jury agreed. They returned the petitions to the court "under the full persuasion that 'the peace, tranquility, and safety,' of the community will be endangered by its reconstruction." Pennsylvania Hall would not be rebuilt.

Garrison reacted immediately. He reprinted an article from the Boston *Daily Advocate* titled "Legal Lynching." It maintained that the grand jury had "committed an outrage upon the laws unheard of in a civilized country." They had indicted some of the "villains" but had negated this act by justifying the mob's action "because some silly white women walked with black ones in Chestnut Street." Noting that the jury called "for the 'frowns of a virtuous community,' not upon the rioters, but upon those they mobbed and plundered," the article reported the recommendation against rebuilding the hall "for fear another mob will tear it down!" Garrison added a note that the presentment was "in all respects characteristic of the foreman, ELLIOT CRESSON!!" [sic] He then reprinted it word for word. A couple of months later he was still fuming, referring to Cresson in one article as a "wolf in Quaker clothing."

The Board of Managers responded by insisting that Cresson's charges against the abolitionists were untrue. They challenged him to "produce the evidence (if any) upon which he ventured to make such high charges." They also asked to see the petitions protesting their plans to rebuild. They were told that the petitions, which had supposedly been given to the clerk of the court, could not be found. Many wondered if they had ever existed. The Pennsylvania Antislavery Society (PASS) reacted similarly. They tried to find out how many jurors concurred in the presentment and to obtain details about the proceedings.

While the abolitionists protested, most of the Northern press agreed with the grand jury. The *Colonization Herald* reported that the jury's sentiments were "in accordance with those entertained by a vast majority of the inhabitants of the city and county of Philadelphia." They enjoyed free expression as much as the next person and, they argued, "there is no better and surer means of preserving freedom of discussion than by an avoidance, or if need be prevention, of inflammatory appeals to passion, and unmeasured denunciation of the constitution and of any portion of the laws made under it."[3]

Suing for Damages

Whether or not the people of Philadelphia cared to acknowledge it, the owners of Pennsylvania Hall had a legal right to compensation for their loss. After a political riot in Philadelphia in 1834 led to the destruction of several houses, the death of three people, and the wounding of fifteen others, the state legislature passed a law making county authorities answerable for such disorder in the future. They passed what amounted to a "riot act" in 1836. It said that anyone who had property destroyed by a riot in the city or county of Philadelphia could apply to local courts for compensation. The court then had to find "six disinterested persons" to hear the case and decide first if the property owner had "any immediate or active participation" in the riot. If not, the court then had to determine the value of the loss and thus the amount of compensation. Such a committee was appointed within a month of the attack on the hall, after David Paul Brown petitioned the Court of Criminal Sessions requesting an inquiry.

The managers of the hall claimed a loss of $120,000. In this figure they accounted for the money they had spent to build the hall as well as the income they would have earned from renting it out. They argued that their hall would have brought at least $8,000 per year. Finally, they included interest from the day of the destruction. They probably realized the court would never give them that amount, but they certainly expected compensation. What they may not have anticipated was just how much trouble the court would have in finding people to serve as examiners.

The first panel of six split over the question of whether or not the hall owners bore responsibility for the riot. Like the police committee and the grand jury, some of them believed abolitionist actions had provoked the assault. Even so, the members awarded the PASS $1,357 for its library of books destroyed in the blaze. This was the group that also awarded Lundy compensation for his losses. As for the hall itself, they would leave that for another jury to worry about.

The court called for appraisers to hear the hall trustees' case and report on their claims in July 1838, but it took until December for them to find six people to agree to serve in that role. Two months later this group reported that they could not come to agreement on the question of whether or not the hall owners had participated in any way in the melee, so they asked to be discharged.

After the second failed attempt at resolution, the Court of General Sessions called for another inquest. This new panel began its investigation in December 1840 and reported its findings the next July—three years after the fire. Five members of this group agreed that the Association had lost $33,000 and ruled that the owners had played no part in the riot. One member dissented and issued a counter-report. Based on the adverse report, the county filed procedural exceptions, which the court upheld in February 1842. Once again the hall owners were denied compensation, this time despite a favorable verdict.

Even so, they were not ready to give up. The lawyer who had taken over the case for the managers motioned that the court call upon county commissioners to "show cause why an inquest should not be made" to determine the owners' loss. In response the Court of Quarter

Sessions appointed yet another committee in September 1842. This group reported the following June that the owners had no part in the riot and had suffered damages of $22,658.27. On the advice of their lawyer, the board of managers accepted the amount awarded even though it came nowhere near their demands or actual losses. They faced many expenses and hoped to pay some of them with this money. Once again, however, they faced bitter disappointment.

The county decided to appeal the decision to the state supreme court. Attorney P. K. Brown argued for the county that the 1836 act under which they were being sued was unconstitutional. It denied the county due process by relying upon an inquest of six out of court rather than an actual jury of twelve in court. He then argued that the Court of Criminal Sessions, which had called the inquest, had no jurisdiction over the matter. He also made a number of narrower claims against the decision of the lower court, eventually charging five exceptions and eleven specifications of error.

The county's ploy did not work. Chief Justice Molton C. Rogers overruled the exceptions on every count and ordered the county to make restitution. The county responded by insisting that all claims against the Pennsylvania Hall Association be settled before it made payment. This was done and the county finally paid the hall owners $27,942.27 in June 1847—almost a decade after their hall was destroyed.[4]

The Nuisance at Sixth and Haines

Those who had counted on using the hall had to find other arrangements, as they waited to see if they could ever return to Sixth and Haines. After losing their offices in Pennsylvania Hall, the PASS moved to a new office at 31 North Fifth Street, where they remained for the next two decades. There they kept a book depository, a reading room, and the editorial office of the *Pennsylvania Freeman*. The Pennsylvania Hall Association continued to meet at Samuel Webb's home for several years after they lost their hall. After that they met at the homes of other members.

For years the lonely skeleton of Pennsylvania Hall stood as a sad reminder of what could have been to the abolitionists and of a shameful act of lawlessness to the public. In September 1838 the gable end of the hall finally came crashing down. After that the hall's remains were more of an eyesore than a safety issue and the managers left them up as a testament to what had transpired on that spot. As the *Christian Herald* reported, the charred walls looked "hideous enough to certain 'gentlemen of property and standing,'" reminding them of the lawlessness they had condoned if not participated in. Of course, the walls also stood as a constant rebuke to city officials. The managers knew this and left them up for just this reason.

By July 1841 the city could take it no longer. They demanded the walls be removed. They sued Samuel Webb for maintaining a nuisance. The walls remained standing until the Association sold the lot to the Odd Fellows fraternity, who used the shell to build their own hall in 1846. That hall stood until the early 1900s, showing just how sound the walls really were. At some point the property passed into the possession of a public radio station—Philadelphia's WHYY.[5]

By the time Pennsylvania Hall was laid to rest, abolitionists from across the nation had been using its story, and its remains, to awaken the public to their cause. Of course, the rioters hoped the hall's fate would remind whites and blacks alike to steer clear of abolitionist agitation. In some sense it did: the destruction showed that racial equality could not be achieved peacefully, even in the city that saw the birth of American abolition. In the end, however, abolitionists were able to turn the tragedy around and gain converts to their cause. That was the final chapter of the Pennsylvania Hall saga.

As John Greenleaf Whittier looked at the ruins of Pennsylvania Hall he saw a temple to free speech that had been ripped apart, beaten, and burned by a desperate mob. He believed that in their haste to appease their Southern slaveholding neighbors, the people of Philadelphia made a sacrifice. In the literal sense they had shown that they would eagerly sacrifice their own rights to free speech and property if that was what it took to make the South happy. In a more literary sense, the poet saw the destruction of the hall as an act that was almost religious—a "smoking sacrifice to the Demon of Slavery." Perhaps he could use this imagery to convince uncommitted Northerners of the dangers of allowing slaveholders to dictate the fate of others. People in the free state of Pennsylvania—and, perhaps more importantly, in the city known as the birthplace of American abolition—had attacked white property owners and deprived them of their liberty. Part of their motivation derived from a desire to appease slaveholders. If he could show the public that such action was leading them to rob themselves and their own neighbors of their constitutional rights, perhaps he could sway them to the cause.[6]

> That Temple now in ruin lies,
> The fire-stain on its shattered wall
> And open to the changing skies
> Its black and roofless hall,
> It stands before a Nation's sight
> A grave-stone over buried Right!
>
> But from that ruin, as of old,
> The fire-scorched stones themselves are crying,
> And from their ashes white and cold
> Its timbers are replying!
> A voice which Slavery cannot kill
> Speaks from its crumbling arches still!
>
> – John Greenleaf Whittier

Other abolitionists also considered the ways in which the mobbing could be used to gain support for the antislavery movement. Some compared the destruction to the martyrdom of Elijah Lovejoy, and others focused on the notion that Pennsylvania Hall had been lynched. Abolitionists had been using this emotionally charged word since at least 1835. In that year, a white mob in Vicksburg, Mississippi, hanged a group of white gamblers after deciding that "no adequate punishment could have been inflicted" on the offenders. According to an account in the *Vicksburg Register*, vigilantes took one of the men into the woods to "*lynch* him—which is a mode of punishment provided for such as become obnoxious in a manner which the law cannot reach." The newspaper account went on to defend the action by arguing that "the laws, however severe in their provision, have never been sufficient to correct a vice which must be established by positive proof, and cannot, like others, be shown from circumstantial testimony." In such a case, according to the writer (who had obviously participated), it became the crowd's duty to step in. The writer argued that the people had dealt with the gamblers' "enormities, until to have suffered them any longer would not only have proved us to be destitute of every manly sentiment, but would also have implicated us in the guilt of accessories to their crimes." Soon after this account appeared, newspapers throughout the country began to carry stories about the Vicksburg "lynchings." The *Vicksburg Register* hoped to justify the action by explaining that "public opinion, both in town and country, is decidedly in favor of the course pursued," but many who read the various press accounts remained unconvinced.

A British newspaper, the *Morning Herald*, pointed to the irony of lynching as part of the "democratic spirit" in North America. According to the reporter, the mode of "justice" known as "Lynch's Law . . . seems likely, as things go in America, to supersede all other law." He added that the appeal to vigilante justice was that it "has the recommendation of being a law in which there is nothing of the 'law's delay'—of being also 'cheap law,' for the Judges administer it without a salary, and even the Executioner operates without a fee." He added that such law also "saves the trouble of deliberation, and excludes all the perplexity which ensues to conscientious Juries on hearing both sides of the case." The reporter then went on to comment about the lynching of two suspected abolitionists and seven slaves in Livingston, Mississippi, just days after the Vicksburg incident. Both of the lynchings were part of a hysterical reaction to an alleged antislavery conspiracy. The Mississippi vigilantism resulted in "Lynch law" and "lynching" becoming household terms. The Southern press hoped that the hangings, which took place in the public streets, would serve as warning to all abolitionists "that they may expect similar treatment all over the South."

Of course, abolitionists knew about these lynchings. A year later, Angelina Grimké wrote about the incident and reported that the "proof" of the victims' ties to abolition had never materialized. She used the violence to argue that "when any community is thrown into such a panic as to inflict Lynch law upon accused persons, they cannot be supposed to be capable of judging with calmness and impartiality." According to historian Christopher Waldrep, abolitionists began to connect Southern lawless mob action to slavery, and some "seized on the word 'lynching,' turning it against their enemies." At this point, three years before the Pennsylvania Hall assault, abolitionists "realized that talking about white southerners' propensity for mob violence helped their antislavery cause." They claimed that "slavery, a lawless institution, encouraged mob violence, lynching, and many other crimes." Waldrep concluded that the abolitionists "knew that many northerners, while indifferent to the plight of black people, could be aroused with reports of mob violence because they disliked the disorder that lynching represented." Little wonder, then, that Garrison was playful, if not exuberant, as he rode away from Philadelphia while Pennsylvania Hall burned in the background.[7]

Five months after the assault, Garrison ran the news of the grand jury's verdict under the heading "LEGAL LYNCHING." To what extent was this fair and accurate reporting? To those who know about the violent lynchings that would take place in the post-Civil War South it hardly seems fair to compare the destruction of a building to the murder and dismemberment of human beings. Of course, Garrison had no idea of the scope of race-based violence that would occur in the South after the 1860s, but he did know of the Francis McIntosh case, in which an African American of light complexion due to mixed ancestry was beaten and then slowly burned to death in front of a large crowd of onlookers. It had occurred in 1836 in St. Louis, Missouri, and he ran an account of it in the *Liberator* almost two years to the day before the Pennsylvania Hall attack. Elijah Lovejoy wrote about the same incident for his own newspaper, and abolitionists argued that it was that story that led to Lovejoy's own martyrdom. As historian Louis Gerteis has shown, abolitionist accounts of the McIntosh lynching and the Lovejoy murder were carefully crafted to emphasize the ways in which slavery led to lawlessness and, ultimately, brutal public murders, or "lynchings." The same could be said for the account of the assault on the hall. By 1838 abolitionists had learned to capitalize on every opportunity to rally otherwise disinterested third parties to their cause, and any "lynching," whether real (as in the McIntosh case) or metaphorical (as with Pennsylvania Hall), served their purposes quite well.

In the years after the attack, images of Pennsylvania Hall as a martyr endured. Because the Philadelphia abolitionists chose to leave the remains of the walls standing as a testament to the attack, several writers effectively used the image of a "skeleton of liberty" and compared the destruction of the hall to Lovejoy's murder. Describing Pennsylvania Hall's fate in such emotionally charged terms offered an image that was both powerful and in some ways accurate. To begin with, like the lynchings that would plague African Americans in the South after the Civil War, the destruction of the building had been justified by both the mob and the grand jury with the argument that racial mixing or "amalgamation" was occurring within its walls. Also, the attack involved tearing the victim apart before burning the victim in a very public manner, with a huge crowd looking on in support. Finally, authorities did little to stop the attack, and by some accounts the sheriff and other officials actually participated. Likewise, the court system would never take the attack seriously, and justice would be slow in coming and begrudgingly administered.[8]

Relics

The city realized that the ruins of Pennsylvania Hall were too power-ful a tool at the hands of the abolitionists and used the guise of public safety to insist that the managers clear the lot. Even if the city could order the removal of the remains, nobody could stop the abolitionists from creating relics that could be shared not only in Philadelphia but throughout the world. Perhaps it was the women who had been speak-ing in the hall the night the attack commenced who came up with the idea to market a variety of goods that they claimed were built from the wood of the hall. Maria Weston Chapman, the woman who made her public speaking debut at Pennsylvania Hall just as the attack was be-ginning, was the driving force behind these fairs. After recovering from the nervous breakdown she sustained on her way home, she continued to make great contributions to the abolition cause, most notable of which was the organization of the fairs. She organized the venues and coordinated the efforts of women throughout the North who made the goods or secured donations.

Newspaper articles and ads that appeared in antislavery newspa-pers mentioned a number of relics from Pennsylvania Hall that were sold at antislavery offices and at the fairs. One of the earliest articles, appearing the year after the attack, vaguely mentioned "relics precious to many, made from the wood of Pennsylvania Hall." Since this fair took place near the time Whittier was presented a cane that was sup-posed to have been made from the wood of Pennsylvania Hall, and since frames that were advertised as being made from the hall's wood were being sold at the Massachusetts Antislavery Society office at the time, canes and frames were likely among these relics.

These relics may also have included inkstands and boxes, both of which were reportedly presented to British abolitionist and Member of Parliament Lord Henry Brougham by Americans. In the first instance a committee sent to England during the World Antislavery Fair presented him "an elaborately carved inkstand," as reported by abolitionist Elizabeth Cady Stanton in her memoirs. In what may be a separate incident or a different take on the same incident, a correspondent to the *Nantucket Inquirer* noted a committee of Americans presenting him with a box made of Pennsylvania Hall wood. Other articles on the fairs mention notecases and a vague reference to wood from the hall along with various types of paperweights. One abolitionist memoir mentions a block of wood from Pennsylvania Hall kept on a mantle, perhaps a block of wood meant to be a paperweight.[9]

Indeed, a variety of relics were available, perhaps a bit surprising given the vivid accounts of all wooden parts of the hall being burned to ash. It is impossible to tell whether the exaggerations were at the hands of those reporting on the fire or the ladies selling the goods. What is important is that, whether genuine or not, these relics held tremendous value to abolitionists like Whittier, and they likely served as curiosities to the average fair shopper, making more people pay attention to what had happened to the hall.

Free Speech and Freedom of the Press

The best way to reach non-abolitionists was to focus on what the attack and destruction of the hall meant for the cause of free speech and freedom of the press. Abolitionist handling of the Pennsylvania Hall incident shows a clever process by which they made the incident as much about freedom of speech as antislavery, realizing that perhaps whites who did not otherwise care about black freedom would care about their own rights.

Whittier offered the first glimmer of hope that something good might come out of the attack. The morning after the hall's destruction he wrote, "Let all men see by what a frail tenure they hold property and life in a land overshadowed by the curse of slavery." Another eyewitness, Bartholomew Fussell, also thought the "conflagration" would open whites' eyes: "I felt nothing like discouragement at the loss of the Hall," he wrote. Instead, he told himself that "every particle of ashes created by this flame shall build up an antislavery hall in the hearts of the people." He heard an associate offer a similar thought: "Every nail that falls from that roof shall clinch through the coffin of slavery."

The editor of the *Massachusetts Spy*, when conveying the news of the attack, pointed out that similar mob action in Boston and Utica had led to backlashes whereby "all class of citizens are now allowed to meet and discuss the same question in the most public manner possible, and even the hall of legislation is thrown open to them for that purpose . . . those who were sustained by the popular voice, in riding, roughshod, over the rights of their fellow citizens, now find themselves in a meager and contemptible minority." The writer forecasted similar changes for the City of Brotherly Love, adding that until that change came, "the friends of liberty and of free discussion have a solemn duty to perform" in helping the proprietors of the hall seek justice: "let them forthwith take measures for raising a new hall, Phoenix-like, on the ruins of the last, before its ashes are yet cold—a hall, like that, sacred to the principles of liberty, and sacred to a 'free discussion of all questions not of an immoral tendency.'" [10]

A number of private letters and journal entries confirm that many abolitionists really believed that the martyrdom of the hall was about more than abolition and would thus ultimately further the cause. Two days after escaping from Philadelphia, as the hall burned in the background, Garrison wrote to his mother-in-law that "Awful as is this occurrence in Philadelphia, it will do incalculable good to our cause; for the wrath of man worketh out the righteousness of God." George H. Stuart expressed a similar idea in his journal immediately upon returning home from the final meeting at the hall and witnessing the attack. As the hall burned blocks away, he recorded his thoughts. "What," he asked, "burn liberty, deter the friends of humanity? No—a loud voice from the east and the west and north says no. . . . Like Gold it will come out of the fire doubly refined . . . the Hall will rise like a Phoenix out of its ashes." Meanwhile, "it shall yet stand up as a rebuke to the haughty slave-driver. . . . Oh what a sight to the friends of liberty! Instead of killing the cause it will advance it twofold."

In many ways the relics were also calculated to emphasize the cause of free speech as well as antislavery. The women who organized the fairs cleverly marketed goods for maximum propaganda value, providing a tempting enough display to bring in those who did not yet understand the need for immediate emancipation and selling them goods that would open their eyes to the cause. New York abolitionist Julianna Tappan, for example, had silk stamped with slave scenes and made into such useful items as workbags. She likely got the idea from famed abolitionist writer Lydia Maria Child, who was known for placing mottoes on many of the items she made for the fairs—including ink blotters, sewing bags, and pincushions. According to one historian, while the sale of these goods brought in money, their creation and use hammered in the basic antislavery message.

The Pennsylvania Hall relics served as clever propaganda in several ways. Though none were perhaps as powerful as the blocks of type rescued and preserved after the attack upon Lovejoy and his press, the hall relics provided a number of symbolic references. For example, Whittier kept his copy of the Declaration of Sentiments of the American Antislavery Society, a significant abolitionist document that he would have revered the way many Americans revere the Constitution, in a frame made of Pennsylvania Hall wood. This had tremendous propaganda value, especially if the women sold the frames with copies of relevant documents. Inkwells and stationery boxes made statements to the value of free speech every time they were put into use by reminding users of the value of the act they were about to take—the expression of their own ideas and opinions. Even the block of wood, when left on a mantle or in a curiosity cabinet, led those who observed it to consider the mobbing and what it meant for the cause of freedom in general. The relics gave tangible evidence that the overall cause of freedom extended past antislavery into free speech and beyond.[11]

In the end, what did the "martyrdom" of Pennsylvania Hall mean for the abolition movement? It is hard to say whether abolitionists won many converts because of the attack, but the image of abolitionists as fighting for freedom in general, rather than just freedom for the slave, gained them respect with some contemporaries. Take, for example, William Ellery Channing. In 1836 he had explained that the true antislavery spirit was best exercised "without passion, or bitterness, and without that fanaticism which cannot discern the true proportions of things, which exaggerates or distorts whatever favours or conflicts with its ends, which sees no goodness, except in its own ranks." In other words, he was not impressed with the "extreme" nature of "modern" doctrine. He was not alone: many who had fought long and hard to end slavery were put off by the same traits of Garrisonian abolition, as made clear in Brown's careful attempt to walk the line between gradualism and immediatism in his keynote speech at

Pennsylvania Hall. The public saw all abolitionists in terms of the Garrisonians, and that put gradualists like Channing in an awkward position: should he speak up against or defend the "modernists"?

Before the anti-abolitionist attacks throughout the North, Channing chose to express his "fervent attachment" to antislavery while making clear his "disapprobation of their spirit and measures," and he hoped to leave it at that. But the behavior of anti-abolitionists led him back into the fray. "Had the abolitionists been left to pursue their object with the freedom which is guaranteed to them by our civil institutions; had they been resisted only by those weapons of reason, rebuke, [and] reprobation with which the laws allow," he insisted, "I should have no inducement to speak of them again either in praise or censure." The violence they faced, however, and their own nonviolent response, transformed them from merely "champions of the colored race" into noble "sufferers for the liberty of thought, speech, and the press." Though continuing to censure their methods, Channing praised their "firm, fearless assertion of the rights of free discussion, of speech and the press," looking upon them with "unmixed respect."

Even so, he was not entirely impressed with their behavior at the opening of Pennsylvania Hall, and he could see why the crowd, rabid with anger over the prospect of "amalgamation," had been driven to violence. After the incident he wrote a lengthy letter defending the rights of free speech and supporting the antislavery cause in general. But, directing his remarks to his "fair abolitionist friends," he felt compelled to add a few words in censure of their "radical" behavior. Essentially telling them to quit with the public displays of interracial cross-gender unity, he called especially upon young female abolitionists to "respect hereafter the usages of society in regard to [your] communications with the other sex." Channing admired the abolitionists' defense of free speech, but his support would only go so far.

It is difficult to tell at this point how many gradualists would have felt the powerful tug to join the immediatists wholeheartedly and how many, like Channing, would have fallen short even with the powerful imagery surrounding the destruction of the hall. Angelina Grimké Weld's long-time nemesis, Catharine Beecher, for one, remained unconverted. She wrote that immediate abolitionists had used "a deliberate and systematized plan . . . to provoke men to anger, so that unjust and illegal acts might ensue, knowing, that as a consequence, the opposers of

Abolition would be thrown into the wrong, and sympathy be aroused for Abolitionists as injured and persecuted men." The abolitionists had "taken the course most calculated to awaken illegal acts of violence" and rejoiced in the violence when it ensued, knowing that it would "advance and strengthen their cause." She concluded that "It is not so much by exciting feelings of pity and humanity, and Christian love, towards the oppressed, as it is by awakening indignation at the treatment of Abolitionists themselves, that their cause has prospered." She contended that many had joined the immediate movement not because they were influenced by abolitionist arguments but "because the violence of opposers had identified that cause with the question of freedom of speech, freedom of the press, and civil liberty."[12]

The destruction of Pennsylvania Hall happened at a key moment in the abolition movement. The people inside the building were struggling to come to terms with changes in the movement and to decide what exactly the new form of abolition known as "immediatism" meant. As they grappled with the changes in their own movement, they came under attack from outside. The story of the hall is about both processes. It has often been discussed in terms of the growing anti-abolition sentiment that occurred after the immediatists entered the antislavery scene. This is correct, but the truth is a bit more complicated. Both gradualists and immediatists helped to collect funds and oversee the construction of the hall, and both groups were represented at the hall's opening. Many who attended different sessions at the opening ceremonies, like David Paul Brown, were unsure themselves just where they fit into the evolving movement. After the attack, however, immediatists were the ones who rallied together and used the event wisely to show otherwise indifferent Americans how closely their own freedom was linked to the freedom of others and to sell relics that would leave a lasting testimony to the precarious nature of free speech.

The violence at Pennsylvania Hall, and the abolitionist reaction to it, also reveals much about the racial reconstruction of the northern United States. Historian Michael J. Pfeifer traced the "genesis of racial lynching" to the Northern states during the Civil War. He suggested that racial violence in the North during the war provided evidence that the North, like the South, underwent a racial reconstruction in which the white population "spurned the extension of racial equality."

He argued further that racial lynchings committed during the war "can be understood as a formative but subsequently sublimated aspect of the history of the construction of northern white racial identity." He was onto something, but the process began even earlier: Northern reconstruction began well before Southern reconstruction, because slavery ended in the North before it ended in the South. In both cases, racial animosity led to violent clashes as African Americans gained their freedom. In the South this happened after the Civil War, but in the North it happened before. Northern society was in the process of reordering to include newly freed blacks in the 1830s, even as the South held firmly to slavery.

The Garrisonian metaphor of a "legal lynching," though exaggerated and imperfect, when put into the context of modern lynching studies, does shed light on the similar circumstances the inhabitants of both sections faced as slavery came to an end and black and white citizens had to coexist in freedom. According to historian Amy Wood, whites in the post-slavery South used the public spectacle of lynching to bolster white supremacy. This was most likely to occur in cities that faced changes that threatened the social order, much like Philadelphia in the 1830s. Though slavery did not end completely in Pennsylvania until the 1840s, most of the states' slaves were free by 1838, and whites in the state were learning to deal with that fact. The "lynching" of Pennsylvania Hall was white Philadelphians' way of resisting changes they thought would destroy their society, just as the lynching of black people at the turn of the twentieth century helped white Southerners feel as if they could preserve their way of life, which rested on white supremacy. In both cases, however, the public display of violence and intimidation ultimately backfired. Just as the abolitionists used poetry and relics to publicize their cause, anti-lynching reformers used graphic photographs and other visual media to draw the public to their outcry against the barbaric behavior.[13]

AFTERWORD

....

B y the time the Pennsylvania Hall case was settled in 1847, the abolition movement had changed drastically. Two years after the mobbing, immediatists divided over issues of women's rights and Garrison's growing emphasis on nonresistance. By that point, even the allies who had once tried to collectively use the hall's destruction to further their agenda could no longer agree on much of anything.

Just as the "women question" played a large factor in the tension that led to the assault, it was also central to the split of the American Antislavery Society (AASS). The first split occurred in 1839. At that point, Garrison and his supporters maintained control of the AASS, continuing to press onward in the quest for women's rights as well as in the fight against slavery. With Garrison's encouragement, women were able to assume important roles in the society. The Tappans and other men who did not agree with this change left to form the American and Foreign Antislavery Society. This group excluded women from membership, instead insisting that those who wanted to support the cause form auxiliary groups. In 1840 another group, consisting of men like John Greenleaf Whittier, who had placed their faith in the American political system to ultimately end slavery, formed the Liberty Party. Since women could not vote, however, it had little room for women, though some did participate as fundraisers. After the schism, the Pennsylvania Antislavery Society (PASS) stayed with Garrison and the AASS despite an internal struggle. While

Pennsylvania immediatists generally had no problem with the issue of women participating fully in the cause, some did take issue with Garrison's refusal to participate in political action. Several Philadelphia leaders would indeed participate in politics—and in the Liberty Party—despite Garrison's disapproval.

After 1845, the PASS became what historian Ira Brown has called "essentially a closed corporation" with an average of about 1,500 members. Most of those members were Hicksite Quakers. Of the 1,500 members, about two dozen or so dominated the proceedings and supplied the officers. James and Lucretia Mott were among these, with James serving as president for 14 years. James Miller McKim and C. C. Burleigh were also part of this group. The group focused mainly on "a many-sided propaganda campaign, designed primarily to persuade *Northern* people to stop condoning and supporting the institution of slavery." It managed to raise an average of $5,000 a year in income from selling publications and collecting donations. It also raised money through annual fairs. Funds raised went mostly to paying for printing costs and paying salaries of traveling lecturers, editors of the *Freeman*, and McKim (who worked as a publishing agent and corresponding secretary) and William Still (who worked as their office clerk). After 1845, the main role of the society was operating the Underground Railroad through the Vigilance Committee, which helped about 100 fugitives a year throughout the 1850s.

In Pennsylvania and throughout the country, female abolitionists continued their work even after the turmoil. They continued and even expanded their petition efforts. They also took an even more active role in fundraising by hosting annual antislavery fairs. These two sources of revenue were crucial to the movement as they helped to fund not only their own societies but also umbrella organizations like the AASS and the PASS. Indeed, women not only remained crucial to the movement but also became increasingly active in fighting against slavery and for women's rights. The one notable exception was Angelina Grimké Weld. After the mobbing she and Theodore Dwight Weld essentially retired. Theodore continued to write and come out of retirement at will, but Angelina did not. It would be easy to see the mobbing as a traumatic event that chased them out of the field, but that is probably not the case. Theodore had already lost his voice and was unable to speak at the hall; the condition remained thereafter.

As for Angelina, William Lloyd Garrison and Henry G. Wright had shown concern before the wedding that this very outcome would result. They were worried that Weld would expect his wife to stay home, but he actually continued to support the idea of women's equality. The reality of life set in, however, and both he and Grimké learned just what it really was like for a woman to try to succeed in both the domestic and public realm. Because the couple was at the forefront of major changes being made to the nation's gender structure, they faced challenges unique to the pioneering generation. Grimké had spoken out about women's rights to speak publicly but she did not challenge the notion that women shouldered the primary domestic duties. Thus, once she married she set out to prove that life outside the traditional female sphere had not ruined her.[1]

The year 1840 also saw the end of Whittier's leadership at the *Freeman*. He remained strongly committed to antislavery, especially the political wing of the movement, but his health was deteriorating. A doctor diagnosed him with a serious heart condition and told him to relax. This meant leaving the paper. He took with him two souvenirs from Philadelphia: his copy of the 1833 Declaration of Sentiments of the AASS, framed in wood from Pennsylvania Hall, and a walking stick also made from the hall's remains. He wrote one of his most famous poems, "The Relic," about that cane. That year his dream was realized with the formation of the Liberty Party.

After the mobbing, African Americans in Pennsylvania also continued to fight for freedom for slaves and for their own civil rights in the North. James Forten died in 1842, but three years later his son-in-law Robert Purvis would become president of the PASS, illustrating how far the abolition movement in the state had come from its early days of gradualism. Even so, Northern racism continued to hold black Americans in secondary positions, and black abolitionists were turning to more militant resistance, primarily through involvement with the Vigilance Committee. Another race riot in the city that year served as a stark reminder that abolition and social reconstruction had far to go. The 1842 riot, referred to as the Lombard Street Riot, began on August 1 when the Young Men's Vigilant Association tried to celebrate West Indian emancipation with a parade and was attacked by a mob. Unlike the Pennsylvania Hall mob, this one has been clearly identified as being composed mostly of Irish Catholic immigrants. As with the Pennsylvania Hall attack, authorities did little to stop the destruction, though the militia was eventually called in this case.

Finally, some of the most lasting changes brought on by the destruction of Pennsylvania Hall had nothing to do with abolition. During a movement to incorporate the various boroughs into the city of Philadelphia in the 1850s, proponents were able to use the chaos at the hall to their advantage. Pointing to the trouble with jurisdictions during the riot and in prosecuting the cases afterward, they argued the need for unified law enforcement. The fire departments underwent similar changes for the same reasons.[2]

Ultimately the assault upon the hall reveals some important parallels between the post-slavery civil rights movements in the North and the South. In both cases, the states underwent a period of reconstruction in which citizens, black and white, had to create a new social order. In both cases, that process was violent as whites worked to keep blacks "in their place" and to maintain their own positions at the top of the social order. One way of maintaining racial dominance in both cases involved lynching. Were abolitionists right, then? Was the destruction of the hall a "legal lynching"? If a building can be said to have been lynched, then it was indeed. The violent and public end of Pennsylvania Hall shed light on the depth of American racism and the need for a clear agenda for social reconstruction after the end of slavery.

NOTES

....

Preface

1. W. L. Garrison to Helen E. Garrison, 12 May 1838 in Louis Ruchames, ed., *The Letters of William Lloyd Garrison, Volume II: A House Dividing Against Itself, 1836–1840* (Cambridge: Harvard University Press, 1971), 358–361; *Liberator* 26 October 1838.

2. *Minutes of the Proceedings of the Twelfth American Convention for Promoting the Abolition of Slavery and Improving the Condition of the African Race, Assembled at Philadelphia, on the ninth day of January, one thousand eight hundred and nine, and continued by adjournments until the twelfth day of the same month, inclusive* (Philadelphia: J. Bouvier, 1809), 15–16. For more about the tensions the PAS was facing, see the Pennsylvania Abolition Society papers at the Historical Society of Pennsylvania, especially, the General Meeting Minutes, Series I, Reels 1, 9, 10 and Correspondence, Series I, Reels 11, 12, 13. See also Beverly Tomek, *Colonization and Its Discontents: Emancipation, Emigration, and Antislavery in Antebellum Pennsylvania* (New York: New York University Press, 2011), 35–38.

3. For recent work on the colonization movement in Pennsylvania and the longevity of the movement, see Tomek, *Colonization and Its Discontents* and Philip W. Magness and Sebastian N. Page, *Colonization After Emancipation: Lincoln and the Movement for Black Resettlement* (Columbia: University of Missouri Press, 2011). See also Eric Burin, *Slavery and the Peculiar Solution: A History of the American Colonization Society* (Gainesville: University Press of Florida, 2008).

4. T. H. Breen, "Creative Adaptations: Peoples and Cultures," in Jack P. Greene and J. R. Pole, eds., *Colonial British America: Essays in the New History of the early Modern Era* (Baltimore: Johns Hopkins Press, 1984), 195–232; Larry E. Tise, *Proslavery: A History of the Defense of Slavery in America, 1701–1840* (Athens: University of Georgia Press, 1987); Joanne Pope Melish, *Disowning Slavery: Gradual Emancipation and "Race" in New England, 1780–1860* (Ithaca, N.Y.: Cornell University Press, 1998).

5. David Grimsted, *American Mobbing, 1828–1861: Toward Civil War* (New York: Oxford University Press, 1998), viii, ix, viii.

Chapter One

1. For more on Gardner (sometimes misspelled as "Gardiner") see Julie Winch, *The Elite of Our People: Joseph Wilson's Sketches of Black Upper-Class Life in Antebellum Philadelphia* (University Park: The Pennsylvania State University Press, 2000), 147–148.

2. For more on Lay and his eccentric behavior and rhetoric, see Srividhya Swaminathan, *Debating the Slave Trade: Rhetoric of British National Identity, 1759–1815* (London: Ashgate Press, 2009).

3. For more on Woolman and Quaker free produce efforts, see Thomas E. Drake, *Quakers and Slavery in America* (Gloucester, MA: Peter Smith, 1965) and Ryan P. Jordan *Slavery and the Meetinghouse: The Quakers and the Abolitionist Dilemma, 1820–1865* (Bloomington: Indiana University Press, 2007).

4. Maurice Jackson, *Let This Voice Be Heard: Anthony Benezet, Father of Atlantic Abolitionism* (Philadelphia: University of Pennsylvania Press, 2009).

5. For the best background on Pennsylvania abolition, see Ira Brown, *Proclaim Liberty! Antislavery and Civil Rights in Pennsylvania, 1688–1887* (University Park, Pennsylvania, 2000). That manuscript is based on a collection of Brown's journal articles, including from *Pennsylvania History:* "Pennsylvania's Antislavery Pioneers, 1688–1776" 55 (April 1988), 59–77; "Pennsylvania, 'Immediate Emancipation,' and the Birth of the American Antislavery Society" 54 (July 1987), 163–178; and "Pennsylvania and the Rights of the Negro, 1865–1887" 28 (January 1961), 45–57, among others; Edward R. Turner, *The Negro in Pennsylvania: Slavery, Servitude, Freedom, 1639–1861* (Washington: American Historical Association, 1911); Richard Newman, "The Pennsylvania Abolition Society: Restoring a Group to Glory," *Pennsylvania Legacies* 5(2) (November 2005), 7; Wayne J. Eberly, "The Pennsylvania

Abolition Society, 1775–1830," PhD Dissertation, Pennsylvania State University, 1973.

6. For the efforts of the founders to avoid using the word "slavery" in the Constitution, see Paul Finkelman, *Slavery and the Founders: Race and Liberty in the Age of Jefferson*, 2nd edition (Armonk, New York: M. E. Sharp, 2001).

7. Pennsylvania Society for Promoting the Abolition of Slavery, *The Oldest Abolition Society, Being a short Story of the Labors of the Pennsylvania Society for Promoting the Abolition of Slavery, the Relief of Free Negroes Unlawfully Held in Bondage, and for Improving the Condition of the African Race* (Philadelphia: Published for the Society, 1911).

8. Gary B. Nash, *Forging Freedom: The Formation of Philadelphia's Black Community, 1720–1840* (Cambridge: Harvard University Press, 1988), 66–68, 98–99, 109–111; Tomek, *Colonization and Its Discontents*, 32–33; Richard Newman, *Freedom's Prophet: Bishop Richard Allen, the AME Church, and the Black Founding Fathers* (New York: New York University Press, 2009), 5, 55–57, 173; Lapsansky-Werner, "Teamed up with the PAS: Images of Black Philadelphia," *Pennsylvania Legacies* 5(2) (November 2005), 11–15; Eberly, "Pennsylvania Abolition Society," 144–162; Pennsylvania Society for Promoting the Abolition of Slavery, "Plan for Improving the Condition of Free Blacks," (Philadelphia, 1789); Tomek, *Colonization and Its Discontents*, 31; Arthur Zilversmit, *The First Emancipation: The Abolition of Slavery in the North* (Chicago: University of Chicago Press, 1969), 163–164; Pennsylvania Society for Promoting the Abolition of Slavery, "Plan for Improving the Condition of Free Blacks."

9. Nash, *Forging Freedom*, 65.

Chapter Two

1. Carol Faulkner, "The Root of the Evil: Free Produce and Radical Antislavery, 1820–1860," *Journal of the Early Republic*, 27(Fall 2007), 377–405; Wendell Phillips Garrison, "Free Produce among the Quakers," *Atlantic Monthly*, 22(132) October 1868, 485–494; Margaret Hope Bacon, "By Moral Force Alone: The Antislavery Women and Nonresistance," in Jean Fagan Yellin and John C. Van Horne, eds., *The Abolitionist Sisterhood: Women's Political Culture in Antebellum America* (Ithaca: Cornell University Press, 1994), 275–297, esp. 278–280; Norman B. Wilkinson, "The Philadelphia Free Produce Attack Upon Slavery," *PMHB* 66(July 1942), 294–313.

2. Wendell Phillips Garrison, "Free Produce," 485–494, esp. 492–493. For the effect on Garrison, see Henry Mayer, *All On Fire: William Lloyd*

> *Garrison and the Abolition of Slavery* (New York: St. Martin's Press, 1998), 51–54.

3. Eberly, *The Pennsylvania Abolition Society*, 120–123; Faulkner, "Root of Evil," 380, 390; Bacon, "By Moral Force Alone," 278–280; Newman, *Freedom's Prophet*, 266–268.

4. James Alexander Dun, "Philadelphia not Philanthropolis: the Limits of Pennsylvania Antislavery in the Era of the Haitian Revolution," *PMHB* 135(1) (January 2011), 73–102.

5. For population statistics, see Julie Winch, "Philadelphia and the Other Underground Railroad," *PMHB* 111 (January 1987), 426–427; Margaret Hope Bacon, *But One Race: The Life of Robert Purvis* (Albany: State University of New York Press, 2007), 17, and Nash, *Forging Freedom*, 136, 142–149.

6. Emma Jones Lapsansky, "'Since They Got Those Separate Churches': Afro-Americans and Racism in Jacksonian Philadelphia," *American Quarterly* 32(1) (Spring 1980), 57–58.

7. Carol Faulkner, *Lucretia Mott's Heresy: Abolition and Women's Rights in Nineteenth-Century America* (Philadelphia: University of Pennsylvania Press, 2011), 37; Bacon, *But One Race*, 17; Winch, "The Other Underground Railroad," 421–443; Tomek, *Colonization and Its Discontents*, 32, 35–36, 139–140; Nash, *Forging Freedom*, 63, 136–158, 172–178, 180–183, 212–219, 254–259; Mayer, *All on Fire*, 173–174; William F. Lloyd, "The Roots of Fear: A History of Pennsylvania Hall," M.A. Thesis, Pennsylvania State University, 1963, 7; Julie Winch, *A Gentleman of Color: The Life of James Forten* (New York: Oxford University Press, 2002), 94–101.

8. Margaret Hope Bacon, "The Pennsylvania Abolition Society's Mission for Black Education," *Pennsylvania Legacies*, November 2005, 22; Eberly, "Pennsylvania Abolition Society," 65–66, 69, 84–85, 88–90, 123; Tomek, *Colonization and Its Discontents*, 35–41, 46–47, 54–55; Newman, *Freedom's Prophet*, 186–206.

9. Howard H. Bell, *Minutes of the Proceedings of the National Negro Conventions, 1830–1864* (Manchester, NH: Ayers Publishing, 1969); Leon Litwack, *North of Slavery: The Negro in the Free States, 1790–1860* (Chicago: The University of Chicago Press, 1961); Philip S. Foner, *History of Black Americans: From the Emergence of the Cotton Kingdom to the Eve of the Compromise of 1850* (Westport, CT: Greenwood Press, 1983); Stephen Middleton, *The Black Laws: Race and the Legal Process in Early Ohio* (Athens, Ohio: Ohio University Press, 2005); Newman, *Freedom's Prophet*, 270–274.

Chapter Three

1. Mayer, *All On Fire*, 51–54, 68, 70.
2. David Walker, *Walker's Appeal in Four Articles: Together with A Preamble, to the Coloured Citizens of the World* (Boston: third edition, 1830), 62.
3. Mayer, *All on Fire*, 71, 91–100.
4. Faulkner, *Lucretia Mott's Heresy*, 60–62; Mayer, *All on Fire*, 100–101, 103–105, 106–115.
5. Brown, "Proclaim Liberty," 77–78; Garrison to Ebenezer Dole, 11 July 1831, in Walter M. Merrill, ed., *The Letters of William Lloyd Garrison, Volume I: I Will Be Heard, 1822–1835* (Cambridge, Mass.: Belknap Press, 1971), 123; Gilbert H. Barnes and Dwight L. Dumond, eds., *Letters of Theodore Dwight Weld, Angelina Grimké Weld, and Sarah Grimké, 1822–1844* (Gloucester, Mass.: Peter Smith, 1965), vol. 2, vii; Garrison to Dole, 11 July 1831, in Merrill, *Letters*, 123; Mayer, *All on Fire*, 120–123; Faulkner, *Lucretia Mott's Heresy*, 63.
6. Mayer, *All on Fire*, 129, 132–133; Garrison to Purvis, 12 May 1832, in Merrill, *Letters*, v. 1, 62; Mayer, *All on Fire*, 170; Sam Bass Warner, *The Private City: Philadelphia in Three Periods of Its Growth* (Philadelphia: University of Pennsylvania Press, 1968) 2nd edition, 129; Mayer, *All on Fire*, 171; Barnes and Dumond, *Letters of Weld and Grimké*, v. 2, vii.
7. Mayer, *All on Fire*, 171; Brown, "Proclaim Liberty," 78–79, quoting Edwin P. Atlee, D. Mandeville, Thomas Shipley, and George Griscom to Arthur Tappan and other Abolitionists of New York 7 October 1833, in the PAS Papers at the HSP.
8. John Greenleaf Whittier, "The Antislavery Convention of 1833," *The Atlantic Monthly* 33(February 1874), 166–172, esp. 166; Brown, "Proclaim Liberty," 79.
9. Whittier, "Antislavery Convention," 167.
10. Brown, "Proclaim Liberty," 79–80, 93–94; *The Abolitionist* 1 December 1833.
11. For McKim's account see Anna Davis Hallowell, *James and Lucretia Mott: Life and Letters, edited by their Granddaughter* (Boston: Houghton, Mifflin, and Co., 1884), 112. Kathryn Kish Sklar, ed., *Women's Rights Emerges within the Antislavery Movement, 1830–1870* (Boston: Bedford St. Martin's, 2000), 9; Faulkner, *Lucretia Mott's Heresy*, 64–65; Whittier, "Antislavery Convention," 168; Mayer, *All on Fire*, 174.
12. Brown, "Proclaim Liberty," 86–87; Whittier, "Antislavery Convention," 169; Barnes and Dumond, *Letters*, v. 2, viii.
13. Mayer, *All on Fire*, 188–89; Samuel T. Pickard, *Life and Letters of John Greenleaf Whittier* (New York: Haskell House Publishers Ltd., 1969)

volume I, 141, 144–152; Elizabeth Gray Vining, *Mr. Whittier: A Biography* (New York: The Viking Press, 1943), 42–44; Archibald H. Grimké, *William Lloyd Garrison, the Abolitionist* (New York: Funk & Wagnalls, 1891), 102–104; Lucretia Mott to Phebe Post Willis 13 September 1834 in Beverly Wilson Palmer, editor, *Selected Letters of Lucretia Coffin Mott* (Urbana: University of Illinois Press, 2002), 29.

14. Warner, *The Private City*, 128.
15. Warner, *The Private City*, 128, 289; Winch, *Gentleman of Color*, 288–289.
16. Winch, *Gentleman of Color*; Lapsansky, "'Since They Got Those Churches,'" 73.
17. Mayer, *All on Fire*, 188–189; Pickard, *Life and Letters*, 141, 144–152; Vining, *Mr. Whittier*, 42–44; Grimsted, *American Mobbing*, ix.
18. Winch, *Gentleman of Color*, 290–292.
19. Mayer, *All on Fire*, 190, 194; L. Mott to McKim, 8 May 1834 in Palmer, *Selected Letters*, 25–26.
20. Mayer, *All on Fire*, 199–203; Grimké, *William Lloyd Garrison*, 106–107.
21. Mayer, *All on Fire*, 206.
22. Mayer, *All on Fire*, 206–209; Grimké, *William Lloyd Garrison*, 111.
23. Mayer, *All on Fire*, 217; Pickard, *Life and Letters*, 144–148.
24. See Leonard L. Richards, *Gentlemen of Property and Standing: Anti-Abolition Mobs in Jacksonian America* (New York: Oxford University Press, 1970), 53 and Grimsted, *American Mobbing*, ix.
25. Benjamin Franklin Morris, *The Life of Thomas Morris: Pioneer and Long a Legislator of Ohio, and U.S. Senator from 1833 to 1839* (Cincinnati: Moore, Wilstach, Keys & Overend, 1856).

Chapter Four

1. Sarah M. Douglass to "Esteemed Friend" 2 April 1844, Grimké-Weld Papers, Clements Library, University of Michigan, cited by Margaret Hope Bacon, "Sarah Douglass and Racial Prejudice within the Society of Friends," A Pendle Hill Lecture delivered to the Friends General Conference of the Religious Society of Friends, accessed at www.fgcquaker.org/library/racism/smd-bacon.php.
2. Sklar, *Women's Rights*, 5–8; Angelina E. Grimké to Sarah Douglass 3 April 1837 in Sklar, *Women's Rights*, 96–97; Bogin and Yellin, "Introduction," in Jean Fagan Yellin and John C. Van Horne, eds., *The Abolitionist Sisterhood: Women's Political Culture in Antebellum America* (Ithaca: Cornell University Press, 1994), 11.

3. Phillip Lapsansky, "'We Abolition Women are TURNING THE WORLD UPSIDE DOWN!': An Exhibit commemorating the 150ᵗʰ Anniversary of the Antislavery Conventions of American Women, 1837, 1838, 1839" (Library Company of Philadelphia, March–June, 1989), 6.

4. Faulkner, *Lucretia Mott's Heresy*, 66–68; Carolyn Williams, "The Female Antislavery Movement: Fighting against Racial Prejudice and Promoting Women's Rights in Antebellum America," in Yellin and Van Horne, *Abolitionist Sisterhood*, 159–177, esp. 164–65; Brown, "Proclaim Liberty," 165–73.

5. Sklar, *Women's Rights*, 17.

6. Lapsansky, "We Abolition Women," 3.

7. Tomek, *Colonization and Its Discontents*, 110–11; Sklar, *Women's Rights*, 27.

8. Faulkner, *Lucretia Mott's Heresy*, 69–70. For the letters see the *National Enquirer* 18 March 1837, 10 June 1837, 17 June 1837, 24 June 1837, 15 July 1837, 20 July 1837, 3 August 1837, 10 August 1837, 26 October 1837.

9. Antislavery Convention of American Women, "Proceedings of the Antislavery Convention of American Women: Held in New York, May 9, 10, 11, 12, 1837" (New York: 1837), 7–8; Sklar, *Women's Rights*, 26.

10. Weld to Grimké, in Sklar, *Women's Rights*, 34.

11. Whittier to Grimkés 14 August 1837 in Sklar, *Women's Rights*, 129–30; Robert H. Abzug, *Passionate Liberator: Theodore Dwight Weld & the Dilemma of Reform* (New York: Oxford University Press, 1980), 176–77, 181.

12. Faulkner, *Lucretia Mott's Heresy*, 74; Sklar, *Women's Rights*, 2; Lapsansky, "Abolition Women," 3.

13. *Pastoral Letter of the General Association of Massachusetts*, June 28, 1837.

14. Ailene S. Kraditor, *Means and Ends in American Abolitionism: Garrison and His Critics on Strategy and Tactics, 1834–1850* (Chicago: Elephant Paperbacks, reprint 1989), 79–80; Stanley Harrold, *American Abolitionists* (New York: Pearson, 2001), 35–36; Pickard, *Life and Letters*, 208; Kraditor, *Ends and Means*, 118–121.

15. Wendell Phillips Garrison, *William Lloyd Garrison 1805–1879: The Story of His Life Told By His Children, Volume 2: 1835–1840* (New York: The Century Co., 1885), 199–200.

16. Brown to Pennsylvania Hall Association, 25 December 1837 in Pennsylvania Hall Association, *History of Pennsylvania Hall, which*

was Destroyed By a Mob on the 17th *of May 1838* (Philadelphia: Merrihew and Gunn, 1838), 12.

17. Other offices included vice presidents David Mandeville and John Sharp, Jr., the latter of which was a PAS member; secretary James S. Gibbons; secretary of domestic correspondence Edwin P. Atlee and secretary of foreign correspondence Thomas Shipley, both major figures in the PAS; and treasurer William J. Wainwright, also with the PAS. The board of managers included Atlee, Isaac Parrish, Charles Gilpin, William A. Garrigues, Dillwyn Parrish, Joseph Cassey, Joshua Coffin, and Charles C. Jackson; all but Cassey, who was African American, and Coffin were or would soon become affiliated with the PAS. The committee included Edwin P. Atlee and fellow PAS members Isaac Parrish, Charles Gilpin, William J. Wainwright, and George Griscom (also a secretary of the PAS) as well as Gibbons. Thomas Shipley, who served as president of both the PAS and the American Convention, was also active in the meeting.

18. *Constitution of the Philadelphia Antislavery Society. Instituted Fourth Month, 30*[th]*, 1834* (Philadelphia: Thomas Town, Walnut Street, 1834).

19. David Paul Brown, *An Oration, Delivered, By Request, Before the Antislavery Society of New York, on the Fourth of July, 1834* (Philadelphia: T.K. Collins & Co., 1834), 3; *First Annual Report of the Board of Managers of the Philadelphia Antislavery Society: Read and Accepted at the Annual Meeting of the Society, July 4*[th]*, 1835* (Philadelphia: Printed By Order of the Society, 1835).

20. *First Annual Report*, 15.

21. *National Enquirer* 3 August 1836 (volume 1 number 1).

22. Brown, *Oration*, 10, 12, 18, 20–9.

23. Brown, "Proclaim Liberty," 117, 142; Pennsylvania Antislavery Society, *Proceedings of the Pennsylvania Convention, Assembled to Organize a State Antislavery Society, at Harrisburg, on the 31*[st] *of January and 1*[st]*, 2*[nd]*, and 3*[rd] *of February, 1837* (Philadelphia: Merrihew and Gunn, 1837), 7.

24. "Pro-Slavery Convention in Pennsylvania!!!," *National Enquirer*, 25 February 1837; "The Friends of the Integrity of Union," *National Enquirer*, 22 April 1837; "Anti-Abolitionist," *National Enquirer*, 15 July 1838.

25. "Our Principals," *National Enquirer*, 4 March 1837; 18 March 1837; "Address from the Antislavery Convention to the Citizens of Pennsylvania," reprinted in *National Enquirer*, 25 March and 1 April 1837; "A Quaker" (from the *Delaware County Republican*), *National Enquirer* 20 July 1837.

26. "J. Blanchard's Speech," *National Enquirer* 20 May 1837; "General Assembly," *National Enquirer* 17 July 1837; "More Sound Doctrine," *National Enquirer* 5 October 1837; "The Time for Action," *National Enquirer* 5 October 1837; "Controversies Among Abolitionists," *National Enquirer* 12 October 1837; "Awake Thou That Sleepest!," *National Enquirer* 12 April 1838; "Clerical Sensitiveness," *National Enquirer* 12 April 1838; Lewis G. Gunn, "General Assembly," *National Enquirer*, 8 July 1837; "Party Politics," *National Enquirer*, 28 January 1837.

Chapter Five

1. Vining, *Mr. Whittier*, 21–32, 52–55; Pickering, *Life and Letters*, 196.
2. Whittier to Ms. Sigourney, January 1833, in Pickard, *Life and Letters*, 112–118.
3. John Greenleaf Whittier, *Justice and Expediency or, Slavery Considered with a View to its Rightful and Effectual Remedy, ABOLITION* (1833); Pickering, *Life and Letters*, 127.
4. Pickard, *Life and Letters*, 129, 133; Vining, *Mr. Whittier*, 38; Whittier to Thayer, 31 March 1837 in Pickard, *Life and Letters*, 157.
5. Pickard, *Life and Letters*, 208.
6. Lloyd, "Roots of Fear," 13–14; Brown, "Proclaim Liberty," 120.
7. *National Enquirer* 1 April 1837.
8. *National Enquirer* 10 August 1837, 21 December 1837, 28 December 1837.
9. Brown, "Proclaim Liberty," 207; PFASS Minutes 12 January 1837, PAS Papers, HSP Reel 30.
10. Other board members included James Mott; Henry Grew; William H. Scott; Joseph Wood; Thomas Hansell; Caleb Clothier, a PAS secretary and bricklayer who provided much of the brickwork; Jacob Haars; Joseph Truman, another PAS secretary; Peter Wright, a PAS treasurer; William McKee; and John H. Cavender. The Executive Committee included Neall, Webb, Truman, Scott, Wright, James Wood, William Harned, William Garrigues, Lewis Beeve, Abraham L. Pennock, and Lewis C. Gunn. John Longstreth served as Chairman of Stockholders, and George M. Alsop was secretary of the board of stockholders.
11. *National Enquirer* 8 July 1838.
12. *National Enquirer* 30 November 1837; Brown, "Proclaim Liberty," 207–208; *National Enquirer* 7 December 1837.
13. *National Enquirer* 7 December 1837.

14. Pickard, *Life and Letters*, 224; Bacon, *Robert Purvis*, 15; Faulkner, *Lucretia Mott's Heresy*, 109.

15. *National Enquirer* 8 March 1838.

16. *Pennsylvania Freeman* 15 March 1838.

17. Lloyd, "Roots of Fear," 15; Pennsylvania Hall Association, *History*, 140.

18. "An Antiabolition Meeting in Philadelphia (1835)," in Jeffrey A. Davis and Paul Douglas Newman, *Pennsylvania History: Essays and Documents* (Upper Saddle River, New Jersey: Pearson, 2010), 179–180.

19. J. Thomas Scharf and Thompson Westcott, *History of Philadelphia, 1609–1884, Volume I* (Philadelphia: L.H. verts & Co., 1884), 642; *National Enquirer* 29 April 1837.

20. *National Enquirer* 25 March 1837; John Runcie, "'Hunting the Nigs' in Philadelphia: The Race Riot of August 1834," *Pennsylvania History* 39(2) (April 1972), 187–218.

21. Warner, *The Private City*, 126–129, 130–131.

22. *National Enquirer*, "Murderous Outrage at Savanna," 4 March 1837. See also *National Enquirer* April, 6 May, and 10 June 1837.

23. *National Enquirer*, "Report of the committee appointed to examine the laws of this commonwealth and the laws of the United States having relation to slavery," 22 April 1837.

24. H. C. Wright, "Pennsylvania a Hunting Ground for Slaveholders," *National Enquirer* 26 October 1837.

25. *National Enquirer* 13 and 27 May 1837; *Niles Weekly Register* 13 May 1837.

26. *National Enquirer* 10 June, 24 June, and 15 July 1837.

27. Pennsylvania Abolition Society, *To the Present State and Condition of the Free People of Color, of the City of Philadelphia* (January 1838), 3–7.

Chapter Six

1. Lovell, "Fall River Report."

2. *Fifth Annual Report of the Executive Committee of the American Antislavery Society* (New York, 1838).

3. Angelina Grimké to T. D. Weld, 6 May 1838 in Barnes & Dumond, *Letters*, vol. 2, 663; William Lloyd Garrison to Helen E. Garrison, 12 May 1838 in Ruchames, *Letters*, vol. 2, 358–361; Grimké to Weld 10 May 1838 in Barnes & Dumond, *Letters*, vol. 2, 675.

4. William Lloyd Garrison to Helen E. Garrison, 12 May 1838 in Ruchames, *Letters*, vol. 2, 358–361.

5. W. L. Garrison to Helen Garrison, 12 May 1838 in Ruchames, *Letters of William Lloyd Garrison*, vol. 2, 358–361; Faulkner, *Lucretia Mott's*

Heresy, 90, citing Maria Mott Davis to Edward M. Davis 3 May 1838 in Mott Manuscripts, FHL, Hallowell, 142. See also L. Mott to A. W. Weston 7 June 1838 in Palmer, *Selected Letters*, 42.

6. Ira Brown, *Mary Grew: Abolitionist and Feminist (1813–1896)* (Selinsgrove, Pennsylvania: Susquehanna University Press, 1991), 19.

7. W. L. Garrison to E. M. Davis in the *National Enquirer* 8 February 1838.

8. Fussell to Fussell, *Friends Intelligencer* 22 February 1896.

9. Pennsylvania Hall Association, Minutes, available at the Historical Society of Pennsylvania.

10. G. Smith to S. Webb and W. Scott 26 December 1837, in Pennsylvania Hall Association, *History of Pennsylvania Hall, which was Destroyed by a Mob on the 17th of May, 1838* (Philadelphia, Merrihew and Gunn, 1838), 7.

11. Pennsylvania Hall Association, Minutes, available at the Historical Society of Pennsylvania.

12. *National Enquirer* 8 February and 15 March 1838; L. Mott to J. M. McKim, 15 March 1838 in Palmer, *Selected Letters*, 39.

13. *Pennsylvania Freeman* 15 May and 5 April 1838.

14. *Colonization Herald*, 30 May 1838; *Liberator* 4 and 25 May 1838.

15. For descriptions of the hall see Lloyd, "Roots of Fear," 20; Bacon, "Pioneer for Peace," 65; Brown, "Proclaim Liberty," 207–208; and Pennsylvania Hall Association, *History*, 7.

16. Pennsylvania Hall Association, *History*, 6–7, 17–18, 29–30, 33, 35.

17. Victor Value, *Arithmetic, Theoretical and Practical* (Philadelphia: Kimber and Sharpless, 1823); *Pennsylvania Freeman* 3 May 1838; James Pollard Espy, *The Philosophy of Storms* (Boston: Charles C. Little and James Brown, 1841).

18. Pickard, *Life and Letters*, 237; Faulkner, *Lucretia Mott's Heresy*, 77.

19. Sarah Grimké to Elizabeth Pease 20 May 1838 in Barnes and Dumond, *Letters of Theodore Dwight Weld, Angelina Grimké Weld, and Sarah Grimké*, volume 2, 678–679; Mayer, *All on Fire*, 243–245; Winch, *Gentleman of Color*, 303.

20. *American Sentinel* 16 May and 18 May 1838.

Chapter Seven

1. Pennsylvania Hall Association, *History*, 63–64, 66, 69; Lovell, "Fall River Report," 8.

2. Mayer, *All on Fire*, 242–243.

3. Pennsylvania Hall Association, *History*, 70–75.

4. Joseph Sturge, *A Visit to the United States in 1841* (London: Hamilton, Adams, and Co., 1842), 45–47; Winch, *Gentleman of Color*, 303.

5. Pennsylvania Hall Association, *History*,136, 77, 81, 91–92.

6. Sleigh to Pennsylvania Hall Managers, 15 May 1838, Pennsylvania Hall Association, *History*, 73–74.

7. Vining, *Mr. Whittier*, 60; Lloyd, "Roots of Fear," 30; "A Southerner and an Eye Witness" to the Editor of the New Orleans *True American*, 18 May 1838, in Pennsylvania Hall Association, *History*, 167–168.

8. Pennsylvania Hall Association, *History*, 96.

9. Walter Forward to the Pennsylvania Hall Association, 10 May 1838, in Pennsylvania Hall Association, *History*, 96.

10. Pennsylvania Hall Association, *History*, 97–100.

11. Lovell, "Fall River Report," 9–10; Brown, *Mary Grew*, 19.

12. Pennsylvania Hall Association, *History*, 112–117; "Opening of the Hall," *Pennsylvania Freeman*, reprinted in the *Liberator* 1 June 1838.

13. Lovell, "Fall River Report," 10–11; Pennsylvania Hall Association, *History*, 117–122.

14. Sleigh to Pennsylvania Hall Managers, in Pennsylvania Hall Association, *History*, 73–74.

15. Pennsylvania Hall Association, *History*, 123; Lovell, "Fall River Report," 11; Mayer, *All on Fire*, 245.

16. "Report of the Committee on Police, on the Circumstances Attending and Connected with the Destruction of the Pennsylvania Hall, and Other Consequent Disturbances of the Peace" (Philadelphia: L.R. Bailey, 1838), 16; Lovell, "Fall River Report," 12.

17. Pennsylvania Hall Association, *History*, 123–127; Faulkner, *Lucretia Mott's Heresy*, 77; Lovell, "Fall River Report," 13.

18. "Address of the Executive Committee of the Pennsylvania State Anti-slavery Society, for the Eastern District," in Pennsylvania Hall Association, *History*, 147; "A." to the *Augusta Georgia Chronicle and Sentinel* 17 May 1838, in Pennsylvania Hall Association, *History*, 169.

Chapter Eight

1. Faulkner, *Lucretia Mott's Heresy*, 78; *Minutes of Proceedings of the Requited Labor Convention, Held in Philadelphia, on the 17th and 18th of the Fifth month, and by Adjournment on the 5th and 6th of the Ninth month, 1838* (Philadelphia: Merrihew and Gunn, 1838), 4; Pennsylvania Hall Association, *History*, 130; Lovell, "Fall River Report," 13.

2. Pennsylvania Hall Association, *History*, 127; Phil Lapsansky, "'We Abolition Women are TURNING THE WORLD UPSIDE

DOWN!': An Exhibit commemorating the 150th Anniversary of the Anti-Slavery Conventions of American Women, 1837, 1838, 1839" (Library Company of Philadelphia, March–June 1989), 22.

3. Lloyd, "Roots of Fear," 4; *Liberator* 25 May 1838.

4. Pennsylvania Hall Association, *History*, 138; *Colonization Herald*, 6 June 1838; Pennsylvania Hall Association, Minutes, 17 May 1838.

5. Pennsylvania Hall Association, *History*, 130, 138; Faulkner, *Lucretia Mott's Heresy*, 78.

6. Bartholomew Fussell to Edwin Fussell, written 23 May 1838 after he returned home to Chester County from attending the convention. Printed in the *Friends Intelligencer* 15 February 1896.

7. Pennsylvania Hall Association, *History*, 139; *Colonization Herald*, 6 June 1838; Williams to Colonel John G. Watmough, 25 May 1838 in *Colonization Herald* 6 June 1838; John G. Watmough, "Address of John G. Watmough, High Sheriff, to His Constituents in Reference to the Disturbances Which Took Place in the City and County of Philadelphia During the Summer of 1838," (C. Alexander, 1838), 6.

8. Pennsylvania Hall Association, *History*, 139, 140.

9. Lovell, "Fall River Report," 16–17; Fussell to Fussell in *Friends Intelligencer* 15 February 1896; Pennsylvania Hall Association, *History*, 135.

10. August Pleasanton Journal, Historical Society of Pennsylvania.

11. Fussell to Fussell, in *Friends Intelligencer* 15 February 1896.

12. Lovell, "Fall River Report," 19.

13. The Mayor's speech is in Pennsylvania Hall Association, *History*, 140.

14. Mayer, *All on Fire*, 246; "Report of Committee on Police," 22; Pennsylvania Hall Association, *History*, 140.

15. Lloyd, "Roots of Fear," 101; Brown, "Proclaim Liberty," 214; Watmough, "Address of High Sheriff," 6–7.

16. Ira Brown, "Racism and Sexism: The Case of Pennsylvania Hall," *Phylon*, 37(2), 130, 134; *Public Ledger* 18 July 1838. For the account from the participant, see the *Liberator* 15 June 1838; Vining, *Mr. Whittier*, 61.

17. "Report of the Committee on Police," 24. For information on the tenants, see the Pennsylvania Hall Association Papers as well as Pickard, *Life and Letters* Volume I, 234 and Volume II, 659–660. For Shotwell's testimony on Yeager's involvement, see the Philadelphia *Saturday Courier* 2 June 1838.

18. Fussell to Fussell, *Friends Intelligencer* 15 February 1896; Pickard refers to "Dr. Parrish" as the source of the disguise. This was likely Dr. Joseph Parrish, an abolitionist and friend of most of the key players in the

Pennsylvania Hall story. Pickard, *Life and Letters* Volume I, p. 234 and Volume II, p. 659–660; Dillon Merton, *Benjamin Lundy and the Struggle for Negro Freedom* (Chicago: University of Illinois Press, 1966), 254.

19. *Liberator* 9 October 1840; Augustus Pleasanton Journal; Lovell, "Fall River Report," 19, 20; Bacon, "Antislavery Women," 287; Lloyd, "Roots of Fear," 46; *Public Ledger* 18 and 24 May 1838; *Pennsylvania Freeman* 17 May 1838; *Niles National Register* 26 May 1838; James Silk Buckingham, *America, Historical, Statistic, and Descriptive* (New York: Harper & Brothers, 1841); Augustus Pleasanton Diary; *Niles National Register* 26 May 1838; Lloyd, "Roots of Fear," 11, 46–47; *Colonization Herald* 23 May 1838; Mayer, *All on Fire*, 246.

20. Faulkner, *Lucretia Mott's Heresy*, 79; Lucretia Mott to A. W. Weston 7 June 1838 in Palmer, *Selected Letters*, 42; William Lloyd Garrison to George W. Benson, 25 May 1838, in Ruchames, *Letters of WLG*, V2, 366. Garrison does not specify which Stonington, but since she was headed home to Massachusetts, Stonington, Connecticut, is a safe presumption.

21. W. L. Garrison to Helen E. Garrison, 12 May 1838 in Ruchames, *Letters of WLG*, V2, 358–361; Edwin Wolf II, *Negro History 1553–1903* (Philadelphia: Library Company of Philadelphia, 1969), 38–39; Robert Purvis to Rowland Johnson, 22 August 1879, in Bacon, *But One Race*, 71. The more dramatic account of the rescue, which includes the story of Garrison taunting the would-be orator and the ghost-ride to New Jersey, is from *The Chicago Tribune* 3 June 1879, p. 6. Titled "Garrison," it appears to be reprinted from the *Philadelphia Times*. This account includes a disclaimer that it comes from the memory of someone who was a child during the actual event, and it includes some material that I have verified as inaccurate, such as the claim that the child who escorted Garrison through the streets was black. Grimké, *William Lloyd Garrison*, verifies the Purvis version of the story. *Liberator* 26 October 1838.

Chapter Nine

1. *Pennsylvania Freeman* 17 May 1838; Fussell to Fussell, *Friends Intelligencer* 22 February 1838.

2. For the origin of the rumor see the *Liberator* 10 August and 16 November 1838. For the accusations pertaining to Pennsylvania Hall see the *Liberator* 20 July 1838. A short-lived Philadelphia newspaper called the *Spirit of the Times* made the strongest assertions that Garrison had defamed Washington at the Hall. Fussell to Fussell, *Friends Intelligencer* 22 February 1896; Lloyd, "Roots of Fear," 52; Pickard, *Life and Letters*,

234; *American Sentinel* 19 May 1838; *Liberator* 25 May 1838, quoting the *Philadelphia Gazette;* Lovell, "Fall River Report," 20, 22; Brown, "Proclaim Liberty," 184; Brown, *Mary Grew*, 20; Faulkner, *Lucretia Mott's Heresy*, 79; Webb to Ritner, 18 May 1838, Pennsylvania Archives, VI, 426. See also Lloyd, "Roots of Fear," 44–51 and Mayer, *All On Fire*, 46; Pennsylvania Hall Association, Minutes, 18 May 1838; Thomas P. Hunt, *Life and Thoughts of Rev. Thomas P. Hunt, An Autobiography* (S. C. Hunt, 1901), 307, 308.

3. Fussell to Fussell, *Friends Intelligencer* 22 February 1896; Brown, "Proclaim Liberty," 215; Augustus Pleasanton Journal, 18 May 1838; Lloyd, "Roots of Fear," 52; Anna Davis Hallowell, *James and Lucretia Mott: Life and Letters, edited by their Granddaughter* (Boston: Houghton, Mifflin, and Company, 1884), 128–129; *Liberator* 23 October 1840 and 12 April 1844; Bacon, "Antislavery Women," 287; *Poulson's American Daily Advertiser* 21 May 1838; *U.S. Gazette* 21 May 1838; *Liberator* 25 May 1838; *Colonization Herald* 23 May 1838; Brown, "Proclaim Liberty," 215; Warner, *The Private City*, 136; *American Sentinel* 21 May 1838.

4. *Philadelphia Inquirer* 19 May 1838; Pleasanton Journal, 18 and 19 May 1838; *American Sentinel* 21 May 1838; Lloyd, "Roots of Fear," 55; *Public Ledger* 24 May 1838; *U.S Gazette* 21 May 1838; *Niles Weekly Register* 26 May 1838.

5. *The U.S. Gazette* 21 May 1838; Lapsansky, "Since they got those separate churches," 54–78; *Colonization Herald* 23 May 1838; Brown, "Racism and Sexism," 132; *American Sentinel* 21 May 1838; London *Morning Chronicle* 17 June 1838.

6. William Lloyd Garrison to Helen E. Garrison, 19 March 1835 in Merrill, *Letters of William Lloyd Garrison*, Volume 1, 469; Lucretia Mott to James Miller McKim 8 May 1834 in Palmer, *Selected Letters*, 25; William Henry Furness, "A Sermon Occasioned by the Destruction of Pennsylvania Hall, and Delivered the Lord's Day Following, May 20, 1838, in the First Congregation Unitarian Church, By the Pastor" (Philadelphia: John C. Clark, 1838), 5, 8, 9; Lloyd, "Roots of Fear," 68; Pleasanton Journal, 20 and 29 May, 10, 11, and 29 June, and 9 and 10 July 1838. For the description of the attack see the 17 May 1838 and 18 May 1838 entries; *U.S. Gazette* 22 May 1838.

7. London *Morning Chronicle* 18 June 1838; *Salem Gazette* reprinted in the *Liberator* 25 May 1838; *Massachusetts Spy* reprinted in the *Liberator* 1 June 1838; *American Sentinel, Pennsylvanian,* New York *Commercial Advertiser,* New York *Morning Herald,* and *Public Ledger.*

8. *U.S. Gazette* 24 May 1838; Daniel Bowen, *A History of Philadelphia, With a Notice of Villages, in the Vicinity, Embellished with Engravings, Designed as a Guide to Citizens and Strangers* (Philadelphia: 1839), 116–117; Lloyd, "Roots of Fear," 81; Winch, *Gentleman of Color*, 304; Scharff and Westcott, *History of Philadelphia*, V 1, 654–655; *Pennsylvanian* 25 May 1838; *Colonization Herald* 23 May 1838; "Report of the Committee on Police," 13–15; Brown, "Proclaim Liberty," 217; Paul Gilje, *The Road to Mobocracy: Popular Disorder in New York City, 1763–1834* (Chapel Hill University of North Carolina Press, 1987), 271, 272; Pleasanton Journal 11, 12, and 23 June and 9 July; Watmough, "Address of High Sheriff," 9.

9. Lloyd, "Roots of Fear," 60; *Liberator* 17 August 1838, 12 April 1839, 24 January 1840, 29 May 1840, 20 August 1848. For other comments on working-class involvement see Brown, "Proclaim Liberty," 214 and Vining, *Mr. Whittier*, 54. For more attempts to reach out to the working class see *Colored American* 11 May 1839 and 3 August 1839; Richards, *Gentlemen of Property and Standing*; Lloyd, "Roots of Fear," 28; Lovell, "Fall River Report," 4; *Pennsylvania Freeman* 24 May 1838; *Pennsylvanian* 15 July 1838; *Liberator* 15 June 1838, 17 August 1838, 19 June 1838, and 18 May 1855; Brown, "Racism and Sexism," 135; Pennsylvania Hall Association, *History*; *Colonization Herald*, 30 May 1838; *Pennsylvanian* 11 June 1838; *Alexander's Weekly Messenger* 13 June 1838; *Liberator* 1 June and 20 June 1838, 13 December 1839, 19 June 1840, 19 August 1842, 24 January 1845. For more assessment of the role of colonizationists in this and other riots, see Tomek, *Colonization and Its Discontents*, 225–227; Fussell to Fussell, *Friends Intelligencer* 15 February 1896; *Colonization Herald* 30 May 1838; *Liberator* 17 August 1838; "Report of Committee," Appendix G, Neall to Committee, 35–36.

10. David Paul Brown, "To the Public," *The Pennsylvanian* 24 May 1838 and the *American Sentinel* 25 May 1838; *U.S. Gazette* 1 June 1838; *Pennsylvania Freeman* 24 May 1838; *American Sentinel* 21 May 1838; *Pennsylvanian* 21 May 1838 and 22 May 1838; *Philadelphia Saturday Courier* 11 August 1838; PAS Papers; Ripley, *Black Abolitionist Papers*, Volume 3, 198; *Colored American* 23 June 1838; Ripley, *Black Abolitionist Papers*, Volume 3, 288; Faulkner, *Lucretia Mott's Heresy*, 80; *Liberator* 10 August 1838; *Minutes of the Proceedings of the Requited Labor Convention, Held in Philadelphia, on the 17th and 18th of the Fifth Month and by Adjournment on the 5th and 6th of the Ninth Month, 1838* (Philadelphia: Merrihew and Gunn, 1838); Brown, "Proclaim Liberty," 215; Brown, "Racism and Sexism," 132–133;

U.S. Gazette 25 May 1838; *The Pennsylvanian* 28 May 1838; *Poulson's American Daily Advertiser* 29 May 1838; *Germantown Telegraph* 30 May 1838; *Liberator* 1 June 1838.

Chapter Ten

1. Reprinted in *Liberator* 15 June 1838; Merton, *Benjamin Lundy*, 225; *Colored American* 22 June 1839.

2. *Rochester Democrat* in *Liberator* 8 June 1838; Brown, "Racism and Sexism," 131, 134; *The National Gazette and Literary Register* 26 May 1838; *Pennsylvanian* 24 May and 5 June 1838; *The American Sentinel* 25 May 1838; *U.S. Gazette*, 26 and 31 May 1838; *National Gazette and Literary Register* 26 and 31 May 1838; *Philadelphia Saturday Courier* 26 May and 2 June 1838; *Germantown Telegraph* 30 May 1838; *Liberator* 1 June 1838; Brown, "Proclaim Liberty," 214; Torbert-Ellegood Collection, Series III, F53, University of Delaware; *Reports of Cases Argued and Adjudged in the superior Court and Court of Errors and Appeals of the State of Delaware, From the Organization of Those Courts Under the Amended Constitution; To Which Are Added Select Cases From the Courts of Oyer and Terminer and General Sessions* Volume III (Dover: S. Kimmey, 1844) 77–79; Grand Jury records, 14 September 1844, Historical Society of Pennsylvania; *Liberator* 26 July 1844; *Hampshire Herald* "Burning of Pennsylvania Hall," reprinted in *Liberator* 18 April 1845.

3. For the first jury, see *Liberator* 25 May 1838; *Colonization Herald* 30 May 1838; Lloyd, "Roots of Fear," 87. For the second jury, see *Poulson's American Daily Advertiser* 9 June 1838; *U.S. Gazette* 6 June 1838; *Germantown Telegraph* 6 June 1838; *American Sentinel* 9 June 1838; *American Sentinel* 12 June 1838; *Pennsylvanian* 13 and 14 June 1838; *Poulson's American Daily Advertiser* 13 June 1838; *U.S. Gazette* 13 and 15 June and 23 October 1838; *Liberator* 26 October and 7 December 1838; *Liberator* 16 November 1838 reprint from *Philadelphia Gazette*; Lloyd, "Roots of Fear," 89; *Colonization Herald* 17 October 1838; Brown, "Proclaim Liberty," 219.

4. Perry K. Blatz, "Boundaries of Responsibility: Philadelphia, Pittsburgh, and the Pennsylvania Riot Damage Laws, 1834–1880," *Pennsylvania History: A Journal of Mid-Atlantic Studies* 76(4) (Autumn 2011) 393–425; *U.S. Gazette* 7 and 8 June 1838; *American Sentinel* 8 June 1838; Lloyd, "Roots of Fear," 92–96; *Colored American* 22 June 1839; *Liberator* 6 July 1838; In Re Pennsylvania Hall, 5 Barr 208–210 (1847); *National Era* 24 June 1847; *The Non-Slaveholder* July 1847.

5. Brown, "Proclaim Liberty," 144; Pennsylvania Hall Minutes; *Colored American* 22 September 1838; *Liberator* 23 and 30 July 1841; *Colored American* 17 August 1839; Pickard, *Life and Letters*, 237.

6. *Pennsylvania Freeman* 17 May 1838.

7. *Liberator* 8 June 1838; *Morning Herald* 25 August 1835; Thomas Ruys Smith, "Independence Day, 1835: The John A. Murrell Conspiracy and the Lynching of the Vicksburg Gamblers in Literature," *Mississippi Quarterly* 22 December 2005; John Johnston, "Judge Lynch," *Catholic World*, 45.269 (1887), 596; *Morning Herald* 25 August 1835; Angelina Grimké, *Appeal to the Christian Women of the South* (New York: American Antislavery Society, 1836), 33; *Vicksburg Register* 9 July 1835, in Christopher Waldrep, ed., *Lynching in America: A History in Documents* (New York: New York University Press, 2006), 48–52.

8. *Liberator* 12 June 1840. See also *The Liberator* 24 June 1840 for another reference to the hall as a skeleton and *Liberator* 7 December 1838 and 19 February 1841 for other comparisons of the hall's burning to the Lovejoy martyrdom. For another reference to the hall as "Liberty's Temple," see *Colored American* 17 August 1838; *Liberator* 21 May 1836; Waldrep, *Lynching in America*, 53–55; "Speech of Thomas Paul," *Liberator*, 19 February 1841; Louis S. Gerteis, "McIntosh and Lovejoy," *Civil War St. Louis* (University Press of Kansas, 2001); *Liberator* 26 October 1838.

9. Julie Roy Jeffrey, *The Great Silent Army of Abolitionism: Ordinary Women in the Antislavery Movement* (Chapel Hill: The University of North Carolina Press, 1998), pp. 108–109; Maria Weston Chapman, "The Mass. Antislavery Fair," *The Liberator* 1 November 1839; "Beautiful Picture Frames," *Liberator* 4 October 1839; "Massachusetts Antislavery Fair," *Liberator* 25 October 1839; *Liberator* 18 December 1840; Vincent Yardley Bowditch and Henry Ingersoll Bowditch, *Life and Correspondence of Henry Ingersoll Bowditch* Volume I (Boston: Houghton, Mifflin & Co., 1902), p. 144; Elizabeth Cady Stanton, *Eighty Years and More (1815–1897): Reminiscences of Elizabeth Cady Stanton* (New York: European Publishing Company, 1898), p. 89; "Miscellany, From the *Nantucket Inquirer*, Old Massachusetts" in *Liberator* 7 January 1842; "The National Antislavery Bazaar, Faneuil Hall" in *Liberator* 26 December 1845; *Niles National Register*, Volume 54, p. 195. See also, *The Friend* Volume 85, p. 236; Julie Roy Jeffrey, *Abolitionists Remember: Antislavery Autobiographies & the Unfinished Work of Emancipation* (Chapel Hill: The University of North Carolina Press, 2008), p. 2.

10. "The Burning of Pennsylvania Hall. Account of an Eye-Witness, Dr. Bartholomew Fussell" *Friend's Intelligencer* 22 February 1896, pp. 125–126. Reprinted in *Liberator* 1 June 1838.

11. William Lloyd Garrison to Sarah T. Benson, 19 May 1838 in Ruchames, Volume 2. 358–361. Stuart's account was printed in an unidentified newspaper in 1916 when his grandson donated a box of his letters to the newspaper. The clipping is in a folder in the Historical Society of Pennsylvania's Pennsylvania Hall Campbell Collection; Jeffrey, *The Great Silent Army*, pp. 122, 117; Henry Tanner, *The Martyrdom of Lovejoy: An Account of the Life, Trials, and Perils of Rev. Elijah P. Lovejoy, who was killed by a pro-slavery mob, at Alton, Ill on the night of November 7, 1837* (Chicago: Fergus Printing Company, 1881); Jeffery, *The Great Silent Army*, p. 100.

12. *Liberator* 19 April 1839; Catharine Beecher, *An Essay on Slavery and Abolitionism, With Reference to the Duty of American Females* (Philadelphia: Henry Perkins, 1837), 35–36.

13. Michael J. Pfeifer, "The Northern United States and the Genesis of Racial Lynching: The Lynching of African Americans in the Civil War Era," *Journal of American History*, December 2010, 621–635; Amy Louise Wood, *Lynching and Spectacle: Witnessing Racial Violence in America, 1890–1940* (Chapel Hill: University of North Carolina Press, 2011).

Afterword

1. Sklar, *Women's Rights*, 42–43; Brown, "Proclaim Liberty," 146–151; Gerda Lerner, *The Grimké Sisters from South Carolina: Pioneers for Women's Rights and Abolition* (New York: Houghton Mifflin, 1967, reprint by Oxford University Press, 1998), 190, 216–218.

2. Pickard, *Life and Letters*, 254; Vining, *Mr. Whittier*, 74; undated newspaper clippings in the Pennsylvania Hall file of the Campbell Collection at the HSP; *Washington Post* 15 March 1908.

INDEX
....